ETHICAL ECONOMICS

Ethical Economics

M. R. Griffiths
Partner in Towers Perrin, Tillinghast
President of the British Chamber of Commerce in Italy

and

J. R. Lucas
Fellow of Merton College, Oxford

First published in Great Britain 1996 by
MACMILLAN PRESS LTD
Houndmills, Basingstoke, Hampshire RG21 6XS
and London
Companies and representatives
throughout the world

A catalogue record for this book is available
from the British Library.

ISBN 0–333–67514–2 hardcover
ISBN 0–333–67889–3 paperback

First published in the United States of America 1996 by
ST. MARTIN'S PRESS, INC.,
Scholarly and Reference Division,
175 Fifth Avenue,
New York, N.Y. 10010

ISBN 0–312–16398–3

Library of Congress Cataloging-in-Publication Data
Griffiths, M. R., 1936–
Ethical economics / M. R. Griffiths and J. R. Lucas.
p.   cm.
Includes bibliographical references and index.
ISBN 0–312–16398–3 (cloth)
1. Economics —Moral and ethical aspects.   2. Business ethics.
I. Lucas, J. R. (John Randolph), 1929–   .   II. Title.
HB72.G745   1996
174'.9339—dc20
                                                            96–25612
                                                            CIP

10   9   8   7   6   5   4   3   2
05   04   03   02   01   00   99   98

Printed and bound in Great Britain by
Antony Rowe Ltd, Chippenham, Wiltshire

The passage on pages 194–5 is quoted by
kind permission of Professor F. G. Bailey.

PREFACE

If our memories serve us right the origins of this book date back to the summer of 1959, when we were reading Aristotle by the banks of the Cam. Book V of his *Nicomachean Ethics* was very difficult, and chapter 5, in which he discusses "commercial justice" particularly unsatisfactory. A better account of justice in economic affairs was clearly needed. We went our different ways, one as an Oxford don, the other into business, ending up as a business consultant in Italy. The project of working together was agreed in principle, but deferred in practice until a term's sabbatical leave from Oxford was spent in Tuscany, with drafts of academic prose being brought down to earth by questions and criticisms grounded in business practice. Businessmen are too busy to have time to think about the underlying principles of business practice, and are usually too committed to the job to challenge assumptions: academics are prone to take off in their search for fundamental principles, and fail to test them against the hard actuality of life, and to avoid facing awkward decisions by withdrawing into cloudy abstractions. We hope to have achieved a high-level over-view, while still keeping our feet on the ground, but must leave to the reader the final verdict on our attempt.

Since the project was first mooted, two tides of fashionable thought have flowed and ebbed. Left-wing egalitarians believed that business was bad, profits immoral, and everyone ought to be paid the same. For many years they occupied the high moral ground, and had the better of right-wing realists, who believed that business was business, the profit motive the only one that could move a rational man, and all moral considerations irrelevant to the proper conduct of business affairs. The collapse of communism, however, has left capitalism triumphant, but many now are unhappy at the selfish individualism it seems to foster, and yearn for a greater recognition of community values. Although the efficiency of capitalism is undeniable, and, more importantly, the security it offers against the totalitarian inclinations of the possessors of political power, it seems abrasively tough-minded about the plight of those who lose out in the competitive market, those who are poor, disadvantaged, or unemployed. Left-wing critics are full of compassion and sympathy, but seem much happier spending other people's money than making their own. Business, though no longer wicked, is still not esteemed. It is like refuse collection and sewage disposal, activities perhaps necessary, but not greatly thought of.

Many people who are partisans of neither side are bewildered. They cannot accept the apparently amoral conclusions of the free marketeers, but shy away from the unrealistic sentimentalism of those who seem to think that hard decisions need never be taken and a caring attitude of mind will make everything come all right in the end. Often they have to take decisions themselves, and would like to take them responsibly and well. They do not want to ignore all moral considerations, although often they believe they are obliged to do so by reason of the very nature of business activity; and they would like not to be regarded as moral lepers simply because they live in a real world and cannot do all that idealists would have them do. They seek guidance, but guidance is difficult to glean from the current debate, which is fast becoming a dialogue of the deaf, the two sides talking past each other, neither appreciating what the other is saying.

Debate is polarised, largely because each side is operating with confused concepts, taking too narrow a view of the variety of human activities, and extending too far the conclusions they draw. We think both sides wrong. We reject the general thrust of egalitarian arguments, and do not hold that it is wrong to be rich or to pay differentials based on principles of distributive justice: but maximising profits is not, and ought not to be, the sole aim of business activity; money, though useful, is a slippery customer, not easy to control or allocate, not worthy to be worshipped. But although we reach some conclusions, we offer no blueprint of what business ideally ought to be, nor offer a Decalogue of *do*s and *don't*s. In the present state of mutual misunderstanding, simple precepts, whether piously platitudinous or realistically hard-nosed, will be heeded only by those already converted. Rather, we have tried to think out the nature of business from first principles, and how it fits in with other forms of social interaction, and to draw fine distinctions about selfishness and self-interest, morality and values, aims and objectives, cooperation and competition, duties and rights, as they relate to business decisions. Our purpose is to appreciate more clearly the nature of business, to delimit more exactly its scope, and to avoid unthinking identifications of profit with selfishness, or prudence with immorality, and thus enable those who are actually taking decisions to work out for themselves the ethical considerations they should take into account.

We therefore argue against the view that businessmen are so much constrained by economic pressures that they have no freedom of action, that there is always No Alternative. Decisions have to be taken because there are alternatives, and in deciding between them, we should be guided by ethical as well as economic considerations. Ethical economics, we argue, is not a contradiction in terms, though often it is difficult to decide in a particular case how different claims are to be balanced against one another.

A responsible businessman is responsive to the wider concerns that form the context within which his business operates, and knowing that business is always done with other people, he recognises the relevance of the other's point of view, and makes fair dealing a cardinal principle of his business life. And because he does this, he can give a good account of himself, and does not need to feel secretly ashamed of the way he earns his living.

M. R. G.
J. R. L.

Tuscany 1994
Oxford 1996

CONTENTS

Chapter 1

The Original Adam

Contents

Abstract

Human beings are not entirely selfish, but are separate centres of decision-making with various values that bear, often in opposite ways, upon the decisions they take. Values can be argued about rationally, and may be changed in consequence; they underlie the aims and objectives we set ourselves, the interests we have, and the needs and wants we recognise. Some of our values we share with other people, but not others, and different forms of association have different decision-procedures in consequence. Some are centralised, but where there is considerable divergence of values held, we have decentralised decision-procedures in which agreements are reached, often by bargaining. These form the model of the business transaction.

§1.1 Benevolence and Self-interest

In a famous passage Adam Smith stresses the importance of self-interest in economic relations:

> It is not from the benevolence of the butcher, the brewer, or the baker that we expect our dinner, but from their regard to their own interest. We address ourselves, not to their humanity but to their self-love, and never talk to them of our own necessities but of their own advantage.[1]

---

[1] *The Wealth of Nations*, 1776, ch.2, p.11 Everyman ed.

1

Although there is some truth in this, it is far from being the whole truth.[2] During the early years of my life I was fed entirely by the benevolence of others, and I owe my education also, in very large measure to the generosity of benefactors now long dead. Often when stranded by the roadside, passers-by have stopped and taken time and trouble to help me loosen a nut, mend a puncture, re-connect a throttle cable. In foreign countries local inhabitants will go out of their way to set the stranger on the right road, often at considerable inconvenience to themselves. Throughout my life I have been the beneficiary of other men's benevolence, and with-out their good offices I should have been often in dire straits. I have been fortunate, but not peculiarly so. Other people have had parents who loved them, and provided them with the necessities of life. Other people have been the recipients of the benefactions of a previous age. At times we have received a helping hand, and may recollect having been ourselves of service to some fellow human being. Concern for others is what makes us human, and we most of us from time to time respond to the needs and wishes of others with no thought for our own advantage.

Nevertheless, Adam Smith had a point. We are conscious of our own self-interest because we are aware of ourselves as individual selves, each one with a mind of his own, peculiarly concerned with his own actions and their consequences. Indeed, it is the fundamental criterion of personal identity that an individual person can make up his mind for himself, differently from anybody else.[3] If you and I are to count as separate persons at all, it must be the case that you do not have to agree with me in every respect. Our interests can diverge. And they not only can, but do. Each of us has a special concern with his own future freedom of action, not necessarily shared by others. Although, as will be argued, we do not have to be selfish in our choices, we are different selves, each one a decision-maker in his own right, making his own decisions in the light of his own assessment of their value as seen from his own point of view.

---

[2] Adam Smith himself recognised this, and had in his earlier *The Theory of Moral Sentiments*, 1759, fully acknowledged the importance of benevolence.

[3] See J.R.Lucas, "A Mind of One's Own", *Philosophy*, **68**, 1993, pp.457-471.

§1.2 Taking Decisions

We constantly have to take decisions. Sometimes the decisions are straightforward, but often there are considerations on either side, for and against a particular action, and it is a difficult matter to ponder them, and decide which considerations are the more weighty. With many considerations there is no doubt that they are relevant, and little dispute about which way they point. We all agree that promises should be kept, valued customers appeased, old employees cherished, profits sought: what is difficult to decide is how much weight to put on these considerations when they conflict. If a valued customer has fallen out with an old employee who has been unwarrantedly rude in return, do I sack the old employee or lose the custom? How frank should I be about my company's deficiencies? Should I continue to honour a contract after coming to suspect that the goods are being shipped to a Third-World dictator who will use them to make poison gas? We differ in our priorities, one man stressing the sanctity of contracts, another the sanctity of human life and the awfulness of governments. When after deliberation we arrive at a decision, we cite in justification the considerations that supported it, passing over, and usually forgetting, those that militated against it. Our account after the event makes the decision seem much easier and more inevitable than it really was. By citing only the arguments on one side, we give the impression that they were conclusive, and that all we had to do was to subsume the particular case under some more general code which laid down unambiguously what in such a situation was to be done. But codes, though valuable, as we shall see, do not and cannot cover every case.[4] Often cases have some features that would suggest applying one principle, and other features that would suggest applying another principle, and the point at issue is to decide which; and on this point codes tend to be silent.

Our reasoning, therefore, is not, as it appears in retrospect, deductive, citing some principle enshrined in a code, and subsuming the particular case under it, but "dialectical", in which we have arguments and counter-arguments, *prima facie* cases and objections to them, the objections themselves being sometimes rebutted by further considerations. Typically at the end of our deliberations, we have not come across a conclusive argument, which leaves no

---

[4] See ch.9, §9.1.

room for further doubt, but only one that carries the day in the
absence of further considerations. Other things being equal, we
conclude that one course of action is better than the other, but
recognise that other things may not be equal, and if so, we may
have to reconsider our decision. But we have to decide. We cannot
afford the luxury of an academic suspension of judgement. In the
world of practical affairs decisions have to be taken, almost always
under conditions of imperfect information. We are quite likely to
be wrong, and our mistakes may cost us dear. But it is not given us
amid the pressures of practical life to have certainty that what we
are doing is the right thing. We only know that we have to decide,
and that not to decide is in fact to decide, and nearly always to
decide badly.

We have to decide. Our decisions show what sort of person
we are, what our values are. When it came to the crunch, some
arguments, some considerations, carried the day. These are our
values.

§1.3 Values

Businessmen do not often talk directly about the values on which
their business activities are based. They talk more readily about
aims and objectives, missions, ideals, interests, strategies, priorities and targets. These words are used in a number of different,
sometimes overlapping, ways. They all have the important logical
feature that they are "non-privative", that is, one person's having
them does not preclude another's having them too, in contrast to
material objects, which are "privative", that is, one person's having
them does preclude another's having them too—they are private
to him, and his having them deprives anybody else's having them
too. We can share values, objectives, ideals, without either of us
having less than we would if we did not share them; whereas if we
share some cake with each other, we each have less. I cannot have
my cake and give it, whereas I can give you an aim in life and still
have it myself.

We can draw rough distinctions between the terms, some being
more general than others, some more focused. 'Mission' refers to
the underlying purpose of the business; for example, the mission
of a pharmaceutical company may be to serve the community by
providing more effective drugs to improve health—and to obtain a
good return on the shareholders' investment. The word 'objective'

is widely used in business, but is open to philosophical niggles;[5] the word 'aim' can be used instead, but, together with 'objective' carries the suggestion of aiming at some particular end result at some particular time. This is sometimes the case, but not always. Some of our values are realised not by bringing about a particular state of affairs, but by maintaining some general condition. Instead of attempting to achieve an aim, we look round and hold ourselves in readiness to take whatever steps are needed to counter unexpected alterations in the situation, and restore the desired sate of affairs.[6] We aim at victory, but having achieved that we seek to maintain peace. Peace would be an ideal, as would harmony between people and nations, self-fulfilment, the flowering of artistic or literary culture. Our usage is fluid. Except in the case of interests, no great harm results from our using these words imprecisely, or in some other sense. The important thing is that they can be shared by more than one agent, and issue in action. The word 'value' will be used in this book as a general term to cover all such shareable reasons for action. Shared values are the basis of joint action, and associations are able to act together on the basis of the values they have in common. What will be of crucial importance is the distinction between those associations that share relatively many values, and can reach fairly simple decisions about how to act, and other associations where there is a much greater divergence of values, with only rather few being held in common, which complicates the way decisions can be arrived at.

Values differ from material objects not only in their logical shape but in metaphysical status. Many thinkers have thought that they have the same reality as tables, chairs and mountains, and that we should all acknowledge the same values, and it is only due to ignorance on the part of individual agents that they do not recognise them. In the ancient world Plato believed in a uniform set of absolute objective values, and in this was followed by the Stoics, who believed in a natural law determining what were the duties of each man in his station, and by the Jews, who believed in a divine law which laid down exactly what the people of the Covenant should do in each situation. The moral law, which, according to Kant, a man of good will would strive to implement,

---

[5] See below, this section, p.8, n.9.

[6] See Sir Geoffrey Vickers, *The Art of Judgement*, London, 1965, pp.31-35; and J.R.Lucas, *Responsibility*, Oxford, 1993, §10.1, pp.205-207.

was similarly objective and absolute; and this is how morality is thought of by most modern people.

But morality thus conceived has always had its critics. As portrayed by Plato and the Stoics, it has seemed cold, impersonal and hard. Jesus castigated the moral Jews of his own generation as whited sepulchres, whose external behaviour belied an unruly self-assertiveness and insensitivity to others in their inner nature. The uniform morality of Kant was criticized by Hegel as being inflexible and by the existentialists as denying the authenticity of moral choice. Many moral people seem to be motivated by a desire to deny themselves and to impose their values on other people; we often sense that if they love their neighbour as themselves, their neighbour is going to be in for a bad time; modern radicals are quick to denounce "authoritarian morality", and many protagonists of the liberal democratic state defend its liberalism from the stand-point of profound scepticism about absolute values—since there is no saying whether an action is right or wrong, the State should not presume to interfere with what the individual is minded to do.

There is much force in these criticisms. The monolithic set of absolute values seems to leave no room for individuality. Each of us is, on that view, simply an agent of the moral law, who ought, in any given situation, to be doing exactly the same as anybody else would: the only way he can be different is by failing to do his duty. But we want to be different. We think of ourselves as unique individuals, not as clones, identical units for realising in their actions an externally imposed set of moral values. But, just though the criticisms are, the critics' overall position is untenable. In the ancient world the great critics of the Stoics—the Epicureans—were unable to formulate a coherent rationale of action; the modern sense of the word 'epicure' shows how the original concern for the human values of freedom and friendship expressed by Epicurus himself degenerated into the sensual gratification of the hedonist. Plato described the decay of morals and the resurgence of the self in the eighth and ninth books of *The Republic*. As men abandon the wholehearted devotion to the Form of the Good, they turn instead first to the worship of their image—the pursuit of honour or *kudos*—and then money, and then permissiveness, and finally, having expelled all values from their nature, become possessed by a demonic self-assertiveness which renders them autistic, incapable of friendship or trust, and in perpetual fear that others will do unto them as they are prepared to do unto them. The twentieth century has proved Plato all too prescient; Hitler, Stalin, and a host of lesser dictators have shown how moral nihilism engenders homicidal madness.[7] We cannot live in a value-free world. If everything is permitted, then nothing is worthwhile, and our life becomes a perpetual search for *divertissement* to relieve our underlying *ennui*, as we seek to kill time until time kills us.[8]

Many people sense the inadequacy of the critical sceptical position for failing to provide an alternative sense of moral direction. There has long been an undercurrent of criticism—though muted during the years of Nazism and Communism—of Western-style political economies for their lack of an inspiring rationale, and the somewhat selfish materialism they seemed to engender. Obviously, if the choice was between American capitalism and Russian communism, American capitalism was the less bad alternative. But many have found themselves uninspired by it. Much though people like to have jeans and hamburgers and consumer durables, such wants are relatively ephemeral, and their fulfilment cannot provide long-term satisfaction. In any case, scepticism is an inherently weak foundation on which to base any defence of freedom—if there are no values I am bound to acknowledge, there is no reason why I should limit my freedom of action in order to respect the rights of other people; I am liberated also from the obligation to be a liberal and to respect the rights of others. And thus many people feel that if this is the only alternative to an authoritarian insistence on absolute values, it is to the latter we must return.

But it is not the only alternative. Jesus criticized moral legalism, but explicitly disavowed any intention to sweep away the moral law. Martin Buber rejected the nihilism of existentialism, and replaced it with a new concept of the value of other people, which required the individual to adopt an "I-thou" rather than "I-it" behaviour towards them. There can be values without their all having to be established *a priori* and the same for all men. An artistic analogy can illuminate. An artist works within a tradition, and needs to observe some constraints on how he expresses himself, or he will be unintelligible to the onlooker, reader, or listener. But a creative artist does not merely work to a formula. He

---

[7] A.Solzhenitsyn, *The First Circle*, tr. M.Guybon, London, 1970, tr. M.Hayward, M.Harari and M.Glenny, London, 1968, 1988.

[8] B.Pascal, *Pensées*; F.A.Dostoievsky, *The Brothers Karamazov*.

adapts, modifies, improvises. Occasionally, but only occasionally, he may contravene some canon hitherto accepted. A writer must observe the grammatical and syntactical rules of his language, but can none the less have his own individual style and may occasionally coin a new word or breach some standard grammatical rule. The Impressionists and the Fauves painted very differently from their predecessors and gave new interpretations to the portrayal of landscapes and people; yet, though bitterly attacked by some art critics at the time, they were still within our artistic tradition, and the scenes they painted were still recognisable. Beethoven broke some of the eighteenth-century rules of musical composition, but abided by many more. The music of Bach and Beethoven is played on the same instruments, with the same scales, and within a limited range of rhythms, but their styles are not at all the same.

Each individual is in his own life like an artist, sometimes not highly original, sometimes not very creative, but individual none the less. There are some canons of behaviour that we all need to conform to, but within them there is a wide latitude of interpretation, and different people fulfil themselves differently, each according to his different capabilities and ideals. I do not have to do the same as you in order to be doing well. I may do my thing and you yours, and we may both be doing well. Not that anything goes. Just as we can criticize an author, composer, painter or sculptor, so we can criticize an individual's actions. I have made many a mistake, and you sometimes rue your actions. The fact that I decided to do something does not mean that it was the right thing for me to do, any more than the fact that you decided in a comparable situation to act differently proves my decision to be wrong.

On this view of values, they are much less external than Plato supposed, and not at all impersonal. Instead of existing out there, entirely independently of us, they are recognised by their appeal to us, and in the way we seek to realise them. But at the same time they are not subjective.[9] I can be wrong. However sincerely and

---

[9] The word 'objective' is often used as a contrast to 'subjective', but has other uses too, and in particular carries connotations of being something material. If we make out that values are material objects, as Plato is supposed to have done, we expose ourselves to easy refutation. John Mackie, *Inventing Right and Wrong*, Penguin, 1977, argues that values must be subjective, since they are clearly not anything like material objects. And although it is important to maintain that values are objective rather than subjective, this is something that has to be argued for, not smuggled in by verbal sleight of hand.

confidently I believe that I ought to preserve the smallpox virus
from extinction, I may be mistaken. It makes sense for you to
say that I am wrong about my moral convictions in a way that it
does not make sense to say I am wrong about my tastes. There,
I am the final authority: if I believe that I like strawberries, and
I can recognise a strawberry when I see one, you cannot, logically,
gainsay me. But the logic of value judgements is such that it is
logically possible for me to be wrong, and hence I am not the final
authority on them. Fallibility precludes subjectivity; that is, if I
am to be proved fallible in my actions or beliefs, there must be an
external reference point against which that fallibility can be judged.
Furthermore, our values are not only fallible, but can be changed
or corrected; that is, they are corrigible. You can not only say that
I am wrong, but sometimes persuade me. I am open to argument.
I am always ready to maintain that I am right, and sometimes,
though only occasionally and reluctantly, I am prepared to admit
that I was wrong. Although, quite rightly, we stick to our settled
convictions, and do not lightly abandon them, even in the face of
serious objections, the possibility of changing our mind is never
ruled out absolutely. Values, although not external, quasi-material
objects, are none the less objective. Although at any one time I am
the ultimate authority on what I do think, I am never the ultimate
authority on what I should think.

It follows that the values we hold at any one time are dynamic.
Our views can change as we develop a better understanding, and
have to change in at least minor respects as we face situations in
which we cannot meet the demands of two conflicting values, and
have to decide their relative priorities. The requirements of freedom
and justice can conflict, and sometimes we abridge freedom for
the sake of justice—as when we hold the accused in prison before
trial—and sometimes abridge justice for the sake of freedom—as
when the guilty escape conviction by invoking a right to silence—
and similarly in the life of each individual his values evolve as he
encounters difficulties and resolves them.

> Values are:
> 1. Shareable
> 2. Not monolithic
> 3. Dynamic
> 4. Creative and individual
> 5. Fallible and corrigible
> 6. Objective, not subjective

If values are, as we claim, in some sense objective and subject to rational discussion and interpretation, with different people acknowledging different values, which they realise in their actions and their lives, important consequences follow. In the first place, freedom is itself a value, in as much as it is the condition for people to realise values.[10] Although sometimes for good reason we abridge freedom, nevertheless there is a general presumption in favour of freedom as an underlying human value.[11]

In the second place, if we view values from the other person's stand-point, we shall be tolerant of his choices independently of our endorsing them, and even when they are wrong. The fact that he has made a choice does not show that it is the right one, but does show that it is his; and although on occasion we may criticize it, and tell him that it is wrong—if he asks our views on it, for instance—often we shall respect his choice, and go along with him, accepting him, warts and all, as the person he is, and not some other person who ought to conform to a world of forms or moral canons and behave as we think he should. In line with this, the word 'value' will be used throughout this book in a descriptive sense, referring to the values people actually espouse, not what they should.

Thirdly, as already indicated, many different associations and relationships will be possible on the basis of the different sets of values held in common by their members. In some there will be relatively many shared values, and only rather few not held in common. In others there will be relatively few shared values as the common basis, and the emphasis will be on the significant differences between associates. A proper understanding of these will prove fundamental for economics and decision-making in business generally.

Values imply:
1. Freedom to express them
2. Tolerance towards the values espoused by others
3. Different forms of association

---

[10] J.R.Lucas, *The Principles of Politics*, Oxford, 1966 and 1985, §1, pp.4-5.

[11] But see below, ch.3, §3.2; see, further, H.L.A.Hart, "Are There Any Natural Rights?", *The Philosophical Review*, **64**, 1955, pp.175-191.

§1.4 Interests

Those engaged in business often talk about their interests. It is a useful concept, but its logic is not well understood, and often gives rise to serious confusion. Interests do constitute reasons for acting, but, unlike most other values, are *assignable*: there is always a party or parties to whom the interests belong. We can always ask 'Whose interest?', but not 'Whose truth?'

Interests have the important, but confusing, feature that they can be used in both a third-personal and a first-personal sense. In the former sense we speak of something being in one's interest, in the latter of one's being interested in something. There are important differences between these two uses of the term. In the third-personal sense I can impute interests to other people. I can look after some one else's interests, taking decisions or putting forward arguments on his behalf. I impute interests to him, assuming that he acknowledges certain values, his life, his health, his liberty, his reputation, his property, his prospects, simply on the basis of his being a person like the rest of us. I do not need to consult him. Often I cannot—there is not time, or I am having to take decisions in his absence—and sometimes it would not be tactful, as when I am putting someone forward for promotion, but know that he is likely to be passed over; I do not want to raise his expectations unrealistically, but urge his merits, doing the best I can for him. I can do this, because I can reckon, without asking him, that more money or greater prestige is what he would like, and without wanting his promotion for myself, can see it from his point of view, and make the judgement he would make. Similarly, the doctor or the solicitor acts in the interests of his patient or client because neither is in a position to know what his interests are, and the doctor or solicitor is.[12] Such vicarious interests are fundamentally third-personal: they are what someone other than the person concerned thinks he needs, not what he himself knows he wants.

First-personal interests, by contrast, cannot be imputed. Only I can say or show what my first-personal interests are. I can be asked what my interests are on a job application form, and say that I like pot-holing, listening to Mozart, singing in the church choir,

---

[12] For a comparable distinction between needs, that can be assessed third-personally, and wants, that are essentially first-personal, see ch.8, §8.9.

and am very keen on saving the whale. Such interests cannot be ascribed to me except on the basis of a first-personal actions or avowals. I am the final judge of what I am interested in.

There is a tension between the interests ascribed third-personally and the values actually avowed first-personally. They can conflict, and sometimes do. I may be interested in doing something which is against my third-personal interests: I may want to go and be a medical missionary in equatorial Africa, at some risk to my health and certain damage to my career prospects. Or I may want to lie abed in the morning, and to smoke and drink, again at some risk to my health and certain damage to my career prospects.

The two senses of 'interest' give rise to two different doctrines. Paternalism is logically possible if interests are construed third-personally. Plato's Guardians, or the Gentlemen in Whitehall, or the Directors of the Company, can know best what is good for you, without consulting you, and even in defiance of your expressed opinion. You may think that cigarettes are good for you, and that it is in your interests to smoke forty a day, but they know better, and acting in your interests, put a tax on tobacco, and establish No Smoking areas everywhere. But if interests are construed first-personally, then the liberal doctrine that each person is the best judge of his own interests is necessarily true. You may think that I ought to be interested in Mozart, but if I deny being keen on Mozart, never go to concerts or operas, never play him on my music centre, you cannot (logically and conceptually cannot) know better than I that really I am interested.

The two senses are often confused. Many liberals hold that a man is necessarily the best judge of his own third-personal interests. But whereas I am necessarily the best judge of whether I am interested in Mozart, I am not necessarily or reliably the best judge of whether it is in my interests to smoke, to invest my savings in an off-shore company specialising in leisure centres, or to serialise my autobiography in the Sunday Times. At best it could be only a rough and ready generalisation that most people most of the time were better able to judge their third-personal interests than any actually available third person. But there are many exceptions. Sometimes we have to say of someone that he is his own worst enemy, and may try for his own sake to thwart his self-destructive plans: we can act against a person's own express wishes in his interests. With children we regularly do, and sometimes with adults also, and perhaps rightly.

Third-personal interests have the further important feature that they carry connotations of self-interest. They are ascribed on the basis of the person concerned being someone whose view systematically differs from the views of other people, and hence the interests ascribed are those that separate him from other people: his life, his health, his reputation, his wealth. We expect each person to value such interests highly, and while we sometimes take care to consider the interests of others, we also suspect that a person's judgement may be biased by his interests. Hence the rules that a person should "declare his interest" before joining in deliberations, and that in some cases where a conflict of interest may arise, a person affected should take no part at all, or else put all his personal affairs into a "blind trust" before taking up public office.

The confusion of the two senses of interest has, as a consequence of this further feature, another unfortunate effect. It colours all talk of interests with a tincture of selfishness. My concerns with my future ability to act, and hence with my life, health, liberty and property, are ones that I necessarily have, and others have only contingently if at all. But my concerns for Plato's philosophy, Bach's music, Christian Aid, or the environment, are not in any way self-centred. It would be quite inappropriate to declare them before joining in a deliberative assembly. Yet they also are my interests. They may move me much more than financial ones.

The confusion infects much of business and public life. It is nearly a tautology that I always pursue my own interests, if we take 'interest' in the first-personal sense—my choices reveal what my real priorities are: but it does not at all follow that, as is often made out, I always act out of self-interest, seeking to further those interests that can be ascribed to me in a third-personal sense. If I go to a Public Inquiry about some future Development Plan, do I have an interest? On one view I do not. I have no *locus standi* because I have no property that might be affected. I have no right to be heard, and in time past such busybodies were not heard, and counsel for the Department of the Environment would sum up by claiming that all the objectors were motivated by self-interest, and the Department alone had the public interest at heart. But on the other view I have an interest, because I am interested in the neighbourhood, and have a view about how it should be treated. But then, if I do make a submission, is it a merely interested one which can be reasonably discounted as merely the expression of a private interest, not to be allowed to obstruct the public interest?

Similarly in wage negotiations the two concepts of interest are often confused. It is in the third-personal interests of employees to receive a fair wage for what they are employed to do, but often what they are actually seeking, and have a first-personal interest in getting, are levels of wages or compensation which would make the business uncompetitive, and deny employment to themselves and others in time to come. A wise negotiator for a trade union may settle for less than his members want, going against their avowed first-personal concerns, but acting in their real third-personal interests.

We need to disentangle the different strands of argument involved in the concept of interest, and to be very cautious in using the word, and to take particular care not to accept the common assumption that because in economic activity we are all pursuing our own interests, it follows that we are all necessarily being selfish. It is helpful to keep in mind those cases where someone in pursuit of a first-personal interest he has adopted argues against some third-personal interest he can be assumed to have: for example, the Treasury official arguing against a pay claim put forward by a civil service union; he is representing the public interest in keeping national expenditure down, but he will be financially better off if he loses, and the pay claim is granted. In time past we could mark this distinction by saying that he was acting disinterestedly (that is, not self-interestedly, not with regard to his third-personal imputed interests), but not that he was uninterested (that is, not bothering to find out relevant facts, not trying to argue the case effectively).[13]

Rather than disentangle, we are tempted to use a linguistic knife, and say simply that there are two entirely distinct senses of the word, and insist that his real third-personal interests are what we know he needs, not what he thinks he wants, which are merely first-personal interests, analogous to wants. But that is a mistake. It denies the significance of the same word being used for each; and as we shall see later,[14] cut off from its first-personal root, the third personal concept withers and dies. Interests ascribed to me by others do not interest me unless by and large and in general I recognise them as concerns that grab me. Needs I do not want are ones I will not own.

[13] In recent years people have been using 'disinterest' and 'disinterestedly' to indicate lack of interest, something done without engagement or commitment—a sloppy usage to be deplored and strenuously resisted.

[14] See ch.8, §8.9.

§1.5 Votes and Vetoes

Associations are based on the values held in common by their members, and the nature of the association and its decision-procedure will vary according as to whether there are relatively many values held in common, or only relatively few. Even where there are many values held in common, it may be difficult to reach agreement about what ought to be done, and as the range of values held in common diminishes, the difficulty increases. Sometimes we can talk it over and form a consensus, but often not everyone is completely convinced. It may be possible to find a compromise, which everyone is prepared to go along with, though not thinking it really the best course. All too often, however, no compromise is available which everyone is really happy with, and then we must reach a decision in some other way. The decision may rest with a single person, the father of the family, the boss of a business, the *caudillo* in a South American republic; or with some group of dominant males, such as the *gerousia* in Ancient Sparta, or the barons in mediaeval England; or, in democracies, with everyone having the vote, and a simple majority being decisive. In all these cases we can see the association as having a centralised decision-procedure by means of a vote, with the vote being possessed by different people in the different cases.

In modern democratic theory it is often held that if everyone has a vote, then a simple majority should be binding, but this fails to accord to each individual a full recognition of his individuality, and can be very unfair. A vote, even if the individual has one, is an inadequate safeguard, since he always may be outvoted on some issue of great importance to himself, though of much less concern to others: others may decide by a large majority that the happiness of the greatest number will be maximised if I am always given the night-shift, and never take my holiday over Christmas and the New Year. They say they are sorry for me, but evidently not nearly so sorry as I am at the prospect of never being able to meet anyone new, and not even to be with my family when they are all together. It is my life: I ought to have a decisive say about what I do.

The only way to meet this difficulty, inherent in any centralised decision-procedure, is to give each person concerned a veto. Unless all the parties concerned are agreed, no decision is reached, and the transaction does not take place. The customer does not buy the goods, the workers go on strike, the peasants do not bring their produce to the market.

To exercise such vetoes, however, is costly; and in many associations where whole-hearted agreement is not possible, rather than have no agreement at all, we strike a bargain. Whereas an agreement has an internal logic and coherence of its own, and is seen as the best way of realising values we all espouse, a bargain trades off quite separate values in order to put together a joint package that each will buy, though for quite different reasons. Bargains are the typical way of reaching decisions in associations in which the values of the parties are significantly different, or in open conflict, whereas some centralised decision-procedure is appropriate in those associations, such as business enterprises or trade unions, where there are many values held in common. In them a consensus is often found, but in addition there is some underlying willingness to go along with a communal decision, even against one's own inclinations or better judgement.

§1.6 Models

Two paradigm models of association have emerged. One is based on there being many shared values, and only rather few not held in common, with a centralised decision-procedure for coming to an agreement which is generally accepted as binding: the other, conversely, on there being relatively few shared values as the common basis of association, with the emphasis on the significant differences between associates, where the striking of a bargain is the way to come to an agreement. Although neither model is fully realised, and there is a wide spectrum of intermediate cases, nevertheless, the two models focus on characteristic features of social interaction, and help us discern the underlying *rationale* of the way decisions are taken.

Neither model is an extreme, pure case. No association can exist if its members have no values in common, and are in total disagreement with one another. This follows simply from the definition of an association, though the consequences that flow from this definition turn out to be quite considerable.[15] And just as one party is never in complete disagreement with another it is doing business with, so we are never perfectly of one mind with one another. No association, not even the most united of families, not even the most dedicated monastery, has its members having absolutely all their

---

[15] See below, ch.3, §3.4, and ch.4, §4.3.

values in common: it is, as we have seen,[16] part of the criterion for being a separate individual that one can make up one's mind for oneself, differently from everybody else, and this being so, each individual has a necessary concern with his own future freedom of action, which is only contingently of concern to others. Even if we do not compete for money or women, we aspire to achieve, and seek the opportunity of achieving great things. Sons would like to emulate their fathers, novices dream of one day being abbot, the junior accountant of becoming finance director. The whole team rejoice when they win, but I even more if I scored the winning goal, or my hat trick made me the man of the match. Man does not necessarily or always act only from self-interest, and may care greatly for the interests of others: but he is necessarily interested in himself as an agent who has to decide what actually to do, and must have a special concern for those actions for which he is responsible. The old Adam is with us yet as autonomous agents, though not invariably selfish ones.[17]

---

[16] See above, §1, p.2.

[17] For fuller discussion, see ch.12, §12.1.

Chapter 2
Cooperation

Contents

Abstract

Business transactions are primarily a matter of cooperation, and take place because we can do better if we cooperate than if we do not. The benefits of cooperation are often unevenly distributed, calling for some readjustment if one party is not to be unfairly exploited by the other. Fairness requires that the transaction be viewed from both sides, each taking into consideration the interests of the other. Economic justice is to be understood not in terms of a just price or just wage fixed by some absolute standard, but in terms of a process that recognises the importance, in arriving at decisions, of the other's point of view as well as one's own.

§2.1 Cooperation

We are not always selfish. Against the imputation of universal selfishness it is enough to point to the many indisputable instances of benevolence. But benevolence is not the basis of economic life. It is, rather, cooperation. Aristotle said that man was a πολιτικὸν ζῷον (*politikon zoon*), usually but wrongly translated as 'political animal'; 'social' would be better, but better still, 'cooperative'. We cooperate. We have to. I should not be here unless my ancestors had cooperated over a long period of years in order to raise their young, nor could we have enjoyed the many advantages of civilised life without the concerted efforts of many different people. Cooperativeness is not a matter of pure altruistic benevolence: the un-cooperative man loses out by virtue of being a loner, and though he may sometimes succeed in trading on other men's good nature, he deprives himself of the fruits of cooperative action, and confines himself to the little he can achieve by his own unaided efforts.

18

Prudential arguments for altruism are suspect:[1] but complete un-cooperativeness is certainly a bad policy.

We are naturally cooperative: I lend a hand to help you start your car or lift a heavy weight; I read the map while you drive the car; I translate something for a colleague. When we cooperate we bring about a new state of affairs which the different cooperators can evaluate. It may be one that would realise some value we all hold in common. If we are members of a team in a sporting competition, we all want to win. All the members of the family on Christmas Eve help to prepare the Christmas dinner. The Sales Department puts in a lot of work to secure a lucrative contract for the firm. In time of war, we all pull together to save the country from defeat.

But not all outcomes will be of the same value to everyone concerned. Since we differ with regard to some values, some out-comes will have different pay-offs for different people. If I set you on your way, or give you a helping hand in setting up a ladder, I may feel a glow of satisfaction at having made the world a better place than it had been before, but you will be even more sensitive to the betterment brought about. Or again, if I help you to get a job by introducing you to someone who has an opening, or if I stay behind over a week-end to help you meet a deadline, I may be glad to have given you a helping hand, but you will have good cause to be grateful for my help. Many cooperative actions benefit some of those cooperating more than others, so that sometimes we feel that some adjustment is needed if justice is to be done. In cases where the contribution made by those who obtain little ben-efit is itself small, we let the matter go—most people are happy to give strangers directions without any expectation of recompense—but if someone's contribution is costly—if he has spent much time and trouble in helping us, or has forgone the opportunity of doing something else he wanted to do—then we are loath to leave him unrecompensed. We want to say Thank You, and seek to give him some tangible tokens of our gratitude and esteem. It does not have to be money; in some cases, indeed, a pecuniary recompense would be inappropriate: but in many, very many, cases it is appropriate. It shows that we are not trading on the benevolence of the man who has helped us, not taking his contribution for granted, but recognising that he has his own priorities which ought not to be

---

[1] See ch.13, §13.6.

entirely overridden by ours. If we pay him, we see to it that the benefits of cooperation have not been altogether annexed by us, and are making sure that he has his share, so that his contribution served not only our interest but his as well. We are showing proper solicitude for his interest, and considering the whole operation not only from our point of view but from what we take, vicariously, to be his.

The basis of cooperation thus varies with the extent to which we share values.[2] Where we share almost all of them, we cooperate very readily, and are not much bothered about how exactly the benefits of cooperation turn out, because we shall all evaluate them pretty much the same in any case. Where there are significant differences between us, the result of cooperation is not naturally equally good for each of us, and readjustment may be called for, which is characteristically brought about by some monetary payment, the economic recompense without which business associates cannot expect us to cooperate.

§2.2 Business Enterprises

In a family we all pull together because the good of the family as a whole is the good of each one of us individually, and although I may distinguish my own interest from my brother's, I nevertheless rate his good highly, and what is good for him is *eo ipso* fairly good for me too. Families live together and work together, and although some activities benefit some members more than others, there are usually not enough long-lasting conflicts of interest to split the family, and each not only identifies with the family as a whole, but by and large also benefits as regards his own individual interests.

Where we have shared values, we cooperate freely, and hence in most cases, more efficiently. It makes good sense, therefore, to have effective units of cooperation. But we do not share all values, and cannot, without an unhealthy suppression of individuality, merge our own identity in that of some group. Although families do work together, and family farms have survived over many generations,

---

[2] As explained in ch.1, values include interests. The word 'value' is used as the most general term referring to a reason for action. Interests are a sub-class of values that can be assigned to particular persons, and are here the third-personal interests that can be vicariously imputed to others.

there are conflicts, and, especially with the advent of money, awkward questions about how much pocket-money the children should have, how far adults members of the family should be enabled to express their own, possibly idiosyncratic, tastes. These problems can be solved, not only for natural families but for other cooperative units, which will be generically called "enterprises". Business enterprises are, so to speak, artificial families, in which the members are linked not by ties of blood but by their already having in common, or (more often) agreeing to endorse, some set of shared values. The values held in common may be many and wide-ranging, as in a family, a monastery, a regiment, a college, or a mission hospital; or relatively restricted, as in an underwriting syndicate, or a firm of currency dealers. But typically—some families and monasteries excepted—the divergence between the shared values of all and the separate interests of each are accommodated by giving each an economic recompense—a wage or share of the overall profits. Some money goes to the individual and is peculiarly his own. He then devotes himself during his working hours to cooperating in appropriate ways so as to realise the shared values of the cooperative enterprise. In some cases these are values already espoused—in a mission hospital, for example—and the salary is paid largely in order to free him from having to devote time and energy to securing shelter and finding food.[3] In other cases, more common in modern commercial life, there is no natural or antecedent identification with the enterprise's values, but it is adopted in accordance with the contract of employment in return for monetary payment. The degree of identification varies, being fairly low for manual workers expected only to perform set tasks in a conscientious and workmanlike way, to very high for top managers, expected to devote their sleeping as well as their waking hours to worrying about the firm's future and thinking up new initiatives.[4]

Typically, business transactions take place between firms which have significantly different values but are cooperating for their joint advantage, and business life takes place within firms, which have some collective purpose that each member of the firm accepts and makes his own. Ethical problems can arise within a firm as colleagues compete for promotion, or seek to establish their own advantage to the detriment of their colleagues, but, largely because

---

[3] See further below, ch.8, §8.5.

[4] See further below, ch.4, §4.2, and ch.6, §6.3.

the firm is long-lasting and has many values shared by its members, the problems do not seem intractable, and often the family analogy helps. It is different with business transactions between business enterprises. These, it is often asserted, are essentially amoral, since it is the nature of business to pursue its own advantage, maximising profits regardless of others, except in so far as they will be useful in time to come. In order to free ourselves of this misapprehension, we need a closer analysis of business transactions, and a determined effort to rid ourselves of false images which can exert a powerful, because unconscious, distortion on our thinking and our doing.

§2.3 Cooperators' Surplus

We can analyse the problem of business transactions with the aid of the Theory of Games.[5] The Theory of Games provides us with a useful, though dangerous, tool for discussing the different evaluations different people make of the situations that may arise from their actions. What actually happens depends, typically, not only on what I do but on what other people do too. We can construct a matrix in which for each agent involved the available alternatives open to him are listed, together with the results of each combination of choices on the part of each of the agents (the "outcomes"). Different agents will value some particular result differently, and these different evaluations can be represented, at the risk of misunderstanding, by numbers (the "pay-offs" of that outcome for the particular agents under consideration). Where the agents share a common value, then there will be outcomes with the same pay-off for each of them. Otherwise the pay-offs will differ, and outcomes will have different values for different players. But in the case of cooperative activities, though the outcomes differ, the all-in-all total is greater if we do cooperate than if we do not—otherwise we should have no reason at all to cooperate.

In a business transaction there is cooperation: services are rendered, goods handed over, as a result of which the parties are, overall, better off than they were before. It is, in the terminology of the Theory of Games a "Non-Zero-Sum Game". But the benefit does not naturally accrue to them all, and adjustment is called for. There is thus, besides the cooperative activity that has produced the "Cooperators' Surplus", a competitive one—in the terminology of the Theory of Games a "Zero-Sum Game"—in regard to the

---

[5] See Appendix A for a brief account of the Theory of Games.

adjustment to be made.[6] If you service my car, then in the natural course of events, I am better off: if I pay you, then I am less better off, and your position is correspondingly improved. If we focus entirely on the question of how much I should pay you, our interests appear to be totally opposed: your gain is my loss, and *vice versa*: but it is only in the context of there being a gain from the transaction that we could be competing against each other for a larger share of the cake. Economics is often thought by moralists to be entirely a zero-sum game. It is one of the prime tasks of ethical economics to take to heart the fact that it is not entirely that. There is, admittedly, an adversarial aspect to business transactions, which colours many of our perceptions of business, and needs to be taken seriously: but it is set within a wider frame of cooperation, which greatly alters the whole aspect of business activity, since then there is a necessary concern for the other party, which in turn gives entry to considerations of justice in business transactions.

§2.4 Tu and Vous

Although Adam Smith was wrong in basing business transactions exclusively on the self-interest of the parties, he was drawing attention to a valid point, namely that in them there are separate centres of decision-making, each evaluating the transaction from his own point of view. But that evaluation need not be selfish. Hayek cites the case of a mother shopping for her children. She may detest fish fingers, but buy them none the less because they like them. She is deciding on behalf of her family from the family's point of view in accordance with the family's tastes, not her own. So too the bursar of a college or a buyer for a retail store is not selfish, but is evaluating in accordance with the interests of the college or the store. It is like the position of a barrister arguing a case in court or an ambassador representing his country. Neither is being selfish, but both are putting one side of a case. In a business deal the parties are not just putting a case, but deciding. Each party has a veto, and the deal will not go through unless each judges it a good one from the point of view he represents. Although it need

---

[6] We owe to R.B.Braithwaite, *Theory of Games as a Tool for the Moral Philosopher*, Cambridge, 1955, the insight expressed in this paragraph and throughout the rest of this book.

not be a selfish one, it is a partial one; it is only because there is a significant difference in the values espoused by the two parties that their cooperation is a business transaction and not a consensual one. And the partiality excludes the other party's point of view. It is for him to decide, from where he sits, whether the transaction is a good one on his scale of values. In Wicksteed's terminology, a business transaction is "non-tuistic" (from the French *tu*).[7] From this it has been inferred that it is altogether unconcerned with the second person, and is entirely first-personal or third-personal, an I-it relation that is necessarily either selfish or impersonal. But, it will be argued, the inference does not hold: although the transaction is "non-*tu*-istic", it is essentially " *vous*-istic" (from the French *vous*), taking account of the generality of other people in the second person plural, though not of the unique individual in the second person singular with his own special set of values.

Although it is ultimately for the other party to a business transaction to decide what his priorities are, and whether the deal is a good one from his point of view, it does not follow that his values are no concern of mine. For, contrary to the assumption implicit in many classical analyses, almost no business transaction is really a one-off one. Often it is one of a continuous series with the same partner, and almost always it is one of a type with other similar partners. From the former fact many have put forward a prudential argument that it is in my interest that the transaction be in your interest too. If I give good value for money, I may get your custom again, and you may recommend me to your friends, and so I can reasonably hope for further custom in the future. The customer is necessarily right in as much as it is only by vicariously taking to heart his point of view and taking care to give him generally a good bargain that I can reasonably expect to remain in business. This is usually represented as an argument from enlightened self-interest: honesty is the best policy; you can rip off a customer once,

---

[7] Philip H.Wicksteed, *The Common Sense of Political Economy*, London, 1910, Bk.I, ch.5, p.174: we owe this point to Hayek; see F.A.Hayek, *The Constitution of Liberty*, London, 1969, pp.78-80. That non-tuistic decisions need not be selfish ones is a point made persistently by Samuel Brittan, *Capitalism with a Human Face*, Aldershot, 1995. See also J.R.Lucas, *On Justice*, Oxford, 1980, ch.1, pp.15-16, and ch.13, pp.229-230. The distinction is also important for our understanding of our own moral commitments; see further below, ch.13, §13.5.

but only once. But it is not only an argument from enlightened self-interest. It is also constitutive of the businessman's role. Just as a doctor is judged to be a good or bad doctor by how well his patients fare, so a businessman is judged by how he stands in the eyes of those who deal with him. It is a necessary concomitant of the two sides of a business transaction. Classical economists stress the importance of my side of the bargain, and how I want it to be a good one from my point of view: but I cannot reasonably invite you to do business with me on the grounds of my wanting to make a profit out of it; if I am to invite you to do business with me, it must be on the grounds of its being advantageous to you. I must hold myself out as ready to serve the interests, in some respect, of you and others, in the same way as the doctor holds himself out as serving the medical needs of his patients. That is what defines the social role of a doctor, and the grounds on which we judge whether he is a good one. Whether he is a successful one is a different question, to be answered in terms of how well he does financially or socially, rather than in terms of how well his patients do. We can similarly distinguish what it is to be a successful businessman from what it is to be a good one. Although in general bad businessmen are unlikely to be successful any more than bad doctors, the connexion is not a necessary one. We can all too easily imagine success being achieved in business by letting down colleagues, defrauding creditors, swindling investors, defaulting on suppliers, chiselling employees, as we can imagine a doctor whose bedside manner and social suavity enables him to amass a fortune by persuading patients to have unnecessary operations and expensive treatments. We have no hesitation in describing such a doctor as a bad one, however successful, but because of the false image of Economic Man engendered by the classical analysis,[8] we are less confident in similarly describing the corresponding operator in business. But once we recognise the two-sided nature of the business transaction, and the importance of the other side in characterizing the businessman's social role, we have a new ground for arguing whether a businessmen is a good one or not, and the case for a new way of looking at what we mean by economic justice.

---

[8] See below ch.3, §3.5.

§2.5 Economic Justice

Once I recognise that I cannot rationally invite you to do business
with me simply on the grounds that I want to profit by it, but
must, rather, hold myself out as being willing in some way or other
to serve your wants, I have introduced a notion of *alteritas*, concern
for the other, which is the foundation of justice. When it comes
to dividing the cooperators' surplus, our interests are opposed: the
more you get the less there is for me. Unless I altogether forgo any
share of it, the allocation of any part of it to me is at your expense,
and you may reasonably ask why you should be getting less than
you otherwise might. A just man takes this question seriously, and
addresses himself to it, being ready to give reasons to the other
party why the adverse decision should be made. If these reasons
are good, the other party will be mollified; even if he does not
accept them *in toto*, he will see that he was not being chiselled,
that the just man was not simply taking advantage of him, but
was trying to arrive at a distribution that was equitable and fair.
Justice, therefore is of prime importance. It enables men to live
together in amity, even though they have different interests, and
decisions are being taken which are adverse to some of the interests
concerned. In economic affairs it blunts the edge of the inevitably
adversarial aspect of dividing the cooperators' surplus, and enables
different people to work together without either feeling that he is
being exploited and done down by the other.

Important though justice is, many economists deny that justice has any bearing on economic transactions. In part it is, as
we shall see,[9] because their analysis yields a market price which
gives no room for claims that any other one could be the right one.
But also they cite the lawyers' tag, *volenti non fieret injustitia*, itself based on Aristotle's *dictum, ἀδικεῖται δ᾽ οὐδεὶς ἑκών* (*adikeitai
d'oudeis hekon*),[10] that injustice cannot be done to a person who
agrees to what is being done to him, from which it would seem to
follow that provided the bargain was entered into voluntarily, no
claim of its being unfair could be countenanced. But we do talk
of hard bargains being struck, and stigmatize some contracts as
being unfair. We draw a distinction between the genuinely voluntary transactions in which a person chooses one alternative, being

---

[9] See below ch.3, §3.3.

[10] *Nicomachean Ethics* V,9,6, 1136b6; and V,11,3, 1138a12

entirely free to choose another, and those where he has no real alternative. If I go to a shop in a strange town shortly before closing time, I would rather pay the inflated price demanded than go without food that night, but I should be hard done by if the shopkeeper, observing my plight, raised his prices in consequence. So, too, the contracts made between small consumers and public utilities or the motor manufacturers, with pages of small print which the consumer had to accept, or go without gas, electricity, or a car, although in one sense freely entered into, could nevertheless be criticized as unjust.[11] Aristotle's *dictum* needs to be modified to take account of the distinction between genuinely voluntary choices and those taken under some sort of duress, or manipulative propaganda, because the available alternatives are ones we are reasonably reluctant to take. In the former case prior agreement rules out of court any subsequent claim of unfairness: but in the latter case, or where we are considering some general practice rather than an individual choice, questions of justice are not excluded by some semblance of voluntariness.

The fact that economic justice does not give definite and precise answers affords classical economists a third reason for wanting to exclude considerations of justice from their subject. Loose, and sometimes contradictory, considerations of justice mess up the argument, and render it unsusceptible of neat mathematical analysis. If the choice is between a mathematical theory involving clear and distinct ideas, and a confused mishmash of arguments actually used in practical decision-making, the theorist may well prefer the former, even if it has little relevance to what actually goes on in the market place and the board room.

For justice is indeterminate.[12] There are many different sorts of reason that we can give for deciding against someone, and it is perfectly possible for a decision to be just in respect of one basis of allocation and unjust in respect of another. The elder son was unjustly treated when the father responded to the prodigal's need rather than to his own desert. Those who had laboured in the vineyard throughout the day were unjustly deprived of their differentials by the generosity of the master to the late-comers. Examiners sometimes face difficult decisions between one candidate who has

---

[11] See further below, ch.7, §7.1.

[12] For a fuller account, see J.R.Lucas, *On Justice*, Oxford, 1980.

failed to obey the rubric, but is clearly brilliant, and another who is rather dull but has scrupulously conformed to the instructions. It is the same in the case of wage differentials, where the skilled worker may feel that he is not being sufficiently rewarded compared .with the unskilled warehouse loader or factory cleaner. How is one to justify the differential between one grade and another? There are different grounds of justification: we can distribute goods on the basis of desert, merit, need, status, or entitlement. So too, we can require a conformity to a norm, and punish infractions of it, either because the norm is inherently fair or because it has been laid down by positive enactment.[13]

Not only are there different aspects of justice which may conflict with one another, but even within a single aspect there are different decisions which may claim to be just in some situation. Justice needs to be filled out in particular contexts, with particular understandings, particular expectations, particular conventions. We need to know what the Romans do if we are to act justly in Rome, and may on occasion need to promulgate conventions so that everybody knows where he stands. There is nothing in the nature of things that makes it right or wrong to drive on one side of the road or the other, but we need a convention so that we all either drive on the right or drive on the left, so as to avoid collisions. Once the convention is established, it becomes just to abide by it, unjust to flout it; for other people expect us to abide by it, and if we do not, we disappoint their reasonable expectations.

Some conventions grow up, and are enshrined in current practice, others are promulgated by an authority. In either case they could be different, and if they were different our view of what was just and unjust would change accordingly. Justice thus depends, in part, on local parameters, and is different in different places and at different times. Many thinkers have thought otherwise. They have taken it for granted that there is one definite just price, just wage, just solution to every dispute. In part it is due to a misunderstanding of natural law. Natural-law arguments do, indeed, establish criteria for assessing the enactments of positive law, but do not determine in every detail what must be done, and do not

---

[13] The mediaeval philosophers expressed this contrast as that between *jus quia justum* and *jus quia jussum*; right because it is just and right because it is decreed.

do away with the need for positive law altogether. In the economic field, doctrines of an absolutely determinate just price and just wage derive plausibility also from the assumption that goods are material goods, possessing some quasi-physical absolute value, analogous to the objective physical properties that material objects actually do possess. Much of the resistance evinced by businessmen towards business ethics is due to *simpliste* doctrines of the just price and just wage that take no account of particular circumstances and contexts. They fear that if once they allow any talk of ethical considerations in their deliberations, they will be required to pay impossibly high wages or charge ludicrously low prices regardless of the actual circumstances in which they operate. It is important, therefore, to stress that business justice is not a single set of answers worked out by some *rigid rule* for business behaviour, but an *approach* to taking decisions in which one considers those who may lose out as a result, and addresses oneself to them, seeking to show them that the decision, though adverse, was, even from their individual point of view, justified. And in doing this, it may be perfectly fair to point out what the going rate is: at least it shows that the bargain is not exceptionally adverse; if the hotel room states that it is more expensive in the high season, you may think it is too expensive, but at least you are not being cheated.

In saying that justice is indeterminate we are not saying that it is relative in the modern sense in which moral values are said to be relative. Although justice is often relative to the situation and context, it is not just a matter of what I happen to think. It might be unjust in one country, where tipping is the custom, not to give the waiter, the taxi-driver, or the hair dresser, a tip, but entirely fair in another country, where the charge includes an adequate recompense to them for their services. Different societies and different jurisdictions balance out competing claims in different ways, which, though different, cannot be stigmatized as unjust. But that does not make it a matter for personal choice, any more than the fact that people drive on a different side of the road abroad makes it a matter of personal choice which side to drive on either at home or abroad.

Nor does the indeterminacy of justice imply that every determination is equally just. Although the laws of England and the laws of Holland determine what is to count as just in different ways, without either being absolutely just, and with each being reasonably acceptable, it does not follow that the laws of Nazi Germany or of the Soviet Union were reasonably acceptable too. Some customs or laws can be condemned as unjust, even though they are accepted in their societies without question. The indeterminacy of justice does not deny that. It allows that some arrangements may be definitely unjust, but argues that we are not therefore to suppose that there is one single arrangement that is absolutely and uniquely just. Rather, there are many that are possible, and it depends on the circumstances and local understandings at the time, which of those should be generally accepted. Justice rules out some things, but does not of itself determine which of the others should be accepted in preference to all the rest.

Justice, then, instructs us to consider the situation from the other person's point of view—an *alteritas* of attitude—but does not of itself lay down exactly how the balance should be struck. It starts us asking certain questions, without providing us with ready-made answers. Often, indeed, there will be considerations of justice on either side, and it will be difficult to weigh them and strike a proper balance in reaching a decision. But that, for a decision-maker, is nothing new.

Many economists deny justice any role in economics because:

1. The market leaves no room for choice.
2. Business transactions are voluntary, and *volenti non fieret injustitia*.
3. Justice is indeterminate.

BUT

1. The market price is not so precisely determinate as theoreticians make out.
2. We do condemn some bargains as hard, some contracts as unfair.
3. Justice, though indeterminate considered absolutely, can lead, in particular situations, to determinate and definite answers.

Chapter 3

Money and False Images

Contents

Abstract

In order to facilitate cooperation we need some transferable and relatively long-lasting form of wealth. Money, although not the only form of wealth, meets this need. It is, essentially, encapsulated choice. It both presupposes freedom and enhances it. For this reason money has often been construed in terms of freedom alone, to the exclusion of justice, thereby creating a false image of economic activity. Further false images are generated by our supposing money to be, like bullion, a material object with physical properties, by economists' talk of perfect competition, by construing business dealings in terms of one-off transactions in isolation from other business dealings and the rest of life, and by an exegesis of rationality in terms of maximising. These false images lead many to suppose that in business there is little room for moral considerations, and no alternative but to drive the hardest bargain possible, and to ignore all considerations except that of maximising profits.

§3.1 Money and Wealth

If we are to do justice to those who cooperate with us in achieving objectives they do not share, we need to adjust the pay-off of the outcome they have helped us bring about, so that it is valuable to them as well as to us. For this we need money. Money is useful because it can be quantified and is generally valued. But why is it valued? Because it is valued by others. Give me money, and I can use it to buy what I want because other people are glad to take it in return of doing, or giving me, what I want. And it is valued

31

by them because they can use it similarly to purchase the goods or services of their choice, on account of its being valued by others, who again value it because its being valued by yet others makes it a means of their being able to effect what they want. Money is valuable, because, being valuable, it enables its possessor to exercise choice. Money is, we may say, almost by way of definition, standardised, generally recognised, encapsulated choice.

Money, thus understood, is less substantial than generally assumed, and more akin to other elusive concepts, such as power and influence. If money is thought of as being, *au fond*, a stock of silver or gold, it makes sense to think of distributing it according to some principle of allocation, much as food was rationed during the war. But once we recognise that, far from being a physical substance, it is a token taking its value entirely from the way it is used and thought of, we can begin to understand how limited is society's control of it. Just because it is encapsulated choice, it is inherently slippery; and if we seek to regiment it and control it according to some preconceived social agenda, it ceases to lubricate social cooperation, and the economy grinds to a standstill. The communists discovered that. They believed that, extracting from each according to his abilities, they should allocate to each according to his needs, and reckoned, reasonably enough, that needs were different from wants, and could be determined by objective criteria without any regard to people's subjective preferences. People, they reckoned, needed steel factories making ball-bearings or tensile wire, and did not need cosmetics or fancy clothes. But people wanted the reverse. If a Russian ship put into a Western port, the town's stock of after-shave lotion would be bought up in a trice; western-style jeans became pearls of great price on the streets of Leningrad; and the real value of the rouble sank and sank, because, for all the ball-bearings it could purchase, it could not be used to obtain after-shave lotion and Levi jeans.

Because money encapsulates choice, we cannot consider wealth in isolation from other means of obtaining what one wants. Some politicians are honest and do not enrich themselves; but if they are ill, they will get the best medical attention; if they need to travel, they will be conveyed by the Air Force; if they want a particular secretary, she will be appointed and assigned at their behest. The managing director can have the company lay on transport, provide entertainment, duplicate papers, without parting with any money. Other people have influence rather than power: if they say that something should be done, it does not follow immediately that it will be done, but it does follow that many people will think that it should be done, and are quite likely to be successful in securing that it actually is done. Power and influence are not the same as wealth—their exercise is hedged about with conditions, whereas money can be spent freely. Nevertheless, the conditions are often satisfied, so that the powerful and influential can have things their own way quite as much as the newly rich.

Equally important in making a realistic estimate of wealth is access to goods and services. Many people in Britain regard themselves as poor, but if they fall ill they will be treated free by the National Health Service, whereas their better-paid counterparts in the United States could be bankrupted by medical expenses. Surveys sometimes claim to find that 90% of the wealth in Britain is owned by 10% of the population. But although it is better to own a house than to rent it, a tenant of a council house has a roof over his head that he can count on for the rest of his life, and that is a real asset, though not a tradeable one. We need to be wary of estimates of wealth. Because money is inherently countable, it is easy to assume that it is an accurate measure. But there are many other components of wealth (which means well-being) than money in the bank, such as a secure job, the ability to influence the course of events, access to information; and to ignore these is to lose contact with the underlying concept altogether. What is the use of money in the bank? To be able to get the things you want, to be free from financial worry, to be able to cope with emergencies, to be able to help friends and relations. But if one can do and enjoy these things anyhow, one is already rich without any money being involved.

Personal security is one of the great goods. The Swiss farmer may have fewer francs than the New Yorker has dollars, but can walk the streets in safety, and leave his possessions unstolen in unlocked houses, enjoying a level of security that in New York would cost millions to achieve. Far greater still is personal affection, which in the nature of the case cannot be bought for money. Money enables us to secure the cooperation of those who would be otherwise unwilling, but cannot buy the unbought willingness we crave for.

§3.2 Freedom and Impersonality

Money encapsulates choice. It therefore enhances freedom. But there is a price to be paid. My freedom to do what I want implies my being free to ignore you and your wants and interests. The market economy based on individual freedom seems cruelly impersonal and uncaring. Although I am free, I am a nobody, a mere unit, one consumer among millions, one producer among thousands. Freedom can generate an anonymous admass society in which I feel marginalised by others' unconcern.

Freedom to do what one wants can be viewed in terms of the decision-procedures discussed in Chapter 1.[1] It represents the limiting case of decentralisation in the way public decisions are taken by the State, where each individual is a separate decision-maker, external to everybody else. It has the great merit of securing him against the danger of being outvoted by a majority that cares little for his interests. But that exacts its price. We cannot give him an absolute veto on all decisions—a unanimity rule is a recipe for indecision and disaster. If we are to give each person any sort of veto, it must be for only a circumscribed range of matters that particularly concern him. Provided we circumscribe the range sufficiently narrowly, we can, by and large, give each person a veto. I can refuse to do what you want me to do unless you make it worth my while, and if I am a tough bargainer, I can hold out for a high price. But others can too. In this contest each is tempted to use his veto power to pressure others into not using theirs to frustrate his purposes. Economics then seems to be an arena governed by the law of the jungle, in which, although we are free to do what we want, we are under intense, and often almost irresistible, pressure to do what others want. I am free to do what I want, but shall starve unless I take a menial job which alone will give me money to buy bread. It is not given to man to be free from all pressures, at liberty to do exactly what he pleases. Civil liberty is purchased at a price: we are no longer living in fear of others killing, enslaving, or robbing us, but are, instead, constrained by economic pressure, often seeming to be economic servitude.

The impersonality and the pressures of business life often make us want to get away from the harsh uncaring world of modern business, and yearn for a rustic simplicity in which each man is known

---

[1] Ch.1, §1.5.

and valued for himself. But though we listen to the Archers, we do not actually make the break and go to Ambridge. We want the variety, need the stimulus of the wider world. Too much cosiness is claustrophobic. In a small society I am imprisoned in my role, fettered by a set of obligations which leave me no room to develop my personality and become a different sort of person. A rural retreat may be idyllic for a holiday, but we soon miss the busy hum of men among the tower blocks of the workaday world. Our ambivalent feelings about money reflect an ambivalence in our own nature. We want to be loved, nurtured, cherished, respected; but we also want to be free, independent, successful, effective; and we are slow to see how the two sets of desires are incompatible, and how my freedom to decide which restaurant to go to, or which show to see, entirely as I please, without regard to the needs of the restaurant proprietor or impresario for my custom, creates the hard impersonal environment in which their best efforts to succeed may none the less end in failure. Impersonality is the other side of the coin from freedom: being subject to economic pressure is the concomitant of being free from being told what to do by those with political power. In thinking about ethical economics we need to remember that we are liable to strong, but contradictory, attitudes to money stemming from our own nature as autonomous agents seeking the cooperation of others but not always being willing to cooperate with them on their own terms.

§3.3 Money and Competition

Money encapsulates choice. It therefore needs freedom, as well as enhancing it. Unless a large number of people are free to try and satisfy market demand, it will not be satisfied, and money will not buy what people actually want to spend it on, and will lose its value like the rouble. Market economics are typically associated with liberal political systems that afford each individual a large degree of personal freedom. And this gives rise to a different view of human society, in which freedom rather than justice is the dominant ideal. It coheres naturally with the Anglo-Saxon liberal tradition, with its emphasis on individual rather than communitarian values. It makes minimal assumptions about morality, needing only to assume the sanctity of contracts and the abhorrence of violence. And, granted certain further assumptions, offers complete precision.

The precision of the classical analysis depends on competition, assumed to be perfect competition, in conditions of perfect information. It considers one-off transactions, typically the exchange or sale of goods, between two parties, totally external to each other, each trying to get the best bargain he can, constrained only by the existence of competition, so that if he holds out for too much, the deal will be off, because the other party can do better by going to a competitor. Granted these assumptions, the market will determine a price at which services may be rendered and goods sold, because although each party is free to enter into any bargain he wishes, and will naturally—it is assumed—seek the best bargain he can, if he holds out for a better bargain, the other party will go, instead, to a competitor and do business with him. Thus, in theory, the market price will be completely determined, in any particular situation, by the balance of supply and demand; and since this is, in theory, what must happen, all arguments about what ought to happen are beside the point. The iron laws of economics determine what will inevitably be, and we must simply accept them, and go along with the inevitable.

There are great merits in the classical analysis. In the first place, freedom *is* a fundamental value as well as being constitutive of the value of money; and although justice is important, it is much more difficult to deal with, on account of its indeterminacy. The classical analysis also offers a completely determinate account of prices and wages, which is inherently attractive, and often illuminating. Because of its merits, it has exercised enormous fascination over the modern mind, and influences, often unconsciously, the way we think and feel about modern life. But the classical analysis, though like the Theory of Games a useful tool, is dangerously distorting one. It has led to much false thinking about economics and negative attitudes towards business, which is portrayed as essentially non-moral, not to say immoral, in contrast to the professions with their codes of conduct, politics with its high-sounding rhetoric, and personal and family life. Its errors are pernicious, and need to be exorcized if we are to think straight about what we ought to do in economic affairs.

Classical economists mislead themselves by abstracting too much. They consider economic transactions in isolation from one another and from the social and intellectual setting in which they occur; they assume perfect competition and perfect information; and they define rationality in terms of maximising. But all these assumptions are unrealistic. In real life, economic transactions are hardly ever one-off, and always take place in some social and intellectual setting; competition is seldom perfect, and information never so; and we often do not in practice pursue a maximising strategy, and in many cases would be acting irrationally if we did.

Perfect competition hardly ever exists; perfect information is what we never have. Although we sometimes shop around in search of a good bargain, we often do not, and are usually ready to make do with a less good bargain than the Best Buy. And we are rational in so doing. Shopping around takes time and effort, and we often have better things to do with our time. Information is costly to obtain, and often we are sensible to pay the price asked in the near-by corner-shop rather than to look for a better buy. Markets are mostly local and limited; only occasionally, in stock exchanges, or where commodity futures or currencies are traded, is competition nearly perfect. But even there equilibrium is never reached. Always there are new demands—I get hungry and want lunch; I decide to take a holiday abroad, and need some foreign currency—and constantly fresh information arrives which alters the state of affairs. Instead of an equilibrium which determines exactly the price at which goods and services are traded, we have only a tendency—if my price is noticeably above that of my competitors, then, other things being equal—which they seldom are—I shall lose custom to them. Other things being equal, I shall choose to buy in the cheapest market and sell in the dearest market, and if what I am buying or selling is something very standard—foreign currency, petrol, or blocks of chocolate—I may well shop around. But often I will go to my own bank, in order to be sure that I am not given forged foreign notes or because they will buy back my unused currency at a reasonable rate; I go to my own local garage, because it also services my car and repairs it; I go to a reputable grocer rather than a street trader whose wares may well have "fallen off the back of a lorry" and be unwholesome too. I take all sorts of other factors into consideration besides price, and am sensible in not being too price-sensitive. As a tool of analysis the classical account of the perfectly competitive market is illuminating: it highlights certain features, and draws attention to important tendencies. But it does this by abstracting from a lot of other relevant details, and by extrapolating from real tendencies to hypothetical end-results, which impart a spurious air of deterministic inevitability. Market equilibrium is as unreal as metabolic equilibrium, which we reach only when we are dead. In the real world of economic activity we are dealing not with an idealized state in which everything has to be exactly as it is, but with a dynamic process in which decisions are being made indeterminately, that is they are influenced by the extent of cooperation which may exist between the partners, and which it is impossible to predict, since perfect economic equilibrium hardly ever exists.[2]

§3.4 Single Swaps

Classical economists considered the one-off transaction between strangers, exchanging copra for beads.[3] But if we specify that it be between strangers, we ignore the importance of social relations, and if we think of economics in terms of occasional swaps, we miss the influence of repetition. The transaction between strangers is indeterminate. Is it a genuine swap, or are the parties constrained through ignorance or fear? Homer has the question 'Are you a trader or a pirate?',[4] and a native of the South Sea Islands, realising that the white man with his enormous ship wanted copra, might well have given him copra in order to have him depart peaceably. An exchange implies mutual obligations involved in the concept of the transfer of ownership. Only if both parties share some concepts and information, can they be deemed to know that what they are doing is an exchange, and not a gift or a forced surrender.[5] Moreover, as we have argued, almost no business transaction is really a one-off one. Often it is one of a continuing series with the same partner, and almost always it is one of a type with other similar partners. In abstracting from the background setting and generality of economic transactions, the classical analysis leaves out too much. We have to have some moral concepts, of non-coercion and of honesty, in order to make sense of any transaction, and in actual fact have built into it some idea of custom and customer, which further directs our thoughts not only to dealing with them honestly and non-violently, but to treating them fairly in other ways too.

Concentration on the single swap leads to a further error, that of undue materialism. We think too much of the exchange of goods, too little of the rendering of services. The very word 'goods' has material connotations, and we still sometimes talk of money as a

---

[2] See Samuel Brittan, *Capitalism with a Human Face*, Aldershot, 1995.

[3] See F.A.Hayek, *The Constitution of Liberty*, London, 1969, p.136.

[4] Thus Nestor to Telemachus in *Odyssey* 3, 73; compare *Thucydides*, I,5,2.

[5] See further ch.4, §4.7.

"medium of exchange". Besides making us uneasy about the sustainability of economic growth in time to come,[6] we are in danger of reifying economics. Material objects have physical properties, such as weight, volume, chemical composition, which they have independently of us, and it is correspondingly easy to ascribe to them an economic value, a quasi-physical property, as objective as weight. We too readily think of material goods having an absolute value, a ghostly number of pounds sterling, in the same way as they really do have an objectively ascertainable number of *avoir du pois* pounds weight or mass. Many errors have arisen from this reification of value, that is, treating it as a material thing with physical properties. It led earlier thinkers to suppose that each thing possessed a natural price, and that this was the just price which ought to be charged everywhere and under all conditions.[7] It has led modern thinkers to suppose that they can redistribute money, in the way that is conceivable to redistribute land, or to allocate to everyone an equal ration of sugar.[8] We are much less inclined to make those mistakes when we are considering the rendering of services; for they are obviously rendered to someone, and only have value because they are valued by him. We also should order our affairs better if we were readier to recognise that it was worth paying for other things than material goods. Many people will part with their money in exchange for a car or a washing machine, but feel, almost instinctively, that it is a waste of money to pay for information; and they are thus led to make bad purchases, when an initial outlay of money on getting good advice would have resulted in their obtaining much better value for their money.

Instead of taking the exchange of goods as the paradigm economic transaction, we should view it as a special case of cooperation, whereby the two parties become better off after the exchange than they were before. Adam Smith argued that it was the division of labour which made exchange of goods a beneficial operation, and in many cases he is right; but there are examples to show that it is not the sole cause. It is not because I am a practised weight-lifter that you ask me to lend a hand: anyone could do it, and I just happen to be around. Often it is not the possession of a special

---

[6] See further below, ch.11, §11.11.

[7] See above, ch.2, §2.5.

[8] See further below, ch.10, §10.4.

skill but the possession of special information that makes us value someone's cooperation; he knows the lie of the land, knows who to ask, whether there is a demand for some particular service, or what the prevailing custom is. Sometimes it is taking responsibility rather than supplying information that is valued. No exchange of goods or provision of information takes place when a piece of silver is hall-marked or a sporting gun proofed, but the warrant of reliability is valued none the less.

§3.5 Maximising

In the classical analysis Economic Man is a maximiser. He is defined as someone who buys in the cheapest and sells in the dearest market, who always seeks the best bargain he can get. Economists assume that rationality consists in maximising one's pay-off. Even in the real world we seek, other things being equal, better bargains, and the traditional view is that the businessman is motivated solely by the desire to maximise his profits. But in the real world I am not always a maximiser. Greedy though I am, I do not have an insatiable appetite for food. I do not seek to maximise my food input. But perhaps money is different. Although there are natural limits to the amount of food I can eat, there is no natural limit to the amount of money I can own. Money, having been fashioned as a uniform transferable token of value can go on being transferred to me without regard to how much I already have. When wealth took material form I might have some problem pulling down my barns and building bigger ones, but with bank accounts there is no difficulty in adding an extra million to my account. Money is what we can all do with more of. Yet even so, we do not always strive to have more. Often we prefer congenial work, greater leisure, more time with the family. Even businessmen do not always seek to maximise their profits, but on occasion, quite rationally, reckon that long-term stability and prosperity are more important than immediate extra profit. As a description of human activity, the claim that we are all maximisers is simply false.

Faced with awkward facts, economists, like other thinkers, often resort to definition. They define rationality games-theoretically, as maximising one's pay-off. Admittedly, some people appear not to, but then no modern thinker supposes that all men are rational. Or perhaps their pay-offs are not what we took them to be: someone who fails to shop round for the best buy simply values his time more than his money. And businessmen who fail to maximise the long-term value of their company are simply being immoral, if not merely incompetent.[9] But the games-theoretical approach is flawed. Although a useful tool of analysis, it distorts the account of our decision-making in redescribing our values so as to make it true by definition that we maximise them. If I am reasonably benevolent, and do something not because I want it but because I know you do, my values have to be re-jigged to incorporate yours too. On occasion that may be an illuminating redescription, but often it appears to impute selfishness quite gratuitously, for it obliterates the difference between my seeking to do something merely because I want it, and my seeking to do it because you want it, or for some other disinterested reason. Worse, it fails to account for the way in which values develop, and have to develop if rationality is to be preserved. For deep mathematical reasons[10] rationality can never be captured completely in any tight definition, and whatever tight definition we give, we can find some action or inference which is not covered by that definition but is evidently rational nonetheless. To define rationality in terms of maximising one's pay-off is, therefore, a mistake. With regard to economic rationality, the definition fails on three counts: the time horizon, the person considered, and the dynamic nature of the values with respect to which the pay-offs are evaluated. We need to know when the pay-offs are to be considered. Many people live only for the present moment, seeking always immediate gratification of immediate wants. But that, though a maximising strategy, is too limited. It is rational to be prudent, and prudence demands that one concern oneself with the future as well as with the present, and it is difficult to resist extending one's concern to the past as well. I am not an individual

---

[9] See below, ch.5, §5.2.

[10] K.Gödel, "Some Basic Theorems on the Foundations of Mathematics and their Implications", in *Collected Works*, vol.III, ed. S.Feferman, Oxford, 1995, pp.308ff.; J.R.Lucas, "The Philosophy of the Reasonable Man", *Philosophical Quarterly*, **13**, 1965, pp.98-106; J.R.Lucas, *The Freedom of the Will*, Oxford, 1970, esp. p.171; R.Penrose, *The Emperor's New Mind*, Oxford, 1989, pp.64ff.; R.Penrose, *Shadows of the Mind*, Oxford, 1994, chs.1-3; J.Myhill, "Some Remarks on the Notion of Proof", *Journal of Philosophy*, LVII, 1960, p. 462, expresses it well: "Gödel's argument establishes that there exist, for any correct formal system containing the arithmetic of natural numbers, correct inferences which cannot be carried out in that system."

unless I have a past as well as looking forward to a future. But also I am not an individual unless I recognise the existence of other individuals, each one using the word 'I' of himself, and having his own first-personal point of view. I am one of "us". And sometimes, as the Prisoners' Dilemma shows,[11] it is irrational to assess courses of action in terms of my pay-offs alone without regard to those of others. If each one of us tries to maximise his own pay-off irrespective of that of others, we all do worse than if each had forgone immediate advantage for the sake of the general good. It is not rational to try to maximise one's own pay-off regardless of others. Rather, it is rational to be reasonable, identifying to some extent with others, and having some regard for their interests as well as those that are peculiarly one's own.

Rationality is dynamic. The Theory of Games gives a useful snapshot at any one moment, but cannot accommodate the way in which we are impelled to develop our values and widen our range of concern. Because we do this, there are points of entry for arguments of justice, of which it is rational to take cognisance. Many people, in the business world as elsewhere, have tried to be fair in their dealings with other men, but have not been able to articulate an adequate rationale of their actions. Responsible decisions about business have been made much more difficult by reason of the false images we form about human nature in general and economics in particular. If we think of men as inherently selfish, always seeking to maximise their profit, concerned primarily to have and to hold material goods, occasionally engaging in one-off exchanges with parties they neither know nor expect to see again, under conditions of perfect competition and information, in which supply and demand are in exact equilibrium, there will be no scope for deciding to do anything other than what the market dictates, and no grounds on which to base a decision other than immediate pecuniary self-advantage. If, however, we think of men as having some, but not all, their values in common, inclined to cooperate repeatedly and over long periods of time, but evaluating cooperative activities each from his own, somewhat different, point of view, usually subject to some, but imperfect, competition, we shall see that there is typically some latitude within which different decisions may be made, and grounds on which to make them, apart

---

[11] See Appendix A.

from the aim of simply getting the mostest—whether for Number One or for one's shareholders.[12]

§3.6 Justice and Freedom

Considerations of justice lead us to seek some transferable form of value, in order that we can redress the way the fruits of cooperation accrue in many of the cases where they naturally accrue to some cooperators more than to others. Hence we need money. But when we think about money, we are led to exalt freedom at the expense of justice, and to form a false image of economic life which leaves the individual with no room for making any other decisions than those the market dictates, and enjoins him in each and every transaction to drive the hardest bargain he can exact.[13]

But it is a false image, and if we think more clearly, we form a less abstract, and more realistic account of economic activity. It is a form of cooperation where the benefits of cooperation would naturally accrue very much more to the one party than to the other, and it would be unreasonable always to expect the other to contribute for altruistic reasons alone. Although within the family, the firm, sometimes within the nation in times of war, sometimes within humanity in times of urgent medical need or danger to life, the shared values are such that the benefit done to the one party is *per se* valuable to the other, and no further recompense than perhaps a 'Thank You' is called for, there are other cases, and it is with these that economics is concerned. It is when I am cooperating with you in the absence of a shared value which makes the cooperation beneficial to both that we call in aid money to make the transaction none the less mutually beneficial. It follows at once that money is, from a very general moral point of view, a Good Thing. Money facilitates cooperation, and makes mankind generally better off. More importantly, economic activity is not, as the classical analysis suggests, inherently selfish. A closer analysis of the nature of cooperation shows that though each party evaluates it from his own point of view according to his own values, he needs

---

[12] The case of maximising shareholders' value is different in as much as it is often maintained that the specific purpose of a public limited company is to do just this. That is a further false image which distorts our understanding of business. It will be discussed in ch.5, §§5.1 and 5.2.

[13] See above, ch.2, §§2.1 and 2.2; ch.3, §§3.1 and 3.3.

to address himself to the other's, and see things from the other point of view, holding himself out as being not just concerned to do as well as he can for himself, but ready to cooperate to the other's advantage, and willing to take trouble to ensure that the other is well served, and the whole transaction is to the other's advantage as well as his own. Instead of viewing the businessman as a self-interested entrepreneur, a profit-maximiser, essentially out for what he can get for Number One, we should view him also as a cooperator, responsive to the two-party nature of business transactions, and ready to meet the other party's wants and needs. The popular view of the businessman being ruled by the law of the jungle should give way to one that sees him more as a cultivator, who responds creatively to the wants and needs of others, enabling them as well as himself to achieve their purposes. He shares values with others and has a rational regard for their point of view, and is not moved by narrow self-interest alone.

Against the False Images

1. Competition is usually imperfect.
2. Information is always imperfect.
3. Perfect equilibrium is never reached.
4. Prices are not precisely determined.
5. Economic justice is indeterminate: the just price and the just wage do not exist.
6. Money is not a substance, but encapsulated choice, and should not exalt freedom at the expense of justice.
7. The reification of economics diminishes the importance of the person in comparison with the exchange of material things; it also diminishes the importance of service in business transactions.
8. Almost no business transaction is really a one-off swap.
9. Rationality does not require that each person should always maximise his pay-off.
10. The concept of a public limited company does not require that long-term profits be always maximised to the exclusion of every other consideration.
11. Cooperation in economic activity is as important as competition.

Chapter 4

Responsibilities

Contents

Abstract

If it is true that:

1) economic determinism is false (in §3.3);
2) a businessman is not obliged, as a matter of rationality, to maximise (in §3.5); and
3) a businessman is not obliged, by his institutional position, to maximise (in §3.5 fn.);

it follows that a businessman has considerable freedom of action, and hence is responsible for what he does. He can be asked 'Why did you do it?', and in some cases 'Why did you not do something to prevent it?'.

Even when someone is not responsible *to* anyone, he is still responsible *for* what he does, but often responsibility is delegated, and in most business enterprises there is a chain of responsibility, with subordinates being responsible to a superior. Such responsibility never excludes all discretion, and the duty to do what one is told does not override all other duties, legal and moral. Trustees and managers have a duty to look after the interests of their beneficiaries and shareholders, but not to the exclusion of all other considerations. The law lays down some as legal duties, but can never spell them all out completely; and legalism tends to diminish personal responsibility, and to suggest, contrary to the actual practice of businessmen, that morality has no place in business dealings, so long as they do not break the law. The cooperative nature of a business enterprise furnishes certain grounds of obligation, both to those within the organization on the basis of the shared values of the organization, and to those external to it on the basis of justice.

45

§4.1 Responsibility To

Economic determinism is false. The iron laws of supply and demand are not made of iron, and indicate tendencies only, without fixing everything, and leaving no room for choice. In economic affairs we are often faced with decisions, and often can choose between a number of alternative courses of action. Moreover, our choice is not completely foreclosed by canons of alleged rationality that would make it irrational to do anything other than maximise our profits, nor by institutional guide-lines, which would lay that down as our only obligation. It is up to us what we do; we are responsible agents, and may fairly be asked to explain why we did as we did.

Responsibility is a difficult concept. Etymologically, to be responsible is to be answerable, obliged to answer the question 'Why did you do it?',[1] explaining and justifying one's actions by giving the reasons why one did them. Because it is concerned with reasons for actions, responsibility, can be shared, without any of those sharing it having less of it than they would if it had not been shared at all.[2] If we both do something together, each of us is responsible for what we do, whereas if we both share a bottle of beer, each has only what the other does not drink.

The obligation to answer the question 'Why did you do it?' varies. In many institutional contexts, especially in business, one person, usually an employee, may have a specific obligation to answer when asked by some particular person, his superior. In such cases the one is *responsible to* the other. It is often supposed that unless I am responsible *to* someone, I am not responsible at all. But that is a mistake. Even if I am not responsible to anyone, I am still responsible. I am not obliged to answer another's questions, but must still answer my own. A responsible businessman may not be obliged to account for his actions to any superior, but still could; in reaching his decisions, he has taken into account the many considerations in favour and against, and, although he may have difficulty in articulating them exactly, can go some way towards saying what they are. And in explaining them, if only to himself, he justifies them. The actions of a responsible businessman are justifiable, and even if he is not obliged to justify them to anyone, they will stand up under scrutiny none the less.

---

[1] See, more fully, J.R.Lucas, *Responsibility*, Oxford, 1993, pbk. 1995.

[2] Compare values in ch.1, §1.3.

We have chains of responsibility, with subordinates being responsible *to* their immediate superior, and through him to the top management. The superior is entitled not only to ask why actions were done, and to assess the account given and blame the subordinate if it is inadequate, but also to give the subordinate instructions for the future, assigning further duties and responsibilities and saying how they are to be discharged. And, correlatively, because his subordinates are carrying out his instructions, he is responsible to his superiors for what they do. It is his business to see that they do not make a mess of things, and he has to carry the can if they do.

Although a superior is entitled to call his subordinates to account, there are limits both to the extent to which he can require subordinates to justify their actions, and to the instructions he may properly give. He may tell his secretary to go to a stationer and get some paper-clips. In commissioning her, he not only instructs her, but authorises her to use her discretion in carrying out the commission. She is to decide when to cross the road. If the nearest stationer is out of paper-clips, and she takes longer to go on to the next, that, in the absence of an explicit instruction to the contrary, is for her to decide. Provided she comes back with the paper-clips in reasonable time without having dallied, she cannot be taken to task, or asked to justify the myriad of minor decisions she had to take in carrying out the commission. In commissioning her he implicitly gave her discretion to make these minor decisions as she thought best. How much discretion a commission confers depends on the nature of the commission and the circumstances of the case, but always there is some discretion.

It follows that the ultimate responsibility, of the subordinate is never completely abolished. Although normally, if challenged, the secretary can say simply "The boss told me to", the defence of superior orders has limits. It gives the subordinate a *prima facie* adequate answer to the question 'Why did you do it?', but not a conclusive one. There could be a further 'but': 'but he clearly did not mean it', or 'but he would have had second thoughts about it', or 'but it was illegal', or 'but it was immoral'. Although it is the duty of a secretary to do what her superior tells her to do, it is not an absolutely overriding one, but, rather, has to be set in a general context of interpreting his instructions in the light of the situation. In the same way an instruction to contravene the law of the land does not override the duty to obey the law of the land, nor does an instruction to contravene the moral law override the duty to obey that. The secretary may be a subordinate, but she is still a person, who is therefore ultimately responsible for all she does. In commissioning her to carry out any task, she is implicitly given some discretion to use her own judgement is discharging the commission: and in commissioning her to do anything, her autonomous responsibility for all her actions is similarly to be respected. If an amoral tool is wanted, a robot should be bought.[3]

§4.2 Responsibility For

If you do something, you can be asked why you did it. It does not follow that if you do not do something you can equally be asked why you did not do it. Some modern philosophers—utilitarians, for example—miss this point, and argue that we should do a cost-benefit analysis of all the alternatives open to us, and choose the one that will maximise human happiness. In that case we could be asked why we had failed to do all sorts of actions, and blamed unless we could show that they would have produced less happiness than what we actually did. This doctrine of unlimited negative responsibility lands an impossible burden on every decision-maker. There are all sorts of things that might have been done and were not, and some of them, for all we know, might have been productive of much human happiness. Certainly there is much unalleviated human misery. But human beings are limited. No one of us can do everything, or think of everything. We cannot even effectively carry out the injunction to do all we can. If we are to accomplish anything at all, we have to concentrate our efforts, confining our attention to achieving those limited aims that are within our power. Before we can be required to answer the question 'Why did you not do it?', we are entitled to ask 'Why should I?'. We can be blamed for leaving undone those things we ought to have done, but not for all the innumerable things we might possibly have done, which, had we done them, would have turned out well.

Except at the lowest level, businessmen do take on some negative responsibilities. They not only do as they are told, but see to it that nothing goes wrong in the area for which they take responsibility, being always ready to take remedial action to prevent untoward events happening. *Being always ready* implies a certain

---

[3] See further below, ch.6, §§6.2-6.6.

degree of alertness which characterizes the business executive in contrast to the person paid simply to perform routine tasks. The senior executive has to be looking round all the time to see if there is anything arising that he needs to deal with. He can never be completely switched off. The Latin word for business, *negotium*, captures this sense of never being entirely at leisure, which goes with taking on the responsibility for something.[4]

With this commitment to continual wariness goes a wide discretion about what measures to adopt in dealing with events as they occur. If you are responsible for recruitment, it is very largely up to you to take the appropriate steps to attract suitable applicants, interview them, and select the most suitable within fairly broad outlines laid down by the directors. Wide responsibilities and detailed accountability are not compatible. There is always a trade-off between detailed accountability and general responsibility for the success of the commission. If the secretary is told she must go to a particular shop, and it is out of paper-clips, she is not to blame if she returns empty-handed. If she is to be sure she succeeds in getting paper-clips, she must have some discretion over the means she adopts to get them. She should not be called to account for having gone to Rymans rather than W.H. Smith. If asked why she did, she can properly reply "You told me to get some paper-clips, and that is what I did."[5]

The last point has in recent years been forgotten. The word 'accountability' has been much used, without any understanding of its conceptual limitations, or recognition of the wide discretion that great responsibility requires. We can ask questions, but we cannot ask many questions all at once, and need to determine what questions are, and what are not, appropriate to ask in calling someone to account. If we press very detailed questions—'Why did you cross the road at the traffic lights and not at the zebra crossing?'— we withdraw the discretion that normally goes with the commission, and thereby narrow the commission to the carrying out of the more detailed instructions. Conversely, if we give a manager the responsibility for a wide range of matters, we implicitly accept his judgement about how best to deal with them, and provided the

---

[4] See above, ch.2, §2.2.

[5] D.A.Hay, *Economics today*, Leicester, 1989, ch.5, §6, p.204, makes this point with respect to centralised planned economies

things he is responsible for go well, we should not press him to justify further the decisions he took. It wastes time. It engenders a spirit of defensiveness in the person being called to account,[6] because it indicates a certain lack of trust. It is a good practice to delegate responsibility as much as possible, assigning to each person the widest responsibility he is capable of undertaking.[7] Besides respecting the individual's autonomy, and treating him not merely as a means, but as an end in himself, it is also a counsel of prudence—people do not want to do things because they are told to, but would rather decide for themselves what needs to be done—and if we give people more responsibility, they will throw themselves more whole-heartedly into the job.

§4.3 Common Concerns

In deliberating about what to do, and in justifying past decisions, at least to himself if not to any one else, a businessman weighs arguments for and against different courses of action. Some of these arguments arise from the cooperative nature of business. Two grounds of obligation have emerged. In the first place the parties to a business transaction, are never completely external to each other but have some values in common, which constitute some basis for ethical consideration. And, secondly, although the two parties may have significantly different values, the very nature of their transaction is other-directed, and carries with it some concern for the other's point of view.

Once we recognise that the parties to a business transaction always have some values in common, it is easier to accept that such shared values as there are can provide the decision-maker with arguments as to what he ought to do. What these values are depends on the relationship between the parties and the context in which they are dealing with each other. There is a wide continuum of cases, from the relationship between currency dealers for whom honesty is almost the only shared value, to monetary transactions between members of a family or within the same group of

---

[6] See further below, ch.12, §12.2.

[7] Charles Handy, *The Empty Raincoat*, London, 1995, p.115, quotes a papal encyclical, *Quadragesimo Anno*, 1941, "It is an injustice, a grave evil and a disturbance of right order, for a larger and higher organisation to arrogate to itself functions which can be performed efficiently by smaller and lower bodies . . " and says that this is the real principle of "subsidiarity".

firms where the shared values predominate, and money is transferred only to meet expenses or equalise accounts. In between are many cases where there is a long-standing partnership with shared concerns for the good name of the trade, the prosperity of the local community, the non-pollution of the environment, and the like, which afford a common basis on which agreements may be reached.

§4.4 The Other's Point of View

In so far as business relations are external, the grounds of obligation are different. They arise from the fact that economic activity is also other-directed. They are often expressed as counsels of prudence: if I do business with you, I am doing something for you, something you want, and unless I do it to your satisfaction, I shall not long continue as your business partner. But it is also an argument of justice, arising from the two-sided nature of business: I cannot coherently expect you to do business with me solely for my sake. It is built into the concept of a business transaction that it should be for your benefit as well as mine, and if I am to make sense of what I am doing, I must take to heart your point of view as well as mine, and aim to do what should be reasonably acceptable to you as well as to me.

The word 'reasonably' needs to be stressed. Other people might like it if they always got the best of the bargain, and I the worst. That is a liking I do not need to accommodate. What I do need to do is to address myself to each party who may be adversely affected by a decision of mine, and assess the reasons I could give him for the decision I take. Often they are good reasons, though unwelcome to him. I sack the employee because he is negligent; I take the customer to court because he has not paid his bill; I send back the supplier's goods because they are not up to the standard agreed upon. But by the same token, I pay the employee more if he has worked overtime, even though I did not promise to beforehand; I give the customer a replacement or his money back if the goods I sold him are defective or unsatisfactory; I pay the supplier on time, and give him ample warning if I am going to cease buying from him. What exactly my obligations are will depend very much on circumstances and context. Quite often, as we saw in Chapter 1,[8] considerations conflict, and it is difficult to decide between them.

---

[8] §1.2.

That is not denied. Here the only point being made is that they do
arise, and arise from the nature of business. A businessman trying
to decide what to do should consider not only arguments about
costs and profits, but wider arguments too, which are grounded in
the fact that he is doing business with other people, and so needs
to take into account the general point of view that others might be
reasonably expected to have. This does not imply consensus at all
costs, but it does imply at the outset of any business negotiation a
clear declaration of intent on the part of both parties as to where
they stand, that is, what their views are regarding the desired
outcome of the negotiation they are about to begin.

§4.5 Grounds of Obligation

In taking decisions a businessman has many considerations to bear
in mind. Typically now they are structured by the role he occupies as employee, colleague, manager, or director. It was different
centuries ago, when most businesses were run by men who were
their own masters, and were perfectly free to apply on weekdays
the precepts they had heard and adopted on Sundays. It might
be a moral problem whether or not to sack a sick workman, but it
was a simple moral problem, uncomplicated by a structure of roles
and responsibilities. But a manager now does not have the same
absolute discretion. He has duties to his superiors, to his directors,
to his shareholders, which certainly restrict his freedom of action,
and which may seem to leave him no alternative but that of sacking
an unprofitable employee. Yet he feels that the arguments are not
all one way, and would like to be able to think clearly through a
maze of conflicting responsibilities and obligations. Some of them
are directed towards particular classes of person, sometimes called
"stakeholder", and some attach to certain capacities or roles.. C.B.
Handy distinguishes six different sorts of stakeholder, whose interests ought to be considered by those taking decisions: financiers,
employees, suppliers, customers, the environment, and society as
a whole; he argues that these six classes constitute a hexagon,
within which a decision-maker has to balance different, and sometimes conflicting, obligations.[9] Further distinctions may be drawn.

---

[9] Charles Handy, *The Empty Raincoat*, London, 1995, pp.130-131, p.143. In
an earlier generation A.A.Berle and G.C.Means (*The Modern Corporation
and Private Property*, New York, 1935, Book IV, ch.4, p.356) had said

Shareholders are in a different position from other creditors. Obligations to society comprise obligations to the local community, to the nation and perhaps to the international community and the whole of mankind. Many firms also recognise some obligation to their industry or trade. There are certain obligations, as well as certain non-obligations, to competitors.

Obligations to shareholders and employees, as well as obligations of shareholders and employees, are primarily internal obligations, arising out of shared values. Obligations to customers, suppliers and competitors are primarily external obligations, arising from our recognition of the validity of the other person's point of view as a necessary condition of making coherent sense of business activity. But in each of these cases some of the other considerations also apply, and the remainder are evidently mixed cases.

Besides obligations, business transactions may generate non-obligations. This is nothing strange: if I am playing chess with you, I am not under an obligation to point out that if you do not move your queen, I shall be able to fork it next turn;[10] if I am playing rugger, I have no duty to cooperate with the opposing team's efforts to score a try. So, too, I do not have to point out to my competitors their mistakes as I would to a friend or even a casual passer-by. The structure of business, like that of games and competitions, and also like that of the law courts, incorporates an adversarial element which not only alters our obligations, but actually suspends some. We need to recognise the considerations which a businessman can properly put out of mind; else he will be immersed in a babel of arguments, unable to think through them clearly, and liable to subside into either a soft emotional mush or a hard-nosed unconcern with genuine obligations. Like the procedure of the law courts, the world of business takes account of the limited range of the individual's concerns, and licenses individual competition for partial ends within an overall structure aiming at an impartial good. Although the importance of cooperation has been insufficiently recognised in Anglo-Saxon thought, competition

"Neither the claims of ownership nor those of control < *i.e.* management> can stand against the paramount interests of the community", but did not distinguish different sections of the community with their different special interests.

[10] See further below, ch.6, §6.4.

is important also. It would not be fair if the defence lawyer cooperated with the prosecution to the extent of not putting the best case he could for the accused, and American anti-trust legislation protects the consumer against producers cooperating to form cartels. The non-obligations of competition, however, are not absolute.[11] I still have an obligation not to cheat, not to commit fouls, not to commit perjury. Our sense of fair play in games is a useful guide, and the practice of the law courts may illuminate the duty of disclosure as it applies in business.[12]

Obligations, like other considerations, can conflict.[13] A duty of confidentiality to one's employer may conflict with a duty of honesty to a customer. As a father, a friend, a trustee, an executor, an employee, a citizen, a juryman, I may have duties which I should not otherwise have, and which may run counter to ones I normally acknowledge: I cannot as a juryman follow the injunction of the Sermon on the Mount "Judge not that ye be not judged"; I cannot as an employee raid the petty cash for the benefit of a beggar; if I am a trustee or an executor I have a duty not to be generous at the expense of the beneficiaries or legatees; and by a further extension of the same argument the bursar of a college or a treasurer of a charity may feel impelled to allow ribbon development on the land entrusted to his care because his duty is to maximise revenue, not to preserve the environment. We are tempted to resolve these conflicts, by establishing a simple hierarchy of obligations, and by attaching them rigidly to roles. But that is a mistake. Often the circumstances of the case affect the priority to be given to different obligations. A confidential secretary may be under an obligation not to reveal her boss's misdemeanours, even though they contravene the law, whereas a civil servant may be right to blow the whistle when the Government is trying to lie to Parliament.[14] It would be wrong for the bursar of a college or the Church Commissioners to divert their funds to providing low-cost housing for the poor, or some other good cause, but they are properly sensitive to charges that the houses they own are being used as brothels, though sometimes feeling that their duty as trustees really requires them to turn a blind eye to what is going on, provided the shekels keep coming in to pay the vicars' stipends.

[11] See further, ch.7, §7.4.

[12] See further, ch.6, §6.5.

[13] Ch.1, §1.2.

[14] See further, ch.6, §6.6.

§4.6 Trusteeship

The law has been slow to accept the argument of §1 of this chapter that responsibility implies a discretion that cannot be altogether fettered by exact rules, and has sought to circumscribe the discretion of trustees and managers rigidly. The standard legal form of the modern business enterprise, the public limited company, regards directors as trustees, but has taken over an unduly limited view of their role. The story is told of an Oxford don who was accustomed every year to go to Scotland with a trunk full of books to read during the Long Vac. One year a zealous employee of the railway company weighed his trunk, and charged a higher price. The don protested that he had been taking the same load every year and had always been charged less, but after a lengthy altercation was persuaded that the employee was right, whereupon he wrote out a cheque to the company to cover all the underpayments in previous years. The cheque was returned with a courteous letter from the directors, saying that in the special circumstances of the case they were waiving payment for years gone by. The don sent the cheque back with a curt note, saying that the money was not for the directors, but the shareholders. On that view there would be no room for managers to take into consideration any ethical arguments. Provided an action was legal, the only question would be whether it would maximise profits. If it would, it should be done: if not, not.

This view has been developed gradually through a number of stages, some involving *ad hoc* legislation, from earlier concepts of trusteeship, and has been distorted by the fear that if any discretion were allowed, too much would be claimed. In time past it seemed reasonable to charge executors with the duty of carrying out the testator's wishes rapidly and precisely, discharging his legal obligations, and if any further decisions were called for, acting vicariously in his interests, and leaving it to his legatees to do anything else that might seem appropriate. But legal obligations do not exhaust moral obligation,[15] and the concept of interest is not as determinate as has been thought.[16] What if after making his will, the testator had a long and incapacitating illness, in which he was devotedly looked after by a retainer? Should not she have

---

[15] See next section and ch.9, §9.3 below.

[16] See above, ch.1, §1.4.

some recognition from his estate? Is it in the interests of the deceased to have a decent funeral? a tombstone? a good reputation? As we move from the death-bed disposition of worldly goods to the long drawn-out winding up of an estate according to a will made many years earlier, it becomes less reasonable, indeed, less feasible, to limit the discretion of the executors rigidly. We begin to want them to take decisions on behalf of the testator in accordance with his general wishes, but not rigidly tied by the letter of a document drawn up years before and not anticipating the situation actually obtaining at the time of death. The executor does not, and should not, have complete discretion—he cannot decide to give the estate to a dog's home instead of to the heirs, But he has to have some, and it cannot be adequately characterized in terms of vicarious self-interest alone, unless that self-interest is glossed as including a man's concern that actions done in his name are ones he would have been willing to be responsible for and could have happily lived with.

The same is true of trustees, and of devolved duties generally. In commissioning someone to do something we cannot totally exclude either his discretion as to how he should act, or his responsibility for what he does. There are, indeed, many things I can commission you to do, and if asked why you did them, you can properly justify them on the grounds of my having told you to do them. But to some actions there are moral objections which cannot be overridden by any defence of superior orders. Many such objections are enshrined in the law, and it is generally recognised that trustees and agents must act within the law. But the law is necessarily an incomplete articulation of our basic morality, and there are always some actions not actually prohibited by law but evidently wrong none the less, and these we cannot commission another to undertake. It follows that we cannot adequately specify any commission or trust in terms that exclude moral considerations altogether. If I commission you to look after my interests, there is an implicit restriction that what you are to do must be not only legal but moral. For you are a moral agent, and though I can properly ask you to do things you would not otherwise do, and even land you in situations of moral conflict, I cannot ask you to abrogate your status as a moral being.

The degree of moral discretion and autonomous responsibility varies very much with the commission.[17] It is minimal in the discharge of specific tasks over a short period of time—when I tell

[17] See above, §§1,2 of this chapter.

a secretary to go to a stationer and get some paper-clips, there is hardly any point of entry for serious moral argument. But it increases as the commission becomes more wide-ranging and long-term. Trustees and boards of directors cannot be coherently given commissions which appear to exclude all discretion in maximising profits. If they are to be trusted with the assets of the charity or the shareholders, they must be trusted also to forbear on occasion from driving the hardest bargain possible with their employees, from polluting the environment, from devastating the local community. They cannot be coherently asked to exercise their judgement in the one respect without being allowed to exercise it in the other.

But we are chary of opening any loophole. Moral obligations, it is often held, are overriding. But also, it is widely held in the aftermath of logical positivism, that they are simply arbitrary personal commitments. If we allow executors and trustees to exercise discretion, may not they become prey to an overmastering conviction that the care of dogs is the sole duty of man? Many moral principles have been strongly held in the present age, in favour of the environment or vegetarianism, against tobacco or *apartheid*, which are not discreditable, but not part either of the common stock of morality that all reasonable men accept. If trustees and managers are allowed to take moral principles into consideration, they may sacrifice the beneficiaries' interests in the pursuit of moral ideals which the beneficiaries may well not share. And so it seemed right to say that the duty of trustees was to be actuated solely by consideration of what was in the best interests of the beneficiaries, and not to fetter their discretion by any antecedent moral or political decisions.[18] But the best interests are not to be computed in monetary terms alone. Just as my executors would not be serving my interests by cheese-paring on my funeral, or by showing gross ingratitude to those who had cared for me at the end of my life, so generally the interests of beneficiaries cannot be adequately defined so as to exclude all moral considerations. As we shall see, there is no sharp dividing line between morality and enlightened self-interest.[19] This was recognised by the courts. Lord Murray in *Martin v. City of Edinburgh District Council* (1989), said "I cannot conceive that trustees have an unqualified . . . duty simply

---

[18] *Cowan v. Scargill* [1985] Ch.270.

[19] Ch.13, §13.3.

to invest Trust Funds in the most profitable investment available. To accept that without qualification would, in my view, involve substituting the discretion of financial advisers for the discretion of trustees."[20] Lord Murray distinguished the claim that trustees had no discretion from the valid point that their duty was to consider the interests, widely construed, of the beneficiaries, and not impose antecedent moral or political views of their own. Trustees cannot divest themselves of all personal preferences, of all political beliefs, and of all moral, religious or other conscientiously held principles, but should do their best to exercise fair and impartial judgement on the merits of the issue before them. It is a feasible task provided morality is reasonable, and not just a matter of arbitrary choice.[21] So long as they can distinguish in moral, as in prudential, deliberation those reasons that are omni-personal and worthy of acceptance by all reasonable men, they can deliberate vicariously on the part of another, and in seeking his best interests, attempt not simply to maximise pecuniary profit, but, taking into account moral considerations, aim to secure profits in a morally responsible way. The same applies to businessmen in as much as they hold in trust the assets of the company for which they are responsible.

We thus are being led to a fuller concept of the public limited company, and of corporations generally. Corporations may have no souls, but they do have bodies—that is to say, they are incorporate as legal personalities, they are centres of decision-making. We can speak of ICI or General Motors doing something, and can ask why they do it, and assess their answers. In this sense corporations are agents in the same way as individual persons are, and can be held accountable for their actions, and their managers cannot claim that moral considerations should be altogether excluded in reaching decisions on their behalf.

---

[20] *Scots Law Times*, 20 May, 1988, p.334 I, quoted by Richard Harries, *Is There a Gospel for the Rich?*, London 1992, p.146.

[21] See next section

§4.7 Legalism and Morality

Some thinkers will accept the argument of the previous section only in so far as it reports a change in the law, and are unwilling to accept that managers and trustees have some further discretion which the law does not determine precisely. In their view it is the function of the law to indicate the limits of acceptable business practice, and once the law has been laid down, the businessman is free—indeed, obliged—to pursue profits within the limits laid down by law. Thus Milton Friedman says:[22]

> In . . . (a free) economy, there is one and only one social responsibility of business—to use its resources and engage in activities designed to increase its profits so long as it stays within the rules of the game, which is to say, engages in open and free competition without deception or fraud.

It is a view widely held, but mistaken none the less. In the first place, the law needs to be predictable, and hence rigid. Often it is formulated in a code, and like codes in general, suffers from the defect of not covering all cases adequately.[23] Moreover, for reasons which will appear later,[24] the law tends to set a minimal standard. And in any case, reliance on the law is not a substitute for morality, but presupposes it.

Two positivist doctrines, logical positivism and legal positivism, lie behind the rejection of moral responsibility in favour of bare compliance with the law. Logical positivism maintained that moral terms were merely emotive, attempts to manipulate the attitudes of others in some desired direction, and that moral arguments lacked cogency, and could always be ignored.[25] Law, by contrast, is definite and real, a hard external constraint, akin to those of the natural world, and a fit subject of study in the social sciences. Although few philosophers accept the tenets of logical positivism now, it remains a pervasive background to the thought of many others. But it would lie outside the scope of this work to adduce the arguments against it.

---

[22] Milton Friedman, *Capitalism and Freedom*, University of Chicago Press, 1962, p.133; quoted, Elaine Sternberg, *Just Business*, Little, Brown and Company, London, 1994, p.30.

[23] See below, ch.9, §9.1.

[24] In ch.9, §9.3.

[25] They can—at a cost; see below, ch.13, §§13.3 and 13.6.

Legal positivism insists upon the separation of law from morals. It confuses a real distinction with a complete separation: it is true and important that the law is different from morality, but it does not follow that they have no close connexion. We generally acknowledge that there is a moral obligation to obey the law, and that almost every legal system enshrines much moral teaching, and that moral considerations have an important influence on the interpretation and development of the law. To insist that there should be no connexion is to misconstrue the rationale of the law, seeing the law as essentially imposed from outside by the arbitrary will of the sovereign, something we cannot afford to disregard but need not in any sense internalise, or make our own. But to see the law as entirely external is to take too limited a view. It is the view of the Bad Man, who is told by his solicitor what he cannot get away with. For most people, however, the law is not just imposed from outside. Although it needs on occasion to be enforced on those who are recalcitrant, it has developed from within society, and could not work unless most people abided by it and cooperated with it voluntarily. It is only in exceptional cases that the bailiffs have to be called in, and although it is important that in such cases they are available to act as a long stop, hardly any judgements could be enforced if nobody would obey them until actually coerced. We need the uncoerced cooperation of witnesses, judges, magistrates and jurymen, if the legal system is to work at all. So, although it is a tautology that people are legally free to do whatever they see fit to do within the limits set by the law, it is very far from a tautology that they are morally free to do whatever is within the limits set by the law. Society only functions if most people most of the time are guided by the spirit, rather than just the letter, of the law. If people only told the truth when they were under oath in court, and only kept their word when it was set down in a legally enforceable contract, society would break down.

And so would business. The honesty enjoined by business ethics is the honesty understood by ordinary morality, not that whose breach is punishable by law. Even the most external transactions are governed by some moral principles in favour of honesty and against violence.[26] If it were only obedience to law that was required, international trade would be impossible, and in particular the paradigm example of exchanging beads for copra would not

---

[26] Ch.3, §3.4.

make sense. Commerce can only take place within some shared moral understandings, which, though in come cases minimal, are ineliminable.

Moral scepticism and legal positivism have been bad guides. Business, and life generally, would be impossible if people did not keep their word, and could not be relied upon to refrain from bad actions unless constrained by law. We need to unlearn the specious arguments of the present age—the city operator who pleaded that it was only a gentlemen's agreement, and so he was not bound by it, or the head of an Oxford college who said that since the undertaking given to the University constituted only a moral obligation, the college was not bound by it. Such contentions show a lamentable lack of understanding of the responsibilities of engaging in the business of the world. If a man is not a man of his word, his words are idle, and negotiations with him are sham.

Behind these sceptical arguments lies an individualist yearning for freedom from all internal and external constraints. The individualist would like to be free to do whatever he wants to do, without having to internalise all the clinging inhibitions of moral and social life. Such an outlook is possible for Robinson Crusoe, but not for a businessman engaged in commerce with other people, constantly needing to cooperate, and having to take account of those he is cooperating with, often in situations too complicated to be adequately covered by any law or code. A responsible decision-maker has to internalise the considerations that bear on the decisions he is called upon to make. He cannot rely exclusively on a legal code which tells him exactly what he may or may not do in any situation.

§4.8 Duty and Obligation

We are responsible. We cannot brush off the question 'Why did you do it?' by saying 'I had no alternative'. Although market forces limit what a businessman can do, he has some freedom of manoeuvre. And although he is entrusted with the commission of securing profitability, that commission does not override all other obligations, which we identified in §5 of this chapter. It is tempting to describe these as duties. Certainly, we could tax a businessman to explain why he had failed to consider his shareholders, his employees, his locality, his country, or the environment, and if he brushed off the question with 'Why should I? It is none of my business', his defence would sound hollow. But the word 'duty' denotes a stringency of obligation that often does not obtain. The duties of non-violence and of honesty are stringent, but many of the obligations we have identified are *prima facie* only[27] and may be overridden by others. But even though they may be overridden, they remain weighty, and require careful consideration.

—o0o—

The responsibilities of a businessman are to:
1. Shareholders
2. Employees
3. Customers
4. Suppliers and creditors
5. Competitors
6. Industry or trade
7. Local community (= neighbours)
8. Nation
9. Mankind (Third World and Environment)

---

[27] See above, ch.1, §1.2.

Chapter 5
Shares

Contents

Abstract

Contrary to a widespread belief, shareholders do not own their companies in a strict sense, and it is not the sole or overriding duty of managers to maximise owner value in the long term, though sustained profitability is, for almost all companies, a prime purpose, and the case for their having other responsibilities has to be argued.

Tradeable shares are not the only possible way of having a stake in a company, and some alternative might be better, but there are strong pressures for being able to trade shares, since they are financial assets, and if they can be traded some people will trade in them solely in the hopes of making short-term gains. The ownership of shares nevertheless confers responsibilities as well as rights, and the short-termism of the large institutional investors is a serious defect of current financial practice. Shareholders share a general responsibility for what their company does, and the problems of ethical investment are real, but, as in all business transactions, limited by reason of the impersonality of the market place, itself stemming from a recognition of its often being for the other party to make decisions.

§5.1 Limited Liability

The limited liability company is an artificial creation. Its chief purpose was to enable investors to take limited risks with their funds. They could buy shares in a limited liability company without being personally liable for its debts if it became insolvent, as they would have been in a traditional partnership. They might lose their investment, but nothing more. It thus became much less risky to invest, and enormous sums of risk capital were unlocked, which financed the industrial revolution, and made possible the economic prosperity of the present age. The public interest was well served by the invention of the limited liability company.

63

But it remains an artificial creation. If corporations have no souls, they have no natural rights either. Americans believe that human beings have a human right to the pursuit of happiness, which is often understood as the pursuit of money, and the Supreme Court ruled that corporations were persons with a consequent constitutional right to equal treatment in every State of the Union.[1] But it does not follow. It is perfectly fair to treat corporations differently from the way we treat human beings, to tax them differently, and to deny them human rights to equal treatment under the law. They are not human. That is not to say that various principles of justice and equity do not apply. From the very fact that we recognise corporate decisions and corporate actions, certain consequences of public morality and legal principle flow. But the way they apply depends on the way limited liability companies are constituted, and the legal and social framework within which they operate.

It is often supposed that public limited companies are owned by the shareholders, and that therefore the shareholders have a right to have their owner value maximised, and the managers a corresponding duty that overrides all other duties.[2] But the shareholders do not, in a strict sense of the term, "own" the company. The legal position was stated by Lord Justice Evershed, in *Short v. Treasury Commissioners* (1947): "Shareholders are not in the eye of the law part owners of the undertaking. The undertaking is something different from the totality of its shareholdings"[3] And, when we think about it, this is obvious and right. Other corporations—the National Trust, the Consumers' Association, Corpus Christi College Cambridge, the Friends of Durham Cathedral—are not "owned" by

---

[1] See *Metropolitan Life Insurance v. Ward*, 470 U.S. 869 (1985), and the cases there cited; much earlier, in 1869 *Paul v. Virginia*, 8 Wall.168 had held that a corporation is not a person as regards the privileges and immunities clause of Article IV §2 of the Constitution, but later cases held that it was under the 14th Amendment.

[2] Tom Sorell and John Hendry, *Business Ethics*, Butterworth Heinmann, Oxford, 1994, ch.5, p.113f.

[3] Quoted by Charles Handy, *The Empty Raincoat*, London, 1995, p.145, and by Tom Sorell and John Hendry, *Business Ethics*, Butterworth Heinmann, Oxford, 1994, p.137. See also Lord Eustace Percy, *The Unknown State*, Oxford University Press, London, 1944, p.37.

their members. A public limited company is not a natural person but a legally constituted one, by means of articles of association, with the shareholders as members with definite rights and responsibilities, but only those laid down. In particular, the shareholders are not responsible for the debts of the company in the way they would be if they were owners. Their liability is limited: so also are their rights.[4] What shareholders own are shares: these have value on account of those rights, but the relationship is more complicated than that of simple ownership, and will be examined more closely in §4 of this chapter.

§5.2 Duties of Managers to Shareholders

Even if shareholders do not, strictly speaking, actually own their company, it is widely held that the only consideration that should weigh with a manager of a company is to maximise shareholders' value. It is one of the false images that distort our understanding of business. Thus Elaine Sternberg states:

> The defining purpose of business is to maximise owners' value over the long term by selling goods or services.[5]

But if we define business in this way, can we be sure that the term thus defined covers all the transactions we should normally count as business transactions? There are institutions that are not profit-making, and may well do business with each other. In each case there are rights and duties, which we should normally consider under the heading of business ethics: I have duties towards my employer, whether I am employed by ICI or the local comprehensive school.

Elaine Sternberg's definition of business is open to the objection, then, that it leaves out many transactions which we should normally call business transactions. It also fails to cover the actual practice of many ordinary profit-making businesses. Many

---

[4] For a fuller discussion, see Tom Sorell and John Hendry, *Business Ethics*, Butterworth Heinmann, Oxford, 1994, ch.5, and earlier A.A.Berle and G.C.Means, *The Modern Corporation and Private Property*, New York, 1935, esp. Book II, and Book IV, ch.4. Berle and Means regard not the legal limitation of liability, but the effective surrender of control, as the justification for denying shareholders full rights of ownership.

[5] Elaine Sternberg, *Just Business*, Little, Brown and Company, London, 1994, p.32.

businessmen do not act on the principle of maximising profits irrespective of other considerations: they do not strike the hardest bargain they can with their employees, and often make donations to charitable causes. It is often argued that in so doing they are acting in the long-term interests of the company, and that the well-treated employee will work better, or that the public image of the firm will benefit if it sponsors concerts, and this in turn will bring in more business. That may be so. But such considerations are only rationalisations none the less, attempting to justify, under the guise of self-interest, decisions taken on other, wider but none the less relevant grounds. We can see that they are rationalisations by contrasting the care taken, when proposals genuinely based on long-term profitability are under consideration, to assess very accurately the likely costs and benefits, with the cursory justifications given when it is a question of making some donation to, say, a local football club. No careful balance sheet of likely returns to be set against the cost are drawn up. The decision is really taken on quite other grounds, and the claim that it will improve the firm's standing in the community is put forward only to give it an air of business respectability.

The objection that the definition does not fit the facts can be parried by allowing that many businessmen do not act so as to maximise owner value over the long term, but maintaining that they should. Elaine Sternberg is quite clear on this point:

> Managers who employ funds for anything other than the legitimate business objective are simply embezzling: in using other people's money for their own purposes, they are depriving owners of their property as surely as if they had dipped their hands into the till.[6]

But then some argument is needed, not just a stipulative definition.

A duty to maximise profits cannot be read out of some imputed right of ownership, nor from some supposed duty of managers as trustees.[7] The purpose of the company, and the duties of the managers are to be read out, rather, from the articles of association, qualified in the way that fiduciary duties generally are. There could be companies whose sole purpose was to make the greatest profit possible, but most companies are associations for the purpose of

---

[6] Elaine Sternberg, *Just Business*, Little, Brown and Company, London, 1994, ch.2, p.41.

[7] See ch.4, §4.6.

trade, or manufacture, or the provision of services, which implicitly commits them to the responsibilities of that line of business, and authorises the directors and managers to use their discretion in discharging those responsibilities.[8]

Of course, almost all companies seek to make profits. None of the arguments adduced is intended to deny that, or to suggest that profitability is not a prime concern of those engaged in business. All that is being denied is that it is the sole purpose, or that it should override all other considerations. Just as an individual is generally entitled to pursue his own purposes, but needs to consider other people in so doing, and not only should not deceive or defraud them, but place some weight in not putting them out and in not disappointing their reasonable expectations, so should businessmen in their business capacities. The fact that they are employed as managers by public limited companies does not abrogate their being responsible for the way they discharge their fiduciary commission, and the fact that they are commissioned to carry on some business profitably does not occlude or override their peripheral obligations.

Peripheral obligations are peripheral. Behind the mistaken arguments of those who maintain that the managers' sole and overriding duty is to their shareholders is a fear that directors may be tempted to play the *grand seigneur* and disburse their shareholders' money in patronising good causes to their own emotional satisfaction but with little benefit for the shareholders. It is a legitimate worry. Although it is perfectly possible for companies to be run for the benefit of their employees, like the John Lewis partnership, or for the benefit of the locality, or, indeed, in order to promote artistic endeavour, few companies are incorporated for these purposes. In most cases companies are run for profit, and should be managed so as to be profitable. It does not follow that the company must chisel its employees, short-change its customers, or generally seek to screw the last farthing out of all and sundry. And similarly, it does not follow that it must do nothing for the locality, the trade, or the environment. But it does follow that a good case has to be made out before the company disburses its money on any such objects. It is not a matter of the directors' generosity, but of the company's having some responsibility in view of its relations with those concerned, its sphere of operations, or its place in the community.

---

[8] See ch.4, §§4.1 and 4.2.

It is not a coherent commission to make it the obligation of managers and directors to maximise profits at all costs. It is reasonable to commission someone to pursue profits, but incoherent to deny him all discretion to take other factors into account in carrying out the general commission. Directors and managers have duties, fairly complicated ones, to protect shareholders' interests from insider trading, market manipulation, and other forms of double dealing. But they cannot be expected to internalise and honour these obligations and to ignore all others absolutely. Solicitous they should be of their shareholders' interests, but their solicitude towards them should be part of a more general solicitude.

§5.3 Alternatives to Tradeable Shares

Since the limited liability company is an artificial creation, we can consider whether some different invention would serve our purposes better.

> Here is the most urgent challenge to political invention ever offered to the jurist and the statesman. The human association which in fact produces and distributes wealth, the association of workmen, managers, technicians and directors, is not an association recognised by the law. The association which the law does recognise—the association of shareholders, creditors and directors—is incapable of production or distribution, and is not expected to perform these functions. We have to give law to the real association, and to withdraw meaningless privilege from the imaginary one.[9]

In fact, there already are non-profitmaking companies, companies limited by guarantee, and, more importantly, companies whose explicit objective expressed in their articles of association, is to further the interests of some other group of stakeholders—its employees, its customers, or its suppliers.

We are familiar with the Coop. The Cooperative Societies do not have shareholders, but divide their profits among their customers. More recently various producer cooperatives have been established, which market agricultural produce so as to obtain better prices than individual farmers could if each bargained on his

---

[9] Lord Eustace Percy, *The Unknown State*, Oxford University Press, London, 1944, p.38; quoted by D.G.Goyder, *The Just Enterprise*, London, 1987, p.8, and by Charles Handy, *The Empty Raincoat*, London, pbk., 1995, p.163.

own behalf. And it is perfectly feasible to have companies that exist to serve the interests of their employees. Quite apart from some benevolently-inspired institutions such as the John Lewis partnership, there are a number of small companies that exist to exploit the talents of one or a few named individuals. The law allows all sorts of association: it does not have to be for profit, nor need the members of the company be shareholders with tradeable shares.

There are obvious advantages in these other sorts of company, but disadvantages too. The adversarial aspect of the company's dealings with its customers, its suppliers, or its employees, is assuaged, and in particular employees can feel that they have more a stake in the company and the fruits of their labours if they have some share of the profits. But profits do not always happen. There may be lean years in which there are no profits, even losses. Just as the investor may lose his money, so the labourer may find that he has laboured in vain. And labourers are rationally reluctant to take that risk, being less able to stand the loss of the fruits of their labour than the investor the loss of his surplus money. If I have got mouths to feed or a mortgage to repay, I need to have my salary secure, and am wise to forgo the prospect of possible profits for the certainty of a weekly wage. Security has its price. Just as risk-averse investors can buy preference shares, with a more assured return, but missing out on possible profits, so workers may opt for wages, but thereby forgo a greater financial involvement in the fortunes of the firm. Mixed systems in which fixed wages were paid, but lower than the normal, together with some share of the profits have been tried. They avoid the disadvantages of the employees having no stake in the profitability of the firm or of their being too dependent on its fortunes, but raise problems of weighing immediate against future share-outs. Large companies operating over a long time need to invest capital to ensure or enhance future profitability. The tension between the short-term interests of their members in having larger dividends, and the long-term interest of the company and its future employees in having invested more, is eased, up to a point,[10] in an ordinary limited liability company, by the shareholders being owners of their shares, and being able to set future value against immediate dividends. With employees, customers, or suppliers, there is no tradeability to even out the relative advantages of present cash and future profitability: if I am

[10] But see below, this chapter §5.

due to retire next year, why should I accept a reduced dividend now in order that my successor might be able to add more value to his labour in five years' time? It may not matter in small companies, with a high degree of identification with the firm, or in associations where the profits are small, or little capital is required, as in producer cooperatives; in such cases it is equitable to allow easy entrance and not to give those leaving the company any continuing right to share in its profits: but with large manufacturing firms, it would be inequitable not to give those leaving employment something in return for their restraint in not receiving the maximum dividends possible during their years of employment. They need to be given some sort of share, and there are strong pressures to make these tradeable shares of the traditional type. In which case they have a market value, and will be construed by many employees as simply a wage under another name and in a less convenient form.

Pressures can be resisted. Shares can be non-transferable, or non-tradeable. A completely satisfactory solution to these problems has yet to be devised. If one emerges, it could well become the prevailing legal form of future firms. But always there are risks in business, and many people, and especially many employees, are risk-averse, and with good reason. The risks of business enterprise are likely, therefore, to be carried very largely by those who can afford to bear the loss, if things go ill, in return for the lion's share of the profits, if things go well.

§5.4 Ownership and Market Value

Shares are tradeable and traded. Stock markets exist for the purpose. It is characteristic of any market that prices—what is offered for what is being sold—will vary.

The value of a particular share at a particular time is an economic, not an ethical, question. What will the market pay? Much as there is no absolute just price or absolute just wage, so there is no single ethical criterion for what the shares of ICI or the Channel Tunnel should be worth. It will depend on how the market values those companies, in turn depending on different circumstances and predictions, including further predictions of what the market itself is going to do, which can never be entirely determinate.

What, then, is the real value of a company? After all, when take-over bids are in issue, merchant banks and investment analysts make careful assessments. Two factors need to be distinguished. There is the "break-up" value of the company. Almost every company owns some property, some machinery, some assets. If the company were to be wound up, these would be sold, and, in the standard case, the proceeds would be distributed among the shareholders—it is this factor that leads people to suppose that the shareholders own the company in a straightforward sense. But unless the company is very badly run, it is not in order to carve up its dead carcass that people want to have shares in it. It is valued as a going concern, that is likely to generate profits in the future which will in due course be distributed as dividends. The company exists to protect, maintain and create value, and it is on account of its likelihood of doing so in future that shareholders want to have a share in it, and the market sets a value on those shares.

It is quite legitimate for investors to want to have a share in future profits, but with their rights, carefully defined by the law and by the articles of association of their company, come obligations. Not only is their liability limited, but their directors have carefully specified duties towards them, to protect their interests, especially in regard to dealing in shares and when a takeover is in prospect. Shareholders correspondingly have duties, both legal and moral: if a shareholder comes to own a majority of the shares, he must offer the minority shareholders the same price for their shares as he did for those he has already acquired. The aggregate of legal rights and legal duties constitutes what a share is, and what it is to own a share. The moral duties of a shareholder are determined by this concept of share, and the legal rights and legal duties that go with it.

Many shareholders repudiate all such imputations of responsibility: they buy shares simply in order to make money. Elaine Sternberg supports this view:

> There is ordinarily no moral obligation to be, or to continue to be, a shareholder. Being a shareholder is just one of the myriad of roles open to an individual or institution, and the reasons for choosing to be a shareholder are equally diverse. Though some objectives encourage long-term holdings, others do not; they can, however, be equally legitimate reasons for owning shares. And it is the shareholder's objectives for owning shares which should determine if a particular holding is to be bought or kept or sold: the long-term goals appropriate for a pension fund may not be sensible for any given elderly pensioner.[11]

---

[11] Elaine Sternberg, *Just Business*, Little, Brown and Company, London, 1994, pp.205-206.

But this is a confusion. The personal motives different individuals have for their various financial transactions is one thing, the institutional rationale of some particular form of property is another. A doctor may have embarked on the medical profession because he wanted to be rich, or well respected in his local community. His personal motives for being a doctor would not affect his responsibilities, or relieve him of any of his professional obligations.[12] It is illuminating to consider the analogous case of people investing in landed property, because landed property was for many centuries the only form of investment, and our moral intuitions have been sharpened in considering it. It has generally been recognised that although people may invest in landed property for a variety of reasons, those reasons do not override the obligations that go with the ownership of land. One particular instance is telling: it was held to be quite wrong to let houses for immoral purposes, that is, as brothels. It was no defence that the landlord was a charity or a pension fund with a duty to get the best return possible. An exactly similar case obtains today with the holding of shares. Or, to take a contemporary parallel, some pension funds have invested in works of art. That may be a legitimate investment. But it would not justify destroying them if they ceased to have market appeal. Although pension funds sometimes say that their duty is solely to their pensioners, they are wrong. To own is to have obligations. An institution cannot own shares, any more than houses or land or Picassos without having some duties in respect of what they own.

The shareholder has a voice and a vote. He can speak out if the company is pursuing bad policies. He can raise the matter at the Annual General Meeting of the company, and may attract some attention in the press, and this may be enough to shame the directors into mending their ways; but if it not, there is not much more he can do about it. Other shareholders are not interested. It is different in the USA, where shareholders regularly raise questions of principle and general policy, and directors seek to justify their actions in detail. The American practice is better than the British.[13] It is obviously more in accord with the ideal of shareowning democracy, with shareholders exercising responsibility for

---

[12] Tom Sorell and John Hendry, *Business Ethics*, Butterworth Heinmann, Oxford, 1994, ch.5, p.118.

[13] The record of some American institutions is better. CALPERS, the Californian pension fund, has been an active and successful shareholder.

their shares as they do for their society at large. But even from the narrower point of view of protecting one's investment, the British practice does not conduce to good management. Although for the small investor the hassle involved in persuading the firm to improve its practice may not be worth the small share of the increased profit he will ultimately reap, for large investors the benefits are much greater. Enlightened self-interest as well as public responsibility should lead them to devote some effort to improving the record of British business as employers, suppliers, customers and associates.

For the small investor the fact that intervention is unlikely to be effective may constitute a good enough reason for not speaking out, but selling the shares instead. It is the "exit" rather than the "voice" option.[14] That may be the right decision. Exiting exerts economic pressure, whereas voicing one's dissatisfaction does not. But exiting conveys minimal information, whereas the managers are left in no doubt about the complaint if it is voiced. Economists tend to focus on the exit option, politicians the voice option. Neither is very effective: the decision may reasonably go either way. But it is a decision that has to be taken; for the question does arise simply by reason of the shareholder having a voice and a vote. He cannot disclaim responsibility, and say that it is none of his business: it is his business to be concerned; he has the shares; he is a member of the company; he has the right to speak. And although he can plead, plausibly if not entirely convincingly, that his voice is too feeble to be effective, the pension funds and insurance companies can mount no such defence. They have clout. If they do not use it, they are answerable for the failings of the companies in whose direction they have an effective say. Poor performance damages us all in many different respects, not least in inviting further government intervention and putting off potential entrants from seeking a career in business.

The standard response in Britain is to sell shares rather than intervene in the management of a particular company. Sometimes it may be the only available choice—often because the majority of shares in most large companies are held by insurance companies, pension funds, and other large institutions, who are not concerned with what their companies do, but only with what dividends they will pay and what value their shares will have over the next few months—and sometimes it may be the right course. But there are grave objections to it in general, because it reinforces the prevailing tendency to "short-termism".

---

[14] We owe these terms to A.O.Hirschman, *Exit, Voice and Loyalty*, Harvard University Press, Cambridge, Mass., 1970.

§5.5 Short-Termism

Managers and directors often complain of short-termism. Share-holders are only interested, they complain, in short-term gains, either by way of dividends or through increases in the share price, and companies cannot, in consequence, afford to take the long-term view. Shares are bought, simply as a speculation, by managers of funds whose own personal salary is related to how their funds perform month by month, without regard to the longer term, which ought to be the chief responsibility of shareholders.[15]

Shares are tradeable. If I have a house, it may take me a long time to find a purchaser who is prepared to pay the price I reckon it is worth; but because there are many shares, each qualitatively identical with many others, there is a continual market for them, and I can buy and sell them with great ease. The question thus arises of whether the shareholder has any responsibility to the company itself. Is there a duty to hang on to shares when the market suggests that the time has come to sell? The market reflects the judgments of many operators, and, in the view of many, is author-itative. But the market is ill informed. If I am astute I may be able to beat the market. But the astuteness is of a peculiar kind. I do not need to know better than the market what the shares are really worth, only what other people are going to think they are worth. I am dealing with opinions, not realities, and opin-ions tomorrow, not opinions in the fullness of time, when realities will have taken their toll of unjustified expectations. There is a high degree of fleeting unreality built into the stock market. This encourages short-termism. By getting into tomorrow's favourite today and getting out again tomorrow a fund manager can make a lot of money for his fund. Particularly since the Big Bang and the introduction of "performance-related pay" fund managers have sought to make a quick killing on the Stock Exchange, and boards of directors have felt pressured to increase dividend payments at the expense of future investment. Some have called for some form of loyalty lock, to prevent shares being bought and sold like raffle tickets. Others have claimed that there is nothing wrong with spec-ulating in stocks and shares, any more than there is with putting money on horses. But, as Sorell and Hendry point out, the cases are not similar: backing a horse has no effect on the horse, whereas

---

[15] See further, ch.12, §12.4.

buying or selling shares has an effect, albeit only a marginal one
if the purchase or sale is small, on the whole undertaking.[16] For
the small punter the principle *de minimis* applies, but the fund
managers are not small investors, and need to take account of the
overall effect of what they are doing. It is perfectly reasonable
to channel funds from the forced savings of pension schemes into
capital investments that will yield a good return in time to come.
But that is a long-term business, and carries with it a readiness to
forgo immediate returns provided the long-term profitability of the
enterprise is sufficiently enhanced. Moreover, although short-term
fluctuations on the stock market open the possibility of specula-
tors making money, it is essentially a zero-sum game; I may make
a killing if I buy tomorrow's favourites today and sell them to you
tomorrow, but you will make a loss when you try to sell them the
next day, next week, next month, or next year, when the fleeting
appearance of profitability has fled. This is not to say that investors should not be allowed to buy shares in some fund devoted
to speculation, so long as that is made explicit, and they know
that they may get their fingers badly burned: managers of pension and insurance funds, however, are under an obligation to put
safety first, and to follow policies most likely to enhance the value
of investments over the long, rather than the short, term. Short-
term speculation is not a proper activity for pension funds, and
if fund managers are to be paid performance-related salaries, the
performance should be assessed not after a few months but after
thirty years, when the contributors will actually be drawing their
pensions.

Although short-term profitability is what some shareholders
want, it is against the interests of shareholders as a whole considered over a longer period of time. By encouraging managers to
stint expenditure on research and development, in order to boost
immediate profits and interim dividends, it diminishes the firm's
ability to compete in international markets, and promotes the general decline of the British economy.[17] What is a reasonable time-
horizon will vary very much from industry to industry—a year is

---

[16] Tom Sorell and John Hendry, *Business Ethics*, Butterworth Heinmann,
Oxford, 1994, ch.5, p.119.

[17] The unwillingness of British firms to invest in research is also attributable
to their being in a "Prisoners' Dilemma" (see Appendix A) in as much as
the benefits of research do not reliably accrue to those who have incurred
the costs.

a long time in the world of fashion, but of little moment if buying super-tankers. But although in the long run all the shareholders will be dead, their estates will benefit if their shares still have a potential for further profitability, and are in firms with a good reputation and in good standing with the public generally. Except in special circumstances—for example, when there is a takeover bid— the duty to the shareholders is adequately discharged by seeking to make the firm prosper over a long period of time and in a general sense.

§5.6 The Ethical Investor

Much of the concern about business ethics in recent years has centred on the ethics of investment. Although many of the issues are really more fundamental ones of business ethics generally, it is convenient to discuss them in this particular context.

People are ready to feel uncomfortable about investments. The Church used to condemn usury, and the Marxists damned the idle rich. Unearned income seemed immoral. At the time of the Student movement it was customary to demand that colleges and universities should disinvest in South Africa, and should not bank with Barclays. In reaction, many administrators and businessmen maintained that business was business, and ethical considerations should play no part in investment decisions. Their duty was simply to get the best return they could on the money they were investing. But that view cannot be sustained. Ethical considerations cannot be absolutely excluded, even when the prime duty is to use invest the money to provide for some charitable purpose. Shareholders have the right to speak out and vote on company policy, and with that right comes responsibility for what the company is doing. But that responsibility is glossed and limited in a number of ways, often ignored by those who criticize the investment decisions of others.

The fundamental reason why responsibility is limited is that business transactions are non-tuistic, and that it is not my business to determine your priorities or objectives. There is a veil of ignorance, therefore, that is not easily penetrated, and limits my responsibility for the use you make of your share of the cooperators' surplus. I am not my brother's keeper: it is up to him to decide what he will do, and not normally any business of mine. Business is business, and carries with it a proper separation of what is my business from what is none of my business.

Business is business, but not every business is a morally accept-able way of earning money. If I owned a factory, and a Third-world dictator wanted me to supply him with thumbscrews, it would be wrong of me to do so, no matter how lucrative the order. And the same would apply if the factory were owned by a public lim-ited company in which I had shares. Even though he would cer-tainly be able to buy the thumbscrews from some other supplier, and even if the order would make the difference between solvency and bankruptcy, and widespread local unemployment, it would be wrong to make money by such means. Instruments of torture have but one use. They are bloodstained, and the stain extends to the money made from making them. The veil of ignorance is pen-etrated by such instruments, and I neither can be ignorant nor rightly unconcerned with the implications of what we are doing.

Most commodities and many services are less specific in their use, and the veil of ignorance correspondingly more opaque. But a pharmacist might properly refuse to sell a small boy fifteen ounces of potassium nitrate and two ounces of flowers of sulphur, reason-ably suspecting that he was going to make three ounces of charcoal himself and then have the ingredients for gunpowder. It is now common practice not to sell ether to adolescents, though still all right to sell it to elderly car buffs having difficulty in starting their elderly cars. A public limited company would be wrong to sell the specific ingredients of mustard gas to Iraq, though having no qualms in selling the same chemicals to an agricultural research station. Often in the real world such purchases are made through intermediaries; but often also the ultimate destination is known or suspected, and that knowledge can carry with it responsibility for the ultimate outcome. British arms manufacturers who supplied Argentina with arms did not know that they would be used to kill British soldiers, but did know that they were intended to kill.

But knowledge does not always carry responsibility. The phar-macist knows that the heroin he is dispensing to an addict is de-stroying him, but should dispense the prescription none the less. It is the doctor's responsibility to decide, and except when he has rea-son to suspect the authenticity of the prescription or the integrity of the prescriber, the pharmacist's duty is simply to dispense the drugs specified. Much of life is like that. We have to coordinate our activities, and can do so only if each of us does not take it upon himself to decide everything, but conforms to the role expected of him.[18] Often, indeed, we go further, and lay on business enterprises "common carrier" obligations, which preclude their refusing to serve customers even in pursuit of bad ends. In the United States the Mann Act makes it a criminal offence to convey a woman across a State boundary for an immoral purpose; but no railroad corporation or bus line could refuse a ticket to convey a woman who had such a purpose in mind. British Telecom and American Telephone & Telegraph earn some of their money from calls made to call-girls by would-be customers, yet we do not stigmatize the dividends they pay as immoral earnings from prostitution. Indeed, while we may well think it wrong for British Telecom to provide a dial-in pornographic service, we should not think that telephones should be denied to women who might then use them to make assignations.

Business responsibility is not simple. Businessmen are responsible for what they do, but their responsibility is limited. There is a presumption of not being responsible for what the other party to a business transaction does, but this presumption can be rebutted. Even then, when we know that the other party is using our help as a means to a bad end, we may be under a duty not to withhold our cooperation. It is the same as in civil society, where we often have defended the other person's right to be wrong. We are not all agreed, but we still have to live together.

The investor is responsible. If the company is doing one particular thing wrong—advertising in Third-world countries to persuade mothers not to breast-feed their babies, but use the company's products instead—then it is reasonable to protest. But often protest is unavailing, sometimes inevitably so—a tobacco company exists to process and sell tobacco—and then the only recourse is to sell the shares. People sometimes complain that that will not do any good, and only moves the problem to someone else: but it is not to be expected that any single individual will be able to effect much of a change; the case is like that of the manufacturer who refuses to make thumbscrews—he will not stop the Third-world dictator from getting them, but he will have had no part in it. Similarly, a shareholder who sells his shares ceases to be responsible for what that company is doing, and if it is something he disapproves of, it is likely to be his only course. The Bishop of Oxford cites a long

[18] See the Rule of the Road in Appendix A.

list of sensitive issues.[19] Sorell and Hendry describe a number of investment trusts which invest only in companies not likely to make shareholders feel queasy. Typically they do not invest in countries ruled by oppressive regimes, or in which basic human rights are disregarded, nor in companies that pollute or are low-wage employers, nor ones involved in gambling, pornography, tobacco, or alcohol. They claim that it is possible to find investments which do not offend and which provide an adequate yield, though they tend to do less well than investment funds not so restricted in their scope.[20] But the individual investor is under no obligation to keep the shares in order to maximise his return. If I were to invest my time and talents in being a turf accountant, I should be richer than I am, but I am free to earn my living as I think best, and the same goes for investing my money.

The case is altered when it comes to criticizing the investments of others, or deciding what investments some trust or corporate body ought to hold. Even if I disapprove of smoking, it does not follow that I am entitled to condemn you for having tobacco shares. Many of our fellow-countrymen know all about the dangers of smoking, but would rather die at sixty six after a happy life puffing away at the weed than live to a moribund old age in austere asceticism, and if you enable them to carry out their choices, who am I to condemn you? Equally a trustee must not let his ethical sensitivity subvert the purpose of the charity. The charity has a specific purpose, not a general remit to make the world a better place, and if every investment has to be socially responsible, money intended for the healing of the sick may be diverted into providing low-cost housing for ethnic minorities.

Mere disapproval is not enough. Criticisms can be made, but if they are to be heeded need to be even-handed, and to take account of answers that may be given. Many critics are selective in their indignation. In the 1970s and 1980s there was much indignation at the undoubted evils of apartheid, but a complete unworriedness about involvement in the Soviet Union, severe condemnation of Chile, and, until the Falklands war, complete silence about Argentina. It was difficult to take such criticisms seriously. It was

---

[19] Richard Harries, *Is There a Gospel for the Rich?*, London, 1992, pp.144-145.

[20] Tom Sorell and John Hendry, *Business Ethics*, Butterworth Heinemann, Oxford, 1994, pp.132-133.

arguable that we should not dirty our hands with South African gold, but in that case Russian gold was even more blood-stained; if it was acceptable to do business with the Soviet Union in order to maintain contact and wean them away from their wicked ways, then it was equally acceptable to keep in touch with South African liberals, and show South Africans generally that there were better ways of doing things.

It is also incumbent on critics to listen. If they criticize a company for being a low-wage employer, they need to consider the reply that the alternative in the actual situation would be to go out of business and be a no-wage employer. That may not actually be the case. If it is not, then the criticism is justified: but the case needs to be considered. It is reasonable to be worried about nuclear energy, and to fear a repetition of Three Mile Island or Chernobyl. But one needs also to consider whether British or French operators are as irresponsible as American or Russian ones, and to weigh the possible hazards of nuclear energy against the actual damage done by burning coal, and the many lives actually lost in mining coal. In the end a judgement has to be made. But it should be a reasoned and responsible one, not an ill-informed emotional one.

Almost every business activity could offend an ethically sensitive person. We are always engaged with people, some of whom are not very nice. Business transactions are with people who have values significantly different from ours. We may, as in this book, take a benign view of it, and say that it takes all sorts to make a world, but we may take a darker, more Augustinian, view, and see ourselves emeshed in a worldly Babylon, a squalid city far removed from the society of our dreams, and yearn to be free of all its earthy entanglements, and withdraw into monastic seclusion, free to realise our ideals in company with a few like-minded souls. But if we thus separate ourselves off, we leave the world to stew in its own juice, and abandon any real chance of improving it. If we are to enter into the business of the world, it must be on the basis that not everything will be as we would wish it. But then we are not responsible for all its ills. If we cooperate with those we do not agree with, we can sup on the fruits of cooperation with a reasonably long spoon.

Chapter 6
Employment

Contents

Abstract

Work is regarded both as a necessary evil and a fundamental good. Employees want both to be compensated for having to work and to be protected against not having to. The obligations both to and of employees are similarly complex. In most respects the relationship is an internal one, both parties working together in a common enterprise which constitutes the ground of their mutual obligations, tempered by the employer's having the greater say, and therefore the greater responsibility. The identification of the employee with his firm is not, and never should be, complete, and conflicts of loyalty can arise, particularly over questions of confidentiality. As regards wages and other emoluments the relationship is an external one, in which bargaining is best done collectively by trade unions, which also have other important roles. It is a fundamental mistake to think of jobs as goodies, and legislation designed to hand them out to deserving recipients is often counter-productive. Nevertheless, in some circumstances a businessman should consider special claims for employment, and may be able to go some way towards meeting them, although attempts by the State to engineer full employment have patently failed.

§6.1 The Curse of Adam

It is not at first sight evident why people want work. It is not inherently satisfying for most people. It never was. The back-breaking toil of the agricultural labourer, the dirt and danger of mining coal—these do not seem to be things that we ought to want on behalf of our fellow human beings. And yet we hark back to the days when farming provided work on the land for whole villages, and sympathize with the miners when pits close and whole communities lose their *raison d'être.*[1]

Traditionally work has been seen as a means of earning one's daily bread. I need food. It does not sufficiently grow on trees— even if I am a hunter-gatherer, I have to go out and kill my prey or gather my blackberries—and for most of us much labour is required if we are to have a tolerably comfortable existence. But the modern unemployed are not starving. Benefits, though not generous, do keep the fiercest wolves from the door. Rather, it is some question of status, of being someone of consequence, someone who matters, someone who makes a contribution.

There are many ways of making a contribution. Voluntary, that is to say unpaid, work entirely alters the aspect of society. The contribution made by most women is primarily in the home, and arguably more valuable than most of the work done in offices. But although voluntary work, in the home or outside, is what gives significance to many people's lives, many lack a clear vision of what they can do that is worthwhile, and many want to contribute to the economic life of the country and be entitled to some share of its benefits. Paid employment is for them the means whereby they can do something useful; the role of breadwinner is a meaningful one within their reach.

For these reasons it has been widely supposed that people have a right to work, which has been construed as meaning that firms existed in order to provide employment, and that their duties to employees were paramount. That is a mistake. Jobs are not good-ies to be given to people because they need them or deserve them. There is no natural right to work in that sense. Work is essen-tially defined in terms independent of the worker. It is what other people want him to do, need him to do, or recognise it as worth doing; and it is well or ill done according to those standards, not according to his. Once that connexion is severed, we move towards the communist world, where people pretend to work and the State pretends to pay them. This is not to say that it is wrong either for the State or for an individual employer to try to provide work. But great clarity of thought and firmness of purpose are required, when talking about the right to work, and the right of the employer to hire and fire at will.

---

[1] See, for example, *Men without Work: a report made to the Pilgrim Trust*, Cambridge, 1938.

§6.2 Obligations of Employers

Employees cooperate with their employers in profitable activities. In the typical case the employer tells the employee what to do, and, instead of giving him a proportion of the profits, contracts to give him a fixed wage, although sometimes people are paid to tell those paying them what to do, and profit-sharing schemes, in spite of the difficulties noted in the previous chapter, are perfectly possible.[2] But typically the employee is the weaker party, unable to take risks, needing to forgo the possibility of profits for the certainty of wages, and also not knowing fully what to do, and needing to be told. The mutual obligations of employer and employee arise from the interplay of the internal relationship constituted by their being members of the same cooperative association, and hence having its values in common, and of the external relationship constituted by their differing from each other in their natural interests and in the matter of wages, together with the employer's having responsibility for what the employee does in the course of his employment, and, commensurate with his greater responsibility, shouldering a larger part of the burdens, and being entitled to a greater part of the cooperators' surplus.

An employee does what his employer tells him. As we have seen,[3] instructions never exclude all discretion, and sometimes leave it very much up to the employee how he should carry out his commission. Different enterprises require different degrees of delegation. Firm leadership is called for in an army or a factory, but would be entirely inappropriate in a university or a research team. Where the tasks are simple, and the function of the manager is to coordinate the activities of the employees so as to produce a good end-result, crisp decisions are called for, but where each employee is having to exercise considerable judgement in the course of his work, and is likely to have a clearer idea of the difficulties and issues involved, a much more consensual style of management is called for, and rather than tell each employee what to do, the employer needs to facilitate liaison between them.[4] The most fundamental duty

---

[2] In ch.5, §5.3.

[3] In ch.4, §4.1.

[4] See G.B.Richardson, "Some Principles of Economic Organisation", Forthcoming.

of an employer is to determine the degree of direction and delegation appropriate for his enterprise. He owes it to his employees to
recognise them as responsible agents, and to give them as much
responsibility as they can safely be trusted with, but also to accept
himself the over-all responsibility for seeing that they know what
to do, and are enabled to do it.[5]

The employer shares responsibility for what the employee does,
and thus has a duty not to tell him to do anything imprudent or
wrong. Further, he is responsible *for* the employee's not contravening any legal or moral principle, or causing anyone (including
himself) any harm. Many of these obligations have been ham-
mered out and made precise in the common law of master and
servant, and in statutes concerned with safety at work and workmen's compensation. The underlying principle is that both parties
have a shared responsibility, which neither side can opt out of.
This shared responsibility gives rise to a partial identification of
the employee with his employer which is the basis of further obligation. It is characteristically long-term. Although legal contracts
in Britain are often short-term, and there is some casual and temporary labour, most employment is actually for an extended period,
and needs to be—it takes time to learn the ropes, and chaos would
ensue if we all had a different job each week. If the employee is ill,
has a temporary lapse, gets old, there are grounds for not being too
extreme to mark what is done amiss. Human beings do get ill, do
make mistakes, do grow old. The nature of the employment made
it sensible to have employed a human being for a lengthy period of
time, in which he was likely to suffer some ill health, make some
mistakes, and grow appreciably older. In availing myself over the
years of your continued willingness to work for me, I have made use
of your being a temporally extended agent, and so should have some
regard for the concomitants of that temporality. The Japanese go
in for life-long employment, and it does not seem that the Japanese
economy has suffered as a result. There are arguments, however,
against making life-long employment a contractual condition universally: it would be very one-sided, unless the freedom of the
employee to change jobs were very much fettered; it would make it
impossible for employers to adjust to unforeseen changes of circumstance, and so would make them excessively cautious about taking

[5] See further below, ch.12, §12.3.

on employees—"if you can't fire, you won't hire". For some occupations good health and youthfulness are essential: those who join the army or become professional footballers know that they cannot expect to be employed into middle age, and a country which requires its armed services to employ the handicapped is unlikely to retain its freedom long. These obligations, then, are not over-riding, but they are real. We should be reluctant to terminate a long-standing relationship, though recognising that in some cases there are even weightier reasons for doing so.

The identification between employer and employee is not one of responsibility only, but of achievement as well. The enterprise could not prosper without the cooperation of the employees. They contribute to the success of the collective effort, and so should have some share of the fruits of success. In practice, and on grounds of practicality, the employees' shares are primarily paid in the form of wages, partly, as we have seen, because most employees set greater store on a steady income than an uncertain share of fluctutating profits, partly because justice is indeterminate.[6] It is quite proper to have clear and definite agreements about wages, but important to remember that they are set in the context of a collective enterprise, and that notions of distributive justice are widespread and deep. The most contentious issues that arise between an employer and his employees concern money and conditions of service. There are cross-currents between internal arguments, based on their all being together in a joint enterprise, and external arguments ending in a bargain between parties whose interests are opposed. Money paid in wages is potential profit forgone. *Prima facie*, therefore, it is in the employer's interest to pay as little as he can get away with if the job is to be done. Up to a point, however, enlightened self-interest argues the other way. Well-paid and well-looked-after employees tend to identify with the firm more and work better. But only up to a point. In many factories there is not much scope for working better, and if a better-paid work-force is only as productive as a an ill-paid one, competition will drive a good employer out of business. Often the choice has been between offering employees a starvation wage and not offering them employment at all. It is difficult to be happy about employing sweated labour, but if there is one thing worse than being an exploited worker, it is being an unexploited one. The good businessman wants to deal fairly with

[6] See above, ch.5, §5.3, and ch.2, §2.5.

his employees, but, justice being indeterminate, what is a fair wage depends very much on time and circumstance. In many ages and many places the going wage is far below what seems needful and right in the twentieth century Western world. We should not be quick to condemn those operating under other conditions who fail to meet our own ideas of the just wage. But it is seldom that there is no latitude at all, and almost always there are some decisions to be taken which can manifest a just concern for employees or its absence. Consideration does not always cost money, and some costs are not critical.

On issues concerning money and conditions of service the relationship between employer and employee is evidently external. This is sometimes regretted; it would be better, it is thought, if employer and employee were completely at one, and altogether imbued with an identity of interest. But it is important to accept the externality of the relation as a recognition of the individual's individuality, and to extend it, by moderating the demand for identification. In some countries and some cultures the firm takes over almost the whole of the employee's life: and even when they do not expect it of all workers, some firms expect too complete a dedication on the part of their executives. I can be paid to promote Unilever's soap powder rather than Procter and Gamble's, and may, indeed, come to believe that it is better, but I should not be expected to devote myself totally to the firm at the expense of my wife and family or my duties of citizenship. It may be different in some of the professions,[7] but business is based on an assumption of externality. The salesman does not have a natural vocation to sell soap powders, and his individuality is not being respected if he is expected to identify himself unreservedly with soap. He ought to do the best he can for the firm while he is employed by it; and even after he leaves its employment respect its confidentiality, and neither disclose its secrets nor make use of them to compete with it: but he is not obliged to a lifetime's service, and can, without disloyalty, wonder whether he might not better himself by taking his talents elsewhere.

---

[7] See further below, ch.8, §§8.1, 8.4.

§6.3 Obligations of Employees

The double relationship, both external and internal, which employees have with the firms that employ them, gives rise both to obligations and sometimes to conflicts of obligation. They do not have a natural or antecedent identification of interest with their firms, in the way in which professional people do have an antecedent identification with the values of their profession:[8] but, in return for a salary or wage, the employee cooperates in helping the firm to realise some of its objectives. The degree of identification with the firm's shared interest varies: much more is expected of a manager than of a blue-collar worker. Although complete identification should never be demanded, some identification is always required. Even a casual labourer carrying out a specific order accepts responsibility for doing it in a workmanlike manner, and long-term employees, just because they are long-term, come to know much more what is expected of them, and have a correspondingly greater responsibility to work well. Normally it is fairly straightforward what they should do; the very fact of their being employees usually carries with it the existence of a supervisor, foreman, or boss, who can, in all cases of doubt, spell out what actually is required of them. Problems arise, however, if what they are told to do contravenes the perceived values of the firm, or, more generally, if either of the former are in conflict with the public interest, the moral law, the law of the land, or the employee's own individual ideals.

It is not a new problem. In the middle ages the servants of the Crown were sometimes instructed by the King to do things clearly contrary to his interests. They developed a doctrine, sounding quaint to our ears, of the King's two bodies, whereby they could justify, by appeal to the King's better and more ethereal body, disobedience to what they were told by the King's actual and earthly body. Since the employee is a responsible agent, and is never without some discretion in discharging his commission, and is to some extent identified with the business enterprise, he may be in a position to judge that the actual instructions he has been given run counter to the general policy of the firm. More often, however, the conflict is an external one, in which the firm's instructions or policies cannot be reconciled with what he, as a citizen and moral agent, believes to be right. Sometimes the issue is clear. If my employer tells me to go and kill someone, I am under no duty to obey,

---

[8] See below, ch.8, §8.1.

but should, rather, tell the police. But what if, looking through his papers, I find that he is intending to murder his wife? Surely, then, too, I must tell. But if he tells me he is having an affair? We begin to hesitate. Some confidences ought to be respected, even if they are about wrongdoing. The seal of the confessional extends beyond the ordained ministry.

In modern business life dilemmas mostly arise over questions of confidentiality. Many organizations engage in dubious practices. Firms cheat customers, default on suppliers, make dangerous products, damage the environment in the Third World. Governments scheme to get the better of foreigners; Ministers lie to Parliament; schools conceal cases of child abuse. Employees who find out, are in a difficult position. Should they "blow the whistle", publish the wrongdoing, and hope that publication will bring about an amendment of practice? Or is their duty of confidentiality to their employer to override their duty as citizens and moral agents? Although the fact that their relation to their employer is in part external gives grounds for other obligations than those directed towards the firm, it can work the other way, and argue for respecting the privacy and keeping the secrets of an institution other than oneself, and under some conditions accepting a stringent duty of complete confidentiality.

§6.4 Openness, Privacy and Secrecy

Most firms are public limited companies, and the board of directors is under a duty to keep the shareholders in the picture about the activities of the company, for which they are ultimately responsible, and to publish in the press any decisions which could affect the price of shares. Public limited companies are effectively in the public domain. So, too, are schools, colleges, universities, churches and hospitals. Their activities are a matter of legitimate concern for the public, and if journalists ring up to ask questions, they should not be met with a blanket "None of your business". There is a general presumption of openness, and officials of these organizations, like government officials, should take trouble to answer questions properly, and to keep the public informed of what they are doing and why. It matters to the local community if the factory is changing its production schedules, if there has been an outbreak of salmonella poisoning, if the vicar has become a Roman Catholic. There is a general presumption of openness, which may, indeed, be rebutted in special cases for good reason, but only if the reason is sufficiently good to override the normal requirement of keeping everyone in the picture.

Three general exceptions to the requirement of openness can be justified. The first is that we should respect the privacy of private persons. Almost always an organization will have information about its members—addresses, telephone numbers, age and marital status—which they may not wish to be publicised. My telephone number may be ex-directory to save me from nuisance calls from animal liberationists; I may have put in for a job, and not want my present employer to know; I may have been passed over for promotion, and not want my colleagues to know. Although the firm's activities are in the public domain, mine are not, and I am entitled to be shielded in my dealings with it from the publicity that attaches to the firm generally.

The duty to protect personal privacy clearly can override the requirement of openness, but it is difficult to delimit it. The fact that someone is employed can hardly be kept quiet. Unsuccessful applications need not be made public, but often appointments committees do swap notes and comments without its being seen as a breach of confidence. If an applicant specially requests it, his present employer should not be told of his application, but in the absence of a special request, his applying for a job carries with it a willingness to have his merits discussed and assessed by anyone reasonably qualified to do so. His application, and their rejection of it, should not be made public, but neither need it be kept a secret.

Although public limited companies operate in the public domain, they are not public institutions. They have limited objectives, not shared with everyone else, nor with all other institutions. Not only are their objectives different from those they do business with, but typically they are in competition with other firms, seeking to outdo them in getting orders and custom. The competitive and adversarial aspect of business requires an element of secrecy. My new soap powder may not be perfect: but I am entitled to expect my employees not to leak a frank appraisal of its defects to my competitors. Negotiations will be jeopardised if those on the other side of the table are told of our target price in advance. Once it is accepted that not everyone has the same interests or shares the same values, some curtain of separateness is established between different organizations with different interests or pursuing different values. We are not all of one mind, and cannot be required to share information unrestrictedly.[9]

The difficulty comes when the information being kept secret is information which in all honesty ought to be disclosed. It is one thing if my soap powder does not actually wash clothes whiter, another if it damages them, or still worse, if it is injurious to health. Although I do not owe a duty to my competitors to tell them of the former, I do have a duty not to mislead my customers on either of the latter scores. Although the competitive and adversarial nature of business affords an argument for secrecy that overrides the general requirement of openness, it is itself overridden by duties of honesty towards customers, and public responsibility towards all whose health might be affected. The duty of an employee to protect his firm's secrets on the former counts does not extend to covering up its failures on the latter. Ultimately, though not always immediately, and not for merely idiosyncratic reasons, whistle-blowing is justified.

§6.5 Confidentiality

The third reason for abridging the general duty of openness is more difficult to spell out. It depends on human fallibility. We often are not sure of our facts, not sure of our judgement, not sure of our moral duty. We hesitate to speak in public. If my facts are challenged, I may not be able to prove them. My judgement may well turn out to be wrong. I might be ashamed if everyone knew the devious course of action I had in mind. So I keep my mouth shut. I do not think the candidate is trustworthy, but had better not say so, because he denied that there was anything wrong in those dubious transactions at the club, and we did not think the case proved beyond all reasonable doubt. But if we all keep our mouths shut, the wrong decisions will be made. We need full information, not the partial information of what people can prove in a court of law, and are prepared to stand by in public. If we are to be in the best position to decide, we need to have people speak freely and proffer their best judgement without fear or favour. And if we are to have them doing that, we must protect them against the adverse consequences of speaking out. In Parliament and the courts of law, proceedings are public, but what is said is given the defence of

---

[9] See above, ch.4, §4.5.

absolute privilege: in other cases, however, the protection is that of non-publicity; I am free to speak my mind, so long as I do so in good faith and without malice, on the understanding that what I say goes no further than the body I am addressing. The decisions ultimately arrived at may be public, but no statements, views, or opinions, expressed in the course of reaching them may be attributed to any individual.

There is a trade-off between openness and effectiveness. If people are allowed to say what they really think, they may think wrong, and not be corrected. The public are excluded, and some member of the public may be in a position to correct an error or put forward a better proposal. But public proceedings tend to be stilted and unreal. Much goes on behind the scenes that is not said in open court: the smoking room in the House of Commons is reckoned to be more important than the chamber itself. Where local council meetings are open, the real business tends to be done in committee or caucus, being only rubber-stamped at the meetings to which the public is admitted. Instead of expressing my doubts about someone's honesty openly in the appointments committee, I talk privately to those I trust, and together we vote him down. And that, even on the score of openness, is counter-productive: for if I had felt free to express my doubts to the whole committee, someone there might have been able to counter them, and cite further evidence to show the candidate to be trustworthy after all. Insisting on all official proceedings being public leads to real decisions being taken entirely in private. If we want bodies to be effective, we have to protect their proceedings with confidentiality.

The principle extends to managers and officials acting on their own. They need to be able to express their real thoughts unencumbered by publicity. And their real thoughts may not be very good ones. If adverse reports about my soap powder start coming in, my first thought is to suppress them, and hope that they will go away. If I am a Minister, and an opposition member is on to some disgraceful goings on in my department, my inclination is to cover up, throw wool in his eyes, and hope no more will be heard of it. Answers to parliamentary questions are an art form: they are courteous, informative, and give as little away as possible; they should not actually tell lies, but may be economical with the truth, stating many truths that were not asked for, but avoiding the point at issue so far as may be. Within that frame of reference, I may well discuss with my permanent officials just how far we can go in preventing Parliament from finding out what has been going on. And in exploring the bounds of constitutional propriety, I may well, in the written expression of my thoughts, go beyond them. If a memo is leaked, I shall be greatly embarrassed. I was trying to pull a fast one, but I did not want it to be known.

The practice of the law courts is illuminating. Legal procedures are structured competitively and adversarially. Each side is striving to win, putting forward the best arguments it can, and not giving any help to the other side, and entitled to keep its secrets from the other side. But though structured competitively and adversarially, the procedures are intended to serve the course of justice, and there are duties of disclosure where justice demands it. Documents have to be made available. Prior notice of an alibi must be given. Lies must not be told on oath. These are analogues of the duties of honesty firms bear towards customers, and Ministers to Parliament. Beyond these, however, is a further provision: communications between a party and his solicitor are privileged, and need never be disclosed. A criminal can tell his solicitor exactly what he did in complete confidence that it cannot be used against him, and that the solicitor will still help him to mount the best defence he can. We can understand the reason for this. Although the courts want to know the truth, they also want everyone to be able to put his case as best he can, and most people, not being lawyers, can do so only if they can consult a lawyer with complete freedom and security. Absolute confidence is required, even though it derogates from the openness and fullness of information also needed if the courts are to do justice.

Confidential secretaries and personal assistants are in some respects like solicitors. They are privy to their bosses' secrets, even their unadmirable ones. They have a duty of loyalty, much as friends have, that overrides most duties of disclosure. Not absolutely —not if the plan is to murder his wife—but very widely. And the reason is clear: only if he can have complete confidence in his secretary, can the boss do his job reasonably well. Otherwise, he will have to resort to hand-written notes, and super-secret files, which will waste time, and obstruct the efficient discharge of his duties.

But the very reasoning that justifies a high duty of confidentiality on the part of confidential secretaries, also restricts its application. Although some communications are confidential, not all are. The habit of marking all documents "Strictly confidential" is unjustified as well as being counter-productive. The circulation of such documents belies their really being that confidential. A Minister may have one confidential secretary, who will keep her mouth shut even when he is lying to Parliament, but cannot extend the cloak of that degree of confidentiality to the whole Department. The Department is a Department of State, with an overriding duty to abide by constitutional proprieties, and not tell lies to Parliament. Employees are servants of the Crown, not of the Minister. It is right to keep cabinet papers confidential as part of the normal process of government, and to protect the duty of officials to speak their minds freely, but not to cover up ministerial misdemeanour. The same principles apply to the exercise of confidentiality, within the business world, particularly at board level, where confidentiality may conflict with the need to speak out at times when intense struggles for survival, or the maintainance of competitive position, may tempt the board to disregard the law or the City code.

§6.6 Whistle-blowing

The three exceptions to the principle of openness give guidance about what an employee should do when faced with a dilemma, without resolving all dilemmas. There is always an obligation of loyalty. Just as the business enterprise should not expect complete identification on the part of the employee, and should respect the employee's autonomous individuality, so the employee should not expect the business to espouse all his own values and ideals, and should respect the firm's right to be different. If I am a Roman Catholic, I should not take employment with a contraceptives manufacturer; if I am a vegetarian, I should not work for a sausage-maker; if I believe that the government of Britain is a conspiracy to defraud the people of their rights, I should not be a civil servant; or if I conclude that any of these occupations is right for me, I must be guided by the values implicit in my employment, and not use my position to subvert its purposes.

Within the general obligation of loyalty, there are many different cases. Rather few employees are confidential secretaries, who have a special duty of loyalty to particular persons, and should respect their confidences in almost all circumstances. Apart from them, the duty is to the firm, not the managers, and the firm may be presumed to want to keep within the law, and do its duty by its customers, its employees, and the public generally. If it has a mission statement,[10] that will constitute a statement of the firm's values independently of what the managers say on a particular occasion. But the managers may be presumed to want this too, and should be given the benefit of fair dealing in any dubious case. If, for example, some adverse reports are beginning to come in, managers can reasonably hold that time is needed to evaluate the reports before taking what may prove to have been precipitate action. Only if there is a clear breach of duty, and internal approaches have been rebuffed or have proved fruitless, is it right to go public.[11]

§6.7 Collective Bargaining

Conflicts in employment can arise not only between what an employee is told to do and what is in the real interests of the firm, or what is enjoined by law, or what is required by morality, but also between his loyalty to the firm which pays him, and his own personal interests. He would like to be paid more, he would like to negotiate a more favourable deal, or better himself by going elsewhere. These are perfectly proper considerations, but not the only ones. They are balanced by obligations to employers, limited but none the less binding within those limits.

Although, as we have noted, contracts of employment are often short-term, the underlying understanding is for a much longer period;[12] and if it is fair for the employer to give long notice of impending redundancy, it is fair for the employee to give long notice too, so that the employer can find a satisfactory replacement—although, since few of us are absolutely indispensable, it is an obligation that can be overridden by personal circumstance. Again, because the employer has the greater say and greater responsibility, and is generally stronger, he is reasonably required to shoulder a greater burden, often carrying risks because they would fall disproportionately heavily on some individual employees.[13] That is fair.

---

[10] See below, ch.9, §9.1.

[11] Many employees are not in a position to tell whether anything unlawful is being done. Were Calvi's or Maxwell's secretaries competent to know that actions were being undertaken which were to lead to the fraudulent misuse of company funds?

[12] In this chapter, §2.

[13] In addition to the fundamental fact that the employer is risking his capital in providing employment, he may well accept some responsibility for carrying employees through periods of ill health and in old age.

But it carries with it an entitlement to the kind of return which an investor will expect to make on his investment, depending on the risk involved. Although in wage negotiations the parties are external to each other, and justice being indeterminate, it is generally reasonable to be guided by the going market price, that does not conclude the matter absolutely. Just as a freely-negotiated wage may be unfairly low, so it is possible for it to be too high. Although I may, in certain circumstances, be able to extort a very large wage for my services, it is unfair to do so if it leaves my employer with a level of cost that could make the business uncompetitive, carrying all the burdens, and reaping none of the rewards of being an employer.

The issues are sharper when the employees combine to bargain collectively with the employer. The normal disparity of bargaining power is reversed when the employer is not dealing with isolated employees individually, but with a trade union speaking for them all. But with a difference of power goes a difference of obligation. A trade union should understand the economics of the business in which the trade operates, and recognise the employer's need to remain competitive and profitable. Although sometimes negotiations break down, and a strike may be the last resort, every strike represents a breakdown in cooperation, and is likely to be counterproductive in the long run. More especially, whereas rather few employees are actually indispensable, so that if one walks out with no notice, the firm can still cope, the sudden simultaneous withdrawal of labour organized by a trade union is insupportable; many contracts have firm delivery dates, often now reinforced by penalty clauses, and unless managers can be sure that their work will not be disrupted by sudden strikes, they must avoid entering into any contract where timely delivery is essential. A strike may be a last resort when all negotiations have broken down, but wild-cat strikes are unwarranted.

In the years after the Second World War, before Marxism was finally discredited, the trade unions exercised great power, often irresponsibly. They reaped their reward. They made their fellow-countrymen, and in particular their own members, far poorer than they need have been, destroyed whole industries and greatly increased unemployment. Although in the short term a vigorous and unscrupulous trade union can do very well for its members, industries whose profits are sucked away to pay extortionate wages cannot attract capital or afford to innovate, and in due course lose out to other forms of enterprise or to competitors in other countries. The National Union of Miners destroyed the coal industry in Britain, NATSOPA and SOGAT the printing industry; ASLEF and NUR have undermined and marginalised the railways. The need for restructuring these industries in the face of technological change and new competition was ignored in order to preserve customary levels of employment and established work practices at all costs. There was, also, a divide between the *haves* and the *have-nots*, those who have work and those who do not. The trade unions represented the *haves*, and in pressing their interests to the limit, consigned many others to having no work. Although employees have their own interests external to those of employers, they also have obligations to them, and if they disregard them, they become unemployable.

But trade unions have a role. They were called into existence by the disparity of bargaining power between employers and employees, and still are needed to support the individual employee and prevent his being done down. They exist to represent the interests of the employees as against those of the employers, but should also recognise their community of interest with them, and undertake other functions for their members that can only be carried out collectively. There is opening out for them a new role, enabling modern business to develop a more effective mechanism for cooperation and the sharing of information. And they still have their traditional role of ensuring that the externality of the employment relationship is protected by agreements which take account of both the short- and the long-term interests of their members. A trade union should cooperate with the employer in maintaining the skills and competences on which the exercise of the trade is based. Besides its natural concern for increasing wages and protecting jobs, it should envisage increasing productivity and transforming jobs in a changing economy. The printers' unions should have been the first to welcome the electronic revolution and to move into desk-top publishing, opening up many new avenues of employment for their members, which have in fact gone to outsiders.

Trade unions are large, and for that reason can bear burdens and carry risks that would fall disproportionately heavily on individual members. The argument that because in the typical case the employer is large, he should shoulder these burdens, applies equally to the trade unions, and in time past the National Union of Miners provided some care for the sick and the elderly. With the advent of the Welfare State it has seemed that neither employers nor unions need take responsibility any more, but State provision is never likely to be entirely adequate, and there will always be contingencies unprovided for. The unions do much to help members who are in various ways unfortunate, and also have a purely social role, often sneered at, but valuable none the less. Employees pass most of their active life in the workplace, and it is the focus of much of their social and emotional life. But employment is inevitably structured in a hierarchical fashion, with most employees being at the bottom of the pecking order. In the trade union there is no such hierarchy, or at least a different one. A man can be more himself if he can meet his mates with no bosses around. And it is good that he can sometimes be more himself.

§6.8   Jobs

Although jobs are not goodies, they are widely felt to be so. In sacking an employee a businessman is depriving someone of his livelihood, in not taking someone on he is failing to give him a good. These are considerations which may properly be borne in mind, but they are secondary, or even tertiary, considerations, which may well be overridden by the primary ones of ensuring the survival and maintaining the prosperity of the firm, though they may come into play when circumstances permit. The secretary is incompetent, losing letters, failing to enter engagements. But she is an unmarried mother going through an emotional crisis. To sack her will send her further down the slope: to keep her may well land the firm in costly litigation. What is the manager to do? It seems hard to say that he must sack her, or at least move her to a position where she can do no harm, but that is the hard decision he must take. His prime responsibility is to the firm, and it is its welfare he must consider first and foremost. In treating employees he should consider their interests generally, but he cannot give priority to the individual interests of each without failing to put the firm's interests first. It makes sense to give to each employee terms of employment that are in general beneficial to both parties, but not to give to a particular one terms that are tailored solely to her needs and altogether one-sided. What sort of terms are generally beneficial to both parties remains open to debate. To allow some latitude to sick employees or to those who have long given good service is fair: it is taking a wider view of employment, and not confining attention to a single week's work. But what can properly be required of employers along these lines is narrowly confined.[14]

A large employer may well be able to find room for small numbers of disabled people or those from ethnic minorities, because having many places to fill, he can find some that do not require able-bodiedness or complete command of vernacular English. It is good that he should, not as a duty towards existing employees, but as one to the locality or to the wider community in which his firm operates. But, once again, legislation to make employers take on certain categories of workers is misconceived and counter-productive. Doctrines of Equality of Opportunity rapidly become precepts of equality of outcome: if an employer does not have the target proportion of workers of the specified category in his work force, it will be taken as presumptive evidence that he has been discriminating, and the onus of proof will be on him to show that he has not, an onus that will become progressively harder to discharge. But that again strikes at the root concept of employment, that it is centred on performing certain tasks, and that jobs are not desirable things to be distributed to those who are deemed to deserve them, but themselves determine the relevant criteria for selecting the people who should have them. If an employer is biased, and discriminates unfairly against suitable applicants, he will be damaging his own interests. But his job is to discriminate. He has to choose, and in choosing he also rejects. He should discriminate—against unsuitable applicants. However desirable it may be on general social grounds that certain categories should be able to obtain jobs, there are strict limits to what may be required of employers in furtherance of general social policies. Although there is, as we have argued,[15] some indeterminacy in what counts as fair dealing, and correspondingly some room for legislative enactment, nevertheless if the balance is tilted too much against one side, people will avoid entering into one-sided contracts, and the result of the legislation will be to damage the very people it was intended to help.

[14] See below, §6.10 and ch.9, §9.4.

[15] In ch.2, §2.5.

§6.9 Overmanning and Downsizing

One traditional response to unemployment has been to foster a certain degree of overmanning. Often in the National Health Service doctors would get patients they wanted to keep an eye on appointed as orderlies. It got out of hand—in some hospitals there were six times as many orderlies as were really needed, and once the unions moved in, the situation became intolerable, and hospitals now are under extreme pressure not to employ anyone they can manage without. But it is not clear that the previous practice was in principle wrong. Society as a whole is better off if five people are paid a little bit more than unemployment benefit, and turn up in hospital and do some work, than if they are given only unemployment benefit, are made to feel useless, and do not do anything useful at all. Although overmanning can be dangerous and did in fact do great damage in Britain, it is not inherently wrong. Unemployment is a great evil, and overmanning is sometimes a lesser one.

Most overmanning occurs in the public services, and is an issue for politicians rather than businessmen. But the issue can arise for them too, particularly when questions of mass-redundancy arise. Businessmen do not like sacking people. But sometimes there seems no help for it. A firm is in danger of being taken over. It must boost its dividends to persuade shareholders not to sell out. It can only do so by cutting costs so as to increase profits, and the wages bill can be cut. Otherwise, the predator will gain control, and will have no compunction in firing far more.

Managers often have to make hard decisions. That is part of the job. They may have to sack people who have given good service, simply in order to balance the books. The question is whether their reluctance to do so is simply squeamishness, or is evidence of a perfectly proper concern on their part, even though it may be overridden in particular cases by other weightier considerations. Imaginary cases may illuminate. A firm has been chugging along happily for many years, the chief employer in a small town in Ohio, achieving a profit margin of 5% making electrical equipment for a variety of specialist purposes. It is taken over by a firm that requires its managers to achieve a 15% profit margin. This it can do if it withdraws from the lower end of its market, cutting its labour costs by 80%, and concentrates on the top end, where an aggressive pricing policy could hoist prices substantially. At the end of the operation, 80% of the workforce will be unemployed, and the remaining customers will be paying much more for their equipment. We have doubts about the rightness of this course of action. It may raise profits for the parent company, but at a great cost to the employees and the remaining customers.

But it might still be for the best. It is no kindness to employees, it can be argued, to shield them from the cold winds of reality, and leave them living in a fool's paradise, while their industry slowly becomes obsolescent and finally moribund; far better to let them face the facts, and adjust while there is still time. In any case the reality may not be as bad as had been feared; there was great sorrow in Britain when various dying industries were closed down, but a few years later most of the former steel-workers in Wales had found new jobs, and fresh life was apparent where devastation had been feared. In South Wales the Steel Board took great pains to help its former employees find new jobs, but it is not to be supposed in that particular Ohio town that the new holding company will be so solicitous, or that other employment will be easily come by. Some employees are going to suffer quite badly; unemployment in that town is going to be greatly increased. But should that matter? Profits have increased; the firm is concentrating its efforts on the most profitable part of its business, and is not that all-important?

The short answer is No. Maximising profits, though important, is not all-important. The long answer is more difficult. Profits are important. We ought to make the best use we can of our resources. The individual firm cannot take on an indefinitely wide responsibility for providing employment. The obligation of the employer to provide employment is limited by the economic constraints under which he operates. In this situation the need for cooperation between employer and employees and their union representatives becomes paramount, and that cooperation will depend on information being available to employees to enable them to decide how far they may reasonably push their wage demands. But even with full information and good will all round there may still be an unresolved conflict between canons of business efficiency and the interests of the employees; and how to balance these contrary considerations in actual cases is one of the most difficult decisions businessmen have to take.[16]

---

[16] Different cultures attach different weights to the conflicting *desiderata*: the American approach would favour closing the business down; the Japanese and European approach is generally the opposite.

§6.10   Full and Future Employment

Full employment has been one of the stated objectives of public policy in many countries since the Second World War. People had a right to work, and it was the duty of employers and the State to provide employment for everyone. Recently the pendulum has swung the other way, and it was seen as the duty of businessmen to raise productivity, avoiding overmanning and squeezing out unnecessary fat. The number of those recognised officially as unemployed has increased, and now there are about 18 million people unemployed in Western Europe.

Not everyone is happy. It is widely recognised that the postwar policies were misconceived, bringing about stagflation and economic decline, as well as industrial indiscipline and trade-union dictatorship. But the re-emergence of an underclass of people who neither have, nor are ever likely to have, a job adds to the spectre of the 1930s further fears of social unrest. At least when they had jobs young males were not joy-riding, thieving, or vandalising. If we do not employ them, can we really afford to keep them all in prison?

Our present high rate of unemployment is in part the result of bad practices in time past. Many strikes were called in the 1960s and 1970s despite warnings from managers that if deadlines on exports were not met, orders would be lost. Orders were lost, and factories closed down. But in any case competition from South East Asia would have made many traditional industries no longer profitable. Coal seams were bound to be exhausted. And technological change would have altered patterns of employment radically. Only an adaptable workforce can maintain employment in the face of change, and most Western workforces are not sufficiently adaptable. It is partly a lack of training, partly the legal framework and social expectations. By imposing various rigidities, we have improved the position of the *haves*—those who have work—at the expense of the *have-nots*.

Inflation does not work. Although in the short term we can produce a boom by stimulating demand, wages and costs begin to rise too, and inflationary expectations build up, and stifle economic initiative. Economies that have tried to cure long-term unemployment by Keynsean methods have deteriorated over the years, and not avoided unemployment either. Moreover, full employment, engineered by the State, is nearly always full pretend-employment, which may stave off trouble for a season, but is ultimately subversive not only of economic health but even of the self-respect of those paid to do non-jobs. And some people are unemployable. To be employed demands a certain degree of self-discipline, in the way of turning up on time, and paying attention to what one is being told to do, and this is more than some people can manage, and more than others will manage unless there is a realistic threat of their being unemployed, if they do not take a grip on themselves. We cannot abolish unemployment, though we may be able to do things to reduce or ameliorate it, if we devise remedies more closely adapted to the problem facing us.

The demand for labour has changed greatly with mechanization and automation. At the beginning of the century a hundred agricultural labourers went out into the fields to gather the harvest, to reap, to bind, to stook, and to carry: now three or four men with a combine harvester can clear a field in a few hours. In the middle years of the century mass-production lines needed thousands of hands to perform their separate functions: now much skill goes into making and maintaining automatic machines that replace the human eye and hand. The able and intelligent work harder than ever before, but there are far fewer things we want done by the unskilled.

We could want more. We could, as a matter of social policy, develop a public taste for certain labour-intensive products. We could become a high-gardening society, which set great store by gardens, both public and private, and employed many men to garden them. Gardening, though at its best highly skilled, can be done by the unskilled, with considerable job-satisfaction. It would make our cities pleasanter places to live and work in, improving the quality of life as well as easing unemployment, though as yet we are not willing to pay either for the benefit to city life or for not having people needlessly out of work.

We have many other unsatisfied wants, which could be met if only we could match supply with demand. Many old people, many sick people need someone to fetch and carry for them. Our present taxation system makes it difficult for any but the very rich to afford such services. If we had a wider spread of wealth, we should greatly increase the demand for the sort of work the present unemployed could do. Egalitarians think it wrong that one person should serve another, or that one old woman should be able to afford the services of a butler, a footman, a chauffeur, a cook, and a parlour-maid, when others cannot. But once we abandon false images, we should have no more objection to one person's spending money on domestic service at home than to another's spending it on chamber-maids, waiters and ski-instructors abroad.

We should go further in eschewing egalitarian dogma. It is people with money to spare who find ways of satisfying wants not previously noticed. They can afford to devote quite a lot of money to having things just as they would like them, whereas people on tight budgets learn to be content with what they have, and put out of mind the wants they know there is no serious possibility of satisfying. Often the rich pave the way for others being able to acknowledge and satisfy their hitherto unrecognised wants too. But even if they do not, even if very few can ever have private yachts which go for Caribbean cruises, still, new employment is being generated. And even egalitarians might concede that inequality was less bad than unemployment.

Future patterns of work are likely to be very different, and much more flexible. Commuting makes a sharp break between work and the rest of life. It was not always so, and in some walks of life still is not; the owner of a corner-shop, the priest and the academic do not fence off their leisure from their work. But mostly now we expect work to occupy working hours most days of the week. This suits factory production and what is done in some sorts of offices, but is not necessarily or universally what is needed. There may be no jobs of this type available in time to come, but work none the less. The job-sharing schemes adopted by some women are a pointer to one new approach. In the North East of the United States of America some junior academics are "long-vac peasants". During the summer they live in log cabins in New Hampshire or Vermont, writing their theses and cultivating their plots of land, and in the winter they go back to Boston, and earn money writing software. They are not excluded from the variety and fulness of modern life, but are not constrained by the unremitting pressures of continuous employment. In Rio de Janeiro there are millions without jobs, but far fewer totally without work. We should envisage the same happening here in time to come, as computing commuting takes over from the conventional kind, and more people can be gainfully employed in their own time at home.

The pendulum swings. At one time too little concern was given to the problem of unemployment, then too much, and now again, too little.

Chapter 7
Customers, Suppliers and Neighbours

Contents

Abstract

Businessmen have external relations with their customers, suppliers, competitors and neighbours, giving rise to obligations based primarily on a recognition of the difference between the values of the parties, and a respect for the other's point of view, but modified by the fact that money is inherently general, and that each transaction needs to be considered not as a single one but in a context that is generalised with regard to person, circumstance and time. A responsible businessman, therefore, is guided by the principle *caveat vendor* rather than relying exclusively on *caveat emptor*, pays his suppliers promptly, gives more than contractual notice, competes only by fair means, not by foul; and on the basis of the common concerns he does have with those who do not share most of his values, he contributes towards the good of his trade, his locality, and the environment generally.

§7.1 Duties to Customers

Besides its internal involvement with shareholders and employees, a business enterprise has external relations, most notably with customers—those from whom it receives money—and suppliers—those to whom it pays money—which also give rise to mutual obligations. These are based primarily on the canons of justice, a recognition of the other's otherness, *alteritas*, taking into account the other party's point of view. In many cases shared concerns give rise to further grounds for consideration, since business relations, though external, are not entirely so; and where money is involved, special obligations arise from the nature of money, so that instead of viewing each transaction as an isolated, one-off bargain, we should see them in a wider context, ranging over customers in general, with typical needs and wants, and ranging also over time.

104

The customer should not be misled, but helped to make a rational choice in accordance with his needs and values. Although it is up to him to decide what he wants, it is up to the seller to provide goods or services reasonably meeting the standards of the sort of thing asked for. The seller is the expert, and his knowledge should be at the service of the buyer, not used to mislead him. The buyer has to rely on the seller's information, and if the seller is dishonest, needs redress. Even in time past, when buyers and sellers were approximately equal in status, and the goods offered for sale were mostly ones whose quality could be ascertained by the buyer, the principle *caveat emptor*, let the buyer beware, was not always adequate: from early on precious metals were hall-marked, because it was not feasible for the buyer to assure himself that they were not alloyed with base metal; often there were laws against watering milk, and adulterating other foodstuffs; and the Crown took responsibility for seeing that weights and measures in the market place were true. The need for reliable warranties, as a qualification of *caveat emptor*, was required by the courts in the nineteenth century, and was codified in the Sale of Goods Act, 1893. In the twentieth century some manufacturers, notably the motor manufacturers, began to get round the Act by inveigling customers to sign an order form waiving their statutory and common-law rights in return for a "warranty" which left everything to the discretion of the manufacturer. There were many cases of people buying cars which were no good, with engines that did not run smoothly, gear boxes that did not engage, brakes that failed, bodywork that was already rusty under paint that was peeling off. They were being treated dishonestly and unjustly by the motor manufacturers, who had great resources of technical know-how and legal support, and were selling a very complicated product to an individual. At length the Unfair Contract Terms Act was passed in 1977, and a further Sale of Goods Act in 1979, which struck down clauses in contracts waiving the provisions of the Sale of Goods Act. Legislation was also needed to extend the provisions of the Act to cover services as well as goods.[1] Since then the Insurance Companies, which allowed their over-enthusiastic salesmen to pressure people into buying unsuitable policies, have been learning, at an estimated cost of

---

[1] Supply of Goods and Services Act, 1982.

£100,000,000, the moral that the principle *caveat emptor*, is balanced by the complementary principle *caveat vendor*.[2] Although only the buyer can determine his priorities, and make up his mind what he really wants, it is the responsibility of the businessman, as holding himself out as ready to supply what is wanted, to see that the customer really gets what he really wants.

Customers pay for their goods with money, tokens guaranteed to be qualitatively identical though numerically distinct. In return the businessman has some duty to treat all customers equally, and not charge some more because of inexperience, vulnerability, or special need. The foreigner is an easy prey to an unscrupulous taxi-driver, the motorist stranded with a breakdown to the motor mechanic. But just as their money is reliably as good as that of anybody else's, so the prices charged them should be the same as those charged to other people. It is difficult to specify this duty precisely. It is not wrong for suppliers to give discounts to favoured customers or on special occasions, and many contracts are specially tailored in which the businessman is putting himself out to meet the particular needs of his client, and is entitled to charge accordingly. But some principle of open and equal treatment remains. It can be realised in many cases by the prior publication of prices—in many countries hotel rooms have to display the price asked, and taxi-meters similarly assure the passenger that he is being charged only a standard fare. In Germany and Switzerland shops must sell at the same price to all; discounts must be approved by the Government or Canton. In Italy bars must by law display their prices. The businessman is not taking advantage of the customer if he is charging him, and the customer knows he is being charged, only as much as what he charges customers generally. He is thus carrying out his duty of being ready to do business with all comers in the absence of special reasons against, and not using the special needs of their situation as reason for charging more.

In time past most goods were simple, and the retailer could form a judgement about their quality, and provided they were good, he would have no continuing responsibility once they were sold. But many goods now are complex. They arrive heavily packaged, and the retailer has no opportunity of checking their quality. Many

---

[2] Strictly speaking it should be *caveat venditor*, but that is ugly and unnatural, and 'vendor' is used by Latinate lawyers.

may need servicing, even though of good quality when sold. After-sales service and the supply of spares has become critical, and it is the mark of a good businessman that he is not finished with his customer as soon as the money is paid, but accepts a continuing responsibility to ensure that servicing and spares are available. In the newer industries the responsibility is widely recognised; indeed, in some it is beginning to be understood that in buying a car or a computer, the customer is not buying just a piece of hardware but rather many miles of reliable motoring or the reliable execution of software programs. Older industries are slower to realise their continuing obligations—potteries will sell a tea set for a time, and then discontinue it altogether, although in the nature of things some cups or saucers of a wedding present will be broken, and the value of the whole set is diminished if they cannot be replaced.

Our understanding of the mutual obligations of buyer and seller reflects our realisation that they are in different positions. In the modern world the seller, like the employer, tends to be large, and to have greater resources and greater say in the course of events.[3] Besides being naturally responsible for the nature of the goods and services being sold, he is expected also to bear certain risks and shoulder some additional responsibilities, just because his shoulders are broader. The motor manufacturers used to make out that it was just bad luck if someone bought a "lemon". some cars were better than others, and in buying a car one was buying a pig in a poke; usually one was lucky, but a proportion of customers were unfortunate. Quite apart from the implausibility of the claim that manufacturers could not exercise quality control, the argument failed to meet the counter-contention that if there was a statistical probability of a car's being a lemon, the cost should be carried by the manufacturer, who could charge a little more for all his wares, rather than fall on a few individuals, who would have spent a lot of their money on something that was no good. The justification for requiring the Post Office, public utilities and transport companies to provide services at awkward times and in awkward places is similar. There is a burden, in this case not of risk but of public policy, and it seems fair to place it unevenly as between the two parties to the purchase.

But the customer is not in all respects in a weaker position. He alone knows what he really wants, he has the final say whether

---

[3] See above, ch.6, §6.2.

to buy or not to buy. Although in some respects he needs to be protected, it is wrong—and inexpedient—to weight the scales too much in his favour.[4]

§7.2 Advertising

Advertising may contravene good business practice with its power to influence and persuade the buyer whose choice will be determined not by the intrinsic usefulness of the product in itself, but by the way it is advertised and promoted. The advertising industry has aimed to set its own house in order through the setting up of the Advertising Standards Authority (ASA) in 1962 and the publication of an Advertising Code which specifies the principles on which advertising and promotion should be based.

The first principle of the Advertising Code, that advertisements should be "legal, decent, honest and truthful", raises a lot of ethical questions. Is it decent to advertise perfume or lingerie with seductive images of the gratification the consumer may hope to obtain through the purchase of these products? Is it honest to portray the pleasures of certain alcoholic drinks consumed on a Caribbean beach? Is it truthful to advertise cigarettes through images of masculine survival in the wild outback, even if health warnings are clearly footnoted? Answers to these questions are likely to be widely divergent and probably irreconcilable. Who is to be the final arbitrator? A State authority? The individual consumer? The ethical issues are complex, and can be answered only if there are agreed positions on what are the responsibilities of the vendor. The principle of *caveat vendor* extends beyond the quality of the product to the way in which it is advertised.

There are other ethical questions. What about advertisements that stimulate wants not previously experienced? Any form of manipulation runs counter to our ideal of autonomous choice on the part of the consumer, but the ideal may be expressing an unreal view of human nature. Merely to know of a possibility will make some people covet it. And often its value is largely created by the advertising image. It would be unduly puritanical to ban all advertisements for soap, alcohol, or cigarettes, on the score of the unreasonable images they conjure up. And yet the difficulty is recognised by the Advertising Code itself when it states that advertisements should not exploit the "credulity, loyalty, vulnerability,

---

[4] See further below, ch.9, §9.4.

or lack of experience" of children. How is the vendor to determine what is the credulity or vulnerability of his target customers, and should he be responsible for doing so? In terms of the principle of *alteritas* the answer has to be Yes, although this both extends and increases the way in which a businessman will have to take decisions.

Other areas of subverting the freedom of the individual, such as subliminal advertising, are clearer. Clearly we are subverting individual freedom, if the individual is unaware of the underlying message to which he is being subjected. But even though it is right to ban advertisements which appeal to certain fears or prejudices, we should hesitate to censor what people are to see. The responsible businessman will not wish to avail himself of that opportunity to mislead potential customers, but the power and influence of modern media increases his obligations to know what he is doing when he approves the latest creative proposals of his advertising agency.

§7.3 Duties to Suppliers and Creditors

Whereas a businessman's customers are those from whom he receives money, his suppliers are those to whom he pays money. His most important duty is actually to pay them, reliably and promptly; a duty much neglected in many business dealings. A practice has grown up in recent years of large firms failing to pay their suppliers, mostly small firms, over long periods of time, relying on the inefficiency of the legal process, and threatening to withdraw their custom in future if any action is taken to make them honour their obligations. The large firms are, in effect, gaining credit at the small firms' expense. There is nothing wrong in seeking credit if it is done openly and explicitly. I can offer you a contract whereby you deliver next month and get paid next year when my bills have been paid; and you, knowing that payment will be deferred, can quote a price accordingly. But it is entirely wrong for a big firm to enter into a contract whereby it undertakes to pay within thirty days, and not keep to it, reckoning that it will cost the supplier too much to take it to court, and anyhow the court will not get round to giving a judgement for a year or so. Such practice is clearly wrong. It would be good if it were condemned so severely in the business community that no firm could afford to engage in it. The Confederation of British Industry claims to be against the practice, and it could, together with trade associations and local chambers of commerce publish the names of regular late payers. More realistically, the Office of Fair Trading should be authorised to demand from firms suspected of late payment details of invoices and payments, and publish warnings to suppliers not to deliver goods until money has been received. In the last resort legislation may be called for. Legislation, though difficult to enforce, can be effective in changing business practices. For example, in the nineteenth century many employers short-changed their employees by paying them with tied credits, until the Truck Act outlawed the practice. It may be that some similar Act of Parliament is called for now, if only to make interest on late payments a legally enforceable obligation.

Some large firms, by contrast, not only pay their suppliers fully and promptly, but take care to maintain their independence, refusing to take more than a certain proportion of their output, so that if the large firm should cease trading, or for good reason go to another supplier, the small firm would not go under. It is somewhat analogous to making pension rights transferable, so that the employee is reasonably free to seek other employment and not too dependent on his present firm. It is taking the externality of business relations seriously.

Banks and other institutions often supply credit. It must be left very largely to the discretion of the creditor what terms to negotiate, because he stands to lose if things go wrong—though the better the security, the less onerous should be their terms. Because legal contracts often do not represent the real understanding, it is important for both parties to be clear what the real understanding is. Legally an overdraft can be called in at a moment's notice, but since that is not the practice, a bank manager should indicate what sort of notice he will give, so that the business can make contingency plans for obtaining alternative finance, should the bank need to have its money back. There are many cases, with regard to suppliers as well as creditors and debtors, where the parties are, with good reason, unwilling to tie themselves down to a legal duty to give notice or to continue an arrangement, but should recognise in all normal circumstances some obligation to give notice, or not to disappoint reasonable expectations, none the less.

§7.4 Duties to Competitors

It may seem strange to say that we have duties towards our competitors, because on the classical view we are locked in cut-throat competition with them in a zero-sum game, where their gain is our loss. But, as the analogy with games, competitions and the law courts shows, the fact that the exercise is adversarial does not mean that there are no obligations, only that some do not obtain in these situations.[5] The obligations of honesty and fair dealing hold good both in competitive sports and in the market place. Although there is a natural opposition of interest, with each party striving to succeed, even though it will be at the expense of its rivals, there are different ways of competing, and we have a strong intuitive sense of which are fair and which unfair. To provide a better product or render a better service at a lower price is fair: but when British Airways got hold of the names of those intending to fly with their rival, Virgin, and telephoned them offering a comparable flight at a reduced fare, it was properly seen as unethical conduct. They were not competing on a level playing field, but were using information they should not have obtained in order to make special offers, not open to the general public, to persuade just those who had made up their minds to fly with Virgin to change their minds. Rockefeller was defensive, when it emerged that his salesmen were undercutting his rivals and forcing them out of business;[6] and that again was unfair, because the level playing field was skewed, in this case over time rather than person. It would have been different if Rockefeller had continued to sell at a price his competitors could not match, even after they had gone out of business. He would than have shown himself a more efficient competitor, justly entitled to win everyone's custom. But he did not keep his prices down once he had bankrupted his rivals, but, having achieved a monopoly, acted like a monopolist. Many people buy the *Independent*, just in order to frustrate Mr Murdoch's attempts to drive it out of business by selling *The Times* at a loss.

In any case the classical analysis gives a distorted account. If it were true, competitors would shun one another's company, each seeking a corner of the market all of its own. But members of the same trade foregather together in trade associations and guilds:

[5] See above, ch.4, §4.5.

[6] J.Rockefeller, *Random Reminiscences*, London, 1909, pp.59, 62-63.

in many towns they congregate in the same area, in Smithfield, Fisherman's Row, or Chandler's Street, and for good reason. If you want to buy a dress or a curtain fabric, you want as wide a variety of choice as possible. You want to be able to shop around. You will therefore go to where there are many shops in preference to where there is only one. If I am the only milliner in Great Tidworth, I shall have a captive market of all its 800 inhabitants, but few people will come over from Broughton Episcopi, Little Norton, or Plumstead-sub-Hamdon, because the chance of finding what they want is my shop is too small to justify the time and trouble of the journey. I shall do far better if I set up shop in Barchester itself, because though I shall have more competitors, the very fact that they offer greater choice will bring in far more potential customers. Moreover, I can learn from my competitors. I cannot try all innovations by myself. Many will end in failure and I should not be able to stand the loss. But if my competitors are each trying some innovations, I shall be able to observe what happens, and shall be kept on my toes to adopt the ones that catch on. Monopolies usually stagnate, and though they have a captive market, it often becomes a reluctant and resentful one. Competition stimulates improvement and defuses resentment.[7]

Competitors, therefore, have a number of common interests, which constitute grounds for common obligations: moreover, the competitive structure itself, within which they operate imposes duties and non-duties. For the only way to resolve the conflict between respect for the other' point of view and the desire to win, is to accept some system of rules or common practice according to which the conflict may be played out.[8]

---

[7] Thus Albert O.Hirschman, *Exit, Voice, and Loyalty*, Harvard University Press, 1970, p.37, "Competition in this situation is a considerable convenience to the manufacturers because it keeps consumers from complaining; it diverts their energy to hunting for the inexistent improved products that might possibly have been turned out by the competition."

[8] For a fuller discussion of the "good" competitor, see Tom Sorell and John Hendry, *Business Ethics*, Butterworth Heinmann, Oxford, 1994, ch.6, pp.153-154, and the examples of Pilkington Glass and small businesses in Scotland.

§7.5 Duties to Trade

Less controversial than the claim that a firm has duties to its competitors is that it has duties to its trade, or line of business. In some modern industries, especially in newer science-based ones, research will benefit the industry as a whole, but is too expensive to be undertaken by any one firm. Many firms help to provide education for new recruits to the industry. In both cases a partial justification can be made out in terms of enlightened self-interest, but it is evident that this is often only a rationalisation.[9] When a new product is being launched, or a new factory built, very careful estimates are made of the return on the expenditure. But it is more difficult to analyse likely benefits from contributing to a research centre or providing scholarships for students. Sometimes the research pays off, sometimes the students supported subsequently take jobs with the company. But the connexion between money laid out and benefits obtained is tenuous. We cast bread upon the waters, hoping that in many days the return will justify the deed, but reckoning that anyhow it behoves a firm in a particular trade to make some contribution to the good of that trade.

Trades often also seek to maintain standards, to police themselves, eliminating cow-boy operators who cheat the public and bring the whole trade into disrepute. They are right to do so, but care is needed. The mediaeval guilds kept up standards, but tended also to restrict competition. Doctors in the United States manage to be very well remunerated, with the result that medical attention is usually difficult and always expensive to obtain; so much so that it is often beyond the reach of the poor. Many economists have argued that all restrictions in the name of quality control are against the public interest, and that members of the public should be left free to make their own choice.[10] But that is unrealistic. I do not have the knowledge to choose a good doctor, and having only one life, cannot afford to discover by trial and error who is competent to look after my health. Although at first it might seem that an absence of regulation would extend competition by opening the industry to new competitors, if there were a general perception that many operators were shoddy, the end-result would be to put

[9] See above, ch.5, §5.2.

[10] For example, Adam Smith, *The Wealth of Nations*, Bk I, ch.10, pt.2, Everyman ed., vol.1, pp.107ff.

a great premium on having already acquired a reputation for reliability. Some degree of regulation and certification not only gives the public information that it needs about quality, but also can enable new firms to compete with those already established. But the dangers remain. There is a standing temptation to raise standards, ostensibly for the benefit of the public, but actually to restrict competition and increase the remuneration of those already practising. Although it is good to have very highly trained doctor to attend me, it is better to have some less highly qualified medical auxiliary than none at all. In particular, the professions are faced with the problem of deciding what is the correct balance between qualification and the cost of the professional service provided. There is a risk that by setting a long obstacle race for would-be entrants, the profession restricts the number of those who actually qualify. Obviously, the professions need to protect and maintain professional standards, but as professions they have an obligation to demonstrate that the cost of professional services is fair and reasonable, and not distorted by over-qualification.

There is no simple answer to the question of how highly qualified the entrants to a trade should be. What is desirable is that the decision should not be entirely in the hands of established practitioners, whose collective interest has a natural tendency to diverge from the public interest. There needs to be some element of lay control. Adam Smith was suspicious of the confabulations of professionals.

> People of the same trade seldom meet together, even for merriment and diversion, but the conversation ends in a conspiracy against the public, or in some contrivance to raise prices. [11]

If there is always some non-professional present when training programmes, standards of qualification, or codes of conduct are being drawn up, it will be less easy to have a covert conspiracy against the public, and on occasion the lay members may raise the embarrassing question of whether the public might not be better served if there were less well qualified people offering a less good service, but at an affordable price.

The principle of lay control can be implemented in many ways. Most schools and some universities have governing bodies largely

---

[11] Adam Smith, *The Wealth of Nations*, Bk I, ch.10, Everyman ed., vol.1, p.117.

composed of laymen. Many appointments in the Church are made by laymen. Many companies now have non-executive directors from outside the industry, with the purpose of improving corporate governance.[12] It is difficult to get the right balance of expertise—only those well versed in the trade can really understand what is going on—and impartiality—only those from outside can really take the outsider's viewpoint. But in discharging his duty to his trade the businessman needs not only to ensure that the interests of the trade are collectively realised but, paradoxically, that they are confronted, and if necessary challenged, by some wider public interest.

§7.6 Duties to Neighbours

Firms have duties to the local community and to wider ones. The underlying argument is the one already given, that a firm is a corporation, a centre of decision-making, and hence able, and needing, to take into account a wide variety of considerations in arriving at its decisions. In particular, a firm can reasonably be said to be located in the place where it operates. It has the power to alter the way things happen in its locality, just as I have in mine, and questions can be asked about the things it does, which a responsible businessman will want to be able to answer satisfactorily. Contributions to the local community, and society in general, are common practice on the part of many businesses today, and may result in a diminution of profits available for distribution to shareholders.

Three different sets of neighbours may be identified: the local community, the national state, and—perhaps—the whole of mankind. In addition, we can identify a non-personal neighbourhood, the environment, as being also a focus of concern. The responsibilities of business enterprises to the State and to the Third World will be dealt with in Chapters 9 and 11; here we shall discuss only their responsibilities to the local community, and the environment.

To a considerable extent the firm's responsibilities to the local community are commuted into the payment of rates and taxes. But sometimes there are special needs which the local community is unable to meet, or opportunities open only to the firm, and then

---

[12] See Report of the Committee on the Financial Aspects of Corporate Governance, London, 1992. (The Cadbury Report)

there may be good reason for further action. As in other cases, the action can be justified on grounds of enlightened self-interest—if the locality is a good one and the local community flourishing, people will want to work for the firm and to do business with it—but in many cases the underlying motivation is purely moral.

Economic activities often pollute, and businessmen are often asked to take into consideration the effect they are having on the environment. Some feel obscurely guilty, and wonder if there is any way they can obtain a clean bill of health: others are robustly defiant, and say it is up to the legislators to lay down acceptable standards of emissions, and within those limits they are free to do whatever will maximise profits.

Both views are wrong. While it is true that all human activity impinges on the environment, it is not the case that it is necessarily for the worse. The English countryside is the result of centuries of human interaction with the land. pristine state: in Brazil almost all the Atlantic seaboard has been brought under cultivation, and it is right to protect the remaining virgin forest. The Amazon rain forest needs protection because of the extremely destructive exploitation to which it has been subject hitherto.. But not every exploitation is malign: to eliminate malarial swamps or the very existence of the smallpox virus is to make the world a better place, even though a less natural one.

Many industrial processes, however, do have bad effects. Waste products pollute the atmosphere, the water table, or landfill sites. Each ton of coal burnt contributes to acid rain, eroding ancient buildings and destroying forests, and to the greenhouse effect, which may, for all we know, have disastrous consequences in the next century.[13] Such considerations should weigh with anyone taking decisions. The view that it is up to the law to set limits to what may be legitimately done, and that within those limits the businessman is free to do whatever seems most profitable is, as we have seen,[14] a mistake. The law is inevitably too crude an instrument to define accurately what may or may not be done, and often considerations of enforceability or public policy will make it impracticable or inexpedient to enact a law which, on the merits of the case, ought to be enacted. The fact that there is no law against

[13] See further, ch.11, §11.7.

[14] In ch.4, §4.7; see also ch.9, §9.3, and ch.3, §3.5.

sending out sulphur dioxide into the atmosphere is no reason for thinking that it is perfectly all right to do so. Considerations of practicality often also prevent laws actually in force from being enforced. Adverse neighbourhood effects are covered by the law of nuisance, but it is often difficult and expensive to invoke the law. Can an angling association prove in court that the dearth of fish in their stretch of the river is due to the effluent from my factory and not to that from another one higher up the stream? But the doctrine that one can damage one's neighbour so long as the damage cannot be provably laid at one's door is a doctrine that few responsible men would care to endorse.

But the absence of legally enforced restraints is relevant. It determines the context in which the businessman operates, and the competition he has to meet. If everyone else is spewing out sulphur dioxide, I cannot afford to put in expensive apparatus to scrub my emissions—and anyhow it will not make much difference to an atmosphere already much polluted. My customers are not prepared to pay for the privilege of being environmentally pure, and the actual benefit will be marginal. And even if there were laws imposing strict controls on emissions, we should merely lose business to Third-world countries that were not so pernickety.

There is force in these arguments, but they do not conclude the matter. At any one time we are caught up in a situation not of our own devising, and must live in the world as it is, not as we would like it to be. But we need not be completely conformed to the world. Some moves are open, at least to monitor, and perhaps to mitigate, the adverse effects of our activities. Carelessness, rather than economy, is often responsible for the worst pollution. Many effluents can be recycled, or made less noxious before they are released. Often, indeed, they can be degraded biologically, if only we allow time and take trouble to find the bacterium with the right appetite. And the pressure of the best practice is effective over time in raising standards in the locality, or industry, as a whole.

Because some environmentalists are woolly-minded idealists, anxious to save the whale, but altogether unaware of the realities of industrial life, and because the neighbours who suffer from neighbourhood effects are manifestly only neighbours, many businessmen and politicians have responded by rejecting environmental concerns, even against their own interests. But often they need to employ woolly-minded idealists as researchers, or sell to them as customers: one of the key factors in the rehabilitation of the

North of England has been to make it a place where managers and those with rare abilities are willing to have their families grow up. Britain and the United States have been scandalously complaisant over their emissions of sulphur dioxide and nitrogen oxides because Members of Parliament and Congressmen think that Norway and Canada are good places for acid rain to fall, but forget that most of the damage is done to their own buildings and their own woods and lakes. The communists cared little for the environment, and one of the factors that undermined the morale of their ruling *élite* was the evident mess they were making of the world, and the coughs and asthma of their wives and daughters.[15]

---

[15] Just days before the Velvet Revolution, there was a quite big (5,000-10,000) demonstration in a polluted region of northern Bohemia where the crowd (chanting "we want oxygen") defied the police and eventually extracted some local party boss from his headquarters to talk to them.

Chapter 8
The Professions

Contents

Abstract

Transactions with professional people differ in that they claim to be acting disinterestedly and not to be concerned to make a profit. Although it is difficult to give a completely satisfactory account of disinterestedness and benevolence in terms of the Theory of Games, it is clear that such conduct is possible. The professional ideal, however, is difficult to realise, in view of the fact that professional people are human, with human wants and needs, and only limited time and resources available to them. In a monetary economy they need to be paid, sometimes by providing them with a salary from outside sources, sometimes by their charging fees. Both methods have their disadvantages, and can in the course of time lead to a loss of professional idealism. There is a fundamental clash between the professional's fiduciary role, doing what is best in his judgement for the client, patient, pupil, or parishioner, and identifying with the individual so completely as to do what he happens to want. Recent attacks on the professions have emphasized the importance of consumer choice, but failed to recognise the need for reliable guidance and the importance of the fiduciary role.

§8.1 The Professional *Ethos*

The professions present an important contrast with business. The professional man is committed to his profession, independently of financial rewards: it is what he wants to do, often what he has always wanted to do, and he does it because he wants to, or thinks it is what he ought to do, not because he is paid to do it. Whereas business transactions are avowedly bargains between parties with different priorities associating together for the benefit of each, the

119

professional man distances himself from his own self-interest, and tries to do what in his judgement is best from the other's point of view. There are obvious practical difficulties in realising this ideal, but deep theoretical ones, too, in articulating it coherently. In one way it seems to be carrying to its logical conclusion the necessary concern with the other's point of view that is implicit in all business transactions, and many types of business aspire to professional status, and seek to establish themselves as proper professions. But besides difficulties over remuneration, there is the deeper one of how far it is possible to treat a particular individual as a particular individual and to know better than he does what he really wants. Between the *ethos* of the professions and that of business there is a dialectic which brings out not only the weaknesses of the business *ethos*, but also its strengths.

§8.2 Benevolence

Adam Smith erred in denying the effectiveness of benevolence. Although I am the only person who can take the ultimate decision about what I shall do, I do not have to decide selfishly, or pursue my own third-personal interests. Not only may my first-personal interests diverge from the third-personal interests that can be standardly ascribed to me,[1] but I can change the pay-offs I ascribe to outcomes in the light of the pay-offs of others. It had not mattered to me at all where the harassed mother with two toddlers took herself, but when she asked me the way to the bus station, it became an objective of mine to accompany her a short distance and set her on her way. In a family although I may distinguish my own interest from my brother's, I nevertheless rate his good highly, and what is good for him is *eo ipso* fairly good for me too. Cicero wrote to his son, Quintus, that he was the only person in all the world, whom he wanted to do better than himself in all things.[2] It is a familiar theme, difficult to do justice to within the framework of the theory of games. Once we start incorporating into the pay-offs of one the pay-offs of another, we are in danger of embarking on an infinite regress. It may be all right for me to add to my pay-off 90% of my

---

[1]　See above, ch.1, §1.4.

[2]　*Solus es omnium a quo me in omnibus vinci velim*, quoted by St Augustine, in his unfinished *Contra Secundam Juliani Responsionem*; *Opus Imperfectum*, VI, 22.

brother's, and *vice versa*, but we may then each take account of the other's adjusted pay-off, and do so again and again, *ad infinitum*; indeed, if we were each 100% altruistic, we should both adjust to infinite pay-offs. We need to insist on some, slightly artificial, distinction between primary and all-in-all evaluations. In Augustine's primary evaluation it was of prime importance that he, Augustine, should be rich and successful; in that of his son, Adeodatus, it was of prime importance that he, Adeodatus, should be but in Augustine's all-in-all evaluation it was rated even more highly and was of even greater importance that Adeodatus should have lived to be rich and successful. Rather crudely, we can characterize the all-in-all evaluation of the benevolent man as assigning the same pay-offs to outcomes as are assigned by those most concerned. He is, so to speak, the mirror image of a public good, which is an outcome that is assigned the same pay-off by all concerned: (the symmetry is not perfect, because the benevolent man assigns a greater pay-off to outcomes that I value than are assigned by others, different from me and less benevolent than him). But whatever the difficulties in giving a games-theoretical analysis, the practice is easy. Most of us are benevolent some of the time, and many of us have been the beneficiaries of much beneficence from others.

Some benevolence is institutionalised. Charitable associations, notably the Church, set out to minister to the needs of people generally: the Church provides pastoral care and spiritual counsel, and in the ancient and mediaeval world also education and medical care. The modern professions stem from the mediaeval ideal of dedication to providing for the needs of others in certain respects. Whereas in the ordinary business transaction the parties do not naturally have a common objective, and only by means of a transfer of money can they construct a package that both want to bring about, in a professional relationship the professional man and his client have a common objective which they both want to achieve in the ordinary course of events. The doctor and the patient both want the patient to be restored to health; the schoolmaster and the pupil both want the pupil to learn and achieve a proper understanding of the subject; the priest wants the penitent to achieve a right relationship with God as much as the penitent does. The sense of shared objective colours all our perceptions of the professions, and these in turn colour our expectations in other cases, and, in particular, give rise to adverse views about trade, motivated solely by the desire for profit, as contrasted with the professions, animated by motives altogether higher and purer.

§8.3 The Oldest Profession

'Motives altogether higher and purer' sounds good, but then we begin to wonder. Are they really doing it for love? If so, why do they charge fees, sometimes quite substantial ones? There is a suspicion not just of hypocrisy, but of something worse. The butcher's meat is not tainted by his selling it for money, but some actions, those whose value lies in what they signify as much as in what they effect, are compromised, or even corrupted, by being done for money. The Franciscan friar gives freely, demanding no money in return. The priest ministers to his flock for love, not for money. The doctor heals the sick because they are sick. The teacher has an understanding to impàrt, loves the young, and wants them to develop their full potential. These are admirable motives, which we can all respect. We naturally draw a contrast between actions done out of these motives and those done for the sake of money, and begin to look askance at the profit motive, and wonder if those who do things for money are not prostituting their talents— the talented artist or writer who spends his time working for an advertising agency, is he not prostituting himself, in devoting his God-given talents to making money instead of expressing himself unconstrained by thoughts of filthy lucre? A priest who absolves me from my sins and then asks for a fee makes me doubt the validity of his actions. The integrity of the professional's professed dedication is compromised by any mention of money. It must be done disinterestedly if it is to be any good, and disinterestedness is compromised by pecuniary interest.[3]

§8.4 Disinterestedness

The disinterestedness of the professions was expressed in terms of shared values. The surgeon, anaesthetist and nurses set great store on the operation's being successful. Each individual patient's good matters greatly to the doctor; the spiritual welfare of his flock is the prime concern of the pastor; the teacher cares greatly for his pupils' success. There is no significant divergence of values in their ministrations, as there is in the paradigm business transaction. The community of interest makes their association more a family affair than a business one. Although the association may be only temporary, while it lasts they are members of the same community, sharing the same concerns, cooperating together in order to realise the same values.   The pupil in his efforts to learn is pleasing

---

[3] The words 'disinterested', 'disinterestedly' and 'disinterestedness' are being used in their traditional sense of denying a third-personal interest, but not a first-personal one. See footnote §1.4, *ad fin.*, p.15n.

his teacher just as he appreciates his teacher's efforts to help him. They both want him to be able to solve differential equations, write Greek verses, or remember the dates of the Kings of England.

But the community of interest is not complete. As sometimes in a family and always in a firm there are some divergences of values which cannot be completely overlooked. It costs the professional something to render his services. Time is limited. If the doctor attends to me, he is not doing other things he might want or need to do: he is not playing golf, not mending his car, not cooking his supper. Given enough money, he can pay others to mend his car, cook his supper, and in a world where few people are clever enough to be doctors and it takes a long time to train them, it is eminently sensible that doctors should be given enough money to be able to devote the bulk of their waking hours to keeping us healthy. That money must be provided somehow. In Britain it has been, at least until recently, a national concern to provide a health service for everybody. Teachers are commonly employed by schools, and the school constitutes the community which provides enough to free the teachers from the need to earn their living elsewhere. Clergymen of the Church of England hold benefices, originally endowed by the benefactions of long ago, and in return for a (somewhat exiguous) stipend hold themselves in readiness to serve the spiritual needs of any of God's children at any time, and in particular to look after their parishioners. In each case there is some recognition that complete disinterestedness cannot be sustained by a human being over long period of time, because he has needs of his own which must be met if he is to give himself to the implementation of the values of his profession.

In the modern world we often pay stipends to professional men, the difference of terminology signifying the different basis on which it is paid. A stipend is not a reward. It is not performance-related pay. Nor is it a bargain. Rather, it is an enabling: the stipend is paid in order that the person to whom it is paid need not spend time on his personal concerns, but can devote himself entirely to his profession. The difference is shown by the different reactions to not needing to earn a living. Occasionally clergymen, schoolmasters, academics, or doctors have come into a fortune. They do not thereupon throw up their profession, and go to live a life of ease, but continue as before, though in a more affluent way. We find this quite natural, whereas we should be considerably surprised if a car salesman on winning the pools returned to the showroom.

§8.5 Professional Pay

Many people in modern Britain believe that clergymen, nurses, teachers, academics and social workers ought to be content with the bare necessities of life, since they have rewarding jobs. There is some force in this argument. They have the privilege of doing what they would want to do anyhow. They are not in it for the money, so there is no need to pay them. The monks did without money, wife, or family, requiring only food, raiment, and shelter; but though we sometimes expect others to practise apostolic poverty, we are less keen to embrace it ourselves, and there are disadvantages in requiring it of others. People with very little money spend a long time eking it out. The clergyman cannot afford to take his car to the garage to be serviced, so he does it himself, when he might have been visiting the sick. The schoolmaster cannot afford to buy new books, so he waits until he can get them from the public library but finds it closed on the one day he goes into town. Apostolic poverty was a feasible option in first-century Palestine, with a rural economy in which money did not play a crucial role, but is hampering in a twentieth-century society of bus fares and credit cards. If professional people are to play any normal part in society, they have to be monied like everybody else. It is neither sensible nor fair in a rich society to think that because teachers have a vocation to teach, therefore they ought to be paid a pittance.

There is a further difficulty. Many people have a vocation to marriage and family life as well as to some professional calling. And they are understandably reluctant to embrace apostolic poverty on behalf of their wife and future children. It is possible, as in the Church of Rome, to make it a clear choice, and insist on the celibacy of the clergy. Some will then choose marriage rather than the priesthood, and there may be a shortage of those willing to give up all prospect of marriage and children in order to minister to others. If we insisted that dons, doctors, or schoolteachers, should remain celibate, we should be unlikely to staff our universities, health service, or schools. Moreover, as again the Church of Rome has found, those willing to remain celibate do not always fare well. There are genuine advantages of celibacy, in the mission field, in slum parishes, and, quite differently, in the Oxford and Cambridge colleges of yester-year, but disadvantages too. The married clergyman with his family has more points of contact with his parishioners, and a greater experience of the problems of family life, the married schoolteacher less tempted by the advances of precocious adolescents, the married social worker a stable base of normality as a refuge from the intractable problems of the deprived and the depraved. Celibacy, though suitable for a season for some, and as a life-long vocation for others, is neither suitable for all, nor desirable as a general rule in the professions.

But if professional people are not to be celibate, then we ought not to wish on the vicar's family a very low standard of living. We have to adjust the level upwards to some sort of going rate. What that should be is again a matter of dispute. Some think that the families of the clergy and of social workers should be as poor as the poorest of those they minister to, in order to show a greater sense of identification and to secure that those ministered to should not have occasion to envy them their easy life. This may be appropriate in some circumstances, but the considerations adduced are not all that compelling, and we should be chary of vicariously embracing poverty on others' behalf in order to manifest their identification, or to assuage the supposed envy of yet others. Often the standard of comparison should be with other families with less dedicated fathers: "If father had been an income-tax inspector instead of a schoolmaster, we would have been able to go to the pantomime at Christmas" is the line of thought we need to ponder. Precise answers will not be forthcoming: circumstances are too complex and varied for any precise rule to be valid. But questions on behalf of the family may help us not to take professional dedication as a reason for short-changing their families.

§8.6   Benefices and Fees

Two ways of paying professional people have been tried. Both have disadvantages. We may make a rigid separation between the payment of a stipend and the performance of specific duties. We appoint someone to a post, with a definite stipend and a somewhat indefinite job-description attached, leaving it to him to do the best he can. The stipend provides him with, in the terminology of the old Church of England, a "living". Livings, or benefices, often financed by some benefaction of long ago, enable the incumbent to devote himself entirely to his calling without having to concern himself with winning his daily bread. Academic posts are the modern equivalent, and so, until recently, were many jobs in the National Health Service. In each case the service was free at the point of delivery. No money passes, and there is no suggestion of impurity of motive, that the professional only did it for money, and would not have done it if we had not been in a position to pay. The relationship satisfies an ideal of a cashless world of shared values and disinterested action in which there is no conflict of interest or sense of awkwardness.

Such an ideal is intelligible, and can be realised, up to a point. But the old Adam remains active, and over the years the separate interests of the different parties tend to reassert themselves to the detriment of all. We, the beneficiaries, tend to contribute less than we should: nurses, like teachers, give their services free at the point of delivery, and like them are paid less than secretaries and administrators who are not expected to work for love. But also we, the professionals, tend to attenuate the connexion between salary received and services to be rendered, and we may let ourselves off lightly as regards our duties while being zealous in defence of our rights. It happened in the Church of England over the centuries, and in the National Health Service over a few decades, where many employees became keener on keeping up their pay than looking after their patients. Restrictive practices grew up, the unions started to strike, and the patients began to lose out.

The other way of paying professional people is through fees. It also appeals to a moral sentiment, though a different one. The community of interest that underlies the professional relationship is incomplete in two directions: not only does it impose some cost on the professional, but the recipient of professional attention is benefited in a peculiarly personal sense. The surgeon, anaesthetist and nurses set great store on the operation's being successful, but not as much as I do, if I am the patient. I cannot, as an agent, not be concerned with my survival and future ability to do things, whereas they could be. It is out of the goodness of their hearts, not of their self-interest, that they are dedicated to making me better. Even in the case where someone seeks another's good in preference to his own,[4] there is the modal difference, that the concern for the other is a commitment of his that he could have made differently, whereas concern for himself is a necessity of his being. It is this difference that justifies us in imputing third-personal interests even in the absence of consultation or first-personal avowal.[5]

Thus in spite of the shared values that form the basis of the co-operative association between the professional man and his client,

---

[4] See above, this chapter, §2.

[5] See above, ch.1, §1.4.

there is an inevitable imbalance of interest in that the client is obtaining a personal benefit peculiarly his own, and the professional man is giving up time which he could have put to other uses. Greatly though the doctors and nurses valued my coming through the operation, I valued it more, and at the end of my stay I may well want to express my gratitude in words to the doctors and with flowers for the nurses. Monetary payments are a more tangible token of gratitude. And hence corresponding to the need for the professional to be paid enough to live on, there is a willingness on the part of those benefited by his attentions to contribute. In default of other arrangements, the payment of a fee fits both halves of the transaction, and has often proved a reasonably satisfactory basis for professional work.

But we feel uneasy, and often find ways of not handing over cash, as we would to a tradesman. We make a donation to the research fund, the school appeal, the parish funds. Although we have benefited, and the professional man ought to be enabled to live, and indeed, to live well, we fear to contaminate the gift relationship of his disinterested attention to our needs with monetary payment. Even where monetary payment is the accepted practice, professional people like to be very late in sending their bill in, hoping that the time interval will somehow sever the connexion between services rendered and money demanded; and in time past used to render their account in guineas rather than £ sterling, to express the notion that what was asked for was not a crude commercial payment, but a gentlemanly token of gratitude and esteem. There is an awkwardness about fees, not adequately dealt with by most professions. Although, as we shall see, the professional man takes on the obligation of considering the client's interest rather than his own, thus creating the shared value that is the basis of the relationship, when it comes to the payment of fees, it is their interests, not the client's, that are being served. Although it is quite right that one should pay for good advice—far better than to be given it "free" by an financial adviser who is paid a commission on the insurance policies he sells, and has an interest in persuading the customer to buy one—the adversarial element of having to fork out nevertheless sits ill with the community of interests professed.

The adversarial aspect is increased when the client is left in the dark as to what he is letting himself in for. Often, in fact, there is a scale of professional charges, so that there is no bargaining process, and no question of the professional taking advantage of the client's ignorance and generally weak bargaining position. But it does not feel like that if the client does not know where he stands. Some professions set a fixed scale of charges, and publish them: some partnerships take care to state in advance what an initial consultation will cost, and the basis on which other services are charged. These are good practices, and go far to remove the adversarial aspect of their professional dealings with clients.

§8.7 The Fiduciary Role

We are now in a position to refine our account of professional ethics: the ideal of absolute disinterestedness cannot be sustained in our sublunary world in which people have to live; but granted some reasonable and controlled concessions to the need to earn a living, a professional man can be required to subordinate any interest he may have to the interests of his clients. He should occupy a fiduciary role, which stands *caveat emptor* on its head. The professional man, because he has professional knowledge and knows his client's interests better than the client can know them himself, puts his knowledge completely at his clients' disposal, and gives him the advice that is best from his client's point of view, even though it may be against his own personal interests. The rich Arab patient comes to me, a Harley Street surgeon, complaining of pains in his abdomen. I examine him carefully, and come to the conclusion that it is only heartburn due to over-indulgence after the end of Ramadan. I tell him that no treatment is necessary: there is no need for an operation, no need for an X-ray, no need for expensive treatment, although I could have sold him all these; he is still not completely re-assured. I tell him that he could have a barium meal and an X-ray to make absolutely sure that there is no cancer starting up in the oesophagus, although my own opinion is that it is not really necessary. The ultimate decision is his, but the advice he gets from me is in what I take to be his interests, not mine.

Similarly with the solicitor. A would-be client steams in, wanting to sue a taxi-driver for not stopping to pick him up. Although the case is hopeless, it would be quite profitable for the solicitor. But he does not immediately take out a writ. He listens to the client patiently, writes down the taxi's number, the client's name and address, gives him some coffee, and when he has calmed down suggests a letter to the licensing authority instead, gradually bringing out that a court case would have no chance of success. Keeping the client out of court is good for clients, but bad business for lawyers.

In accepting the obligation to look after the client's interests rather than his own, the professional man is not being non-tuistic,[6] but "tuistic", going much further than is expected of a business-man dealing with a potential customer. The businessman should be offering something which would meet the standard requirements a customer could be expected to have, but is not required to go into the detailed personal circumstances of the individual customer, and advise him from his particular personal point of view. The profes-sional man is. Of course, if the advice is rejected, he may then feel obliged to do what the client wants: a solicitor is prepared, ultimately, to act on instructions, but regards it as a failure on his part if he has not succeeded in dissuading the client from an inad-visable course, in which he considers not only his client's pocket, but his reputation, and in some cases his standing as a man of integrity. The doctor will often refuse to treat the patient in a way he regards as unnecessary or hazardous, though pointing him towards another doctor who will give a second opinion, and might be willing to do what is demanded. Some sense of the patient's being an autonomous being ought to be retained. Where there are dangerous or difficult choices, the doctor should take the patient into his confidence, and enable him to choose between treatments, none of them beyond all doubt the correct one. But, this important proviso made, we can say, as a first approximation, that whereas in business transactions the businessman should adopt a *vous*istic, but not a tuistic, attitude, the attitude of the professional man should be not merely vousistic, but tuistic as well.[7]

§8.8 Business Professions

With the shift of emphasis from pure disinterestedness to the fidu-ciary commitment, the modern business professions have come to the fore. Lawyers soon acquired a taste for fees, and it is difficult to maintain a difference in principle between them and accountants,

---

[6] See above, ch.2, §2.4; and ch.,7, §7.1.

[7] In some situations the professional man is not completely at the disposal of one individual, but has to consider others as well: the schoolmaster has to consider other pupils, the clergyman other parishioners. But the obligation of disinterestedness remains.

actuaries, architects and surveyors. In each case there is an identification with the client's interest: the lawyer is satisfied if his client is acquitted, the accountant if his client's tax bill is lessened, the architect if the building wins a prize. But the disinterestedness is more remote: fees are sought, and seldom waived. But the client's interests must come first. This is what distinguishes professional advice from that of salesmen and financial advisers, who receive commissions from insurance companies for the policies they sell. Although I may pay a professional man for his help, it is essential that I can be sure that he has no hidden incentive to direct my choice in one way rather than another. The only money that passes must be money from me.

The essential characteristic of the business professions is self-regulation to secure the integrity and competence of its members. Professional standards and codes of practice, qualifications before entry and disciplinary control afterwards, are all ways in which professions seek to eliminate unprofessional conduct. We can see this in part as a natural development of the professions from their ecclesiastical origins into the modern business world, and in part the growing recognition of the importance of *caveat vendor* within ordinary commercial transactions. Unbridled consumer choice is abridged, because consumers cannot know where their interests lie; and this holds good in the modern complex world of financial and tax advice, as it does in medical matters. Instead of being free to go to any slick salesman, who may con me into buying dud insurance policies, I am guided towards reputable professionals, who will know what is best for me in my situation, and not feather their own nest at my expense.

But there are disadvantages in altogether abrogating consumer choice, and there is an inherent danger of a profession becoming a closed shop more concerned with the interests of its members than of its clients. Doctors, mindful of their own fallibility, are notoriously unwilling to condemn the shortcomings of their colleagues, even though patients' health and lives may be at risk.

§8.9 *Vous* and *Tu*; Needs and Wants

The distinction between *vous* and *tu* is not sharp, or always clear, and parallels the distinction between wants and needs. Many old-fashioned shop-keepers go some way to considering individual customers' particular interests, advising customers not to make purchases that will not suit their personal circumstance. But it is old-fashioned shop-keepers who do, occupying an established *niche* in society, serving customers with known wants or predictable needs. It would not be feasible for a fashion house, or a dealer in CDs or videos, to do this, because he cannot know what they need, and only they can decide what they want.

The parallel between the two distinctions is the root cause also of our problems over payment. As we divorce the provision of professional services from the transfer of money, we also weaken its connexion with actual wants. The professional man acts in the interests of his client because the client is not in a position to know what his interests are. But the vicarious interests the professional man can impute to his client are fundamentally third-personal: they are what someone other than the client thinks the client needs, not what the client himself knows that he wants. And over the course of years the professional view can drift too far out of line with actual wants to be seen as genuine interests at all.[8] Medically, perhaps, I ought to have a painful and debilitating operation that will postpone death by a few months, but actually I would rather die sooner, uncut up, at home. It suits the convenience of the hospital administration that I come into hospital next month, but I would rather go to my daughter's wedding then. The patient has no leverage on services free at the point of delivery. He can take what is offered or leave it, but he is in the position of a needy suppliant who should be grateful for what is given him, but never insist that something else would, actually from his point of view, be better.

Needs and wants are inter-connected. Third-personal imputed interests are not interests at all unless they can, by and large, be seen as such in the end by the person concerned. Some opportunity of exercising idiosyncratic choice, of satisfying wants that are not recognised as needs, must be preserved if the professional service is not to ossify. We can compare the ossification of the National Health Service in our time with the ossification of the Church of England in the eighteenth century, and the growth of British United Provident Association and other private schemes with that of the Methodists and the other dissenting sects. There is no single solution. For the most part we are not conscious of idiosyncratic wants rather than standard needs, and welcome the guidance of the doctor, the priest, the schoolmaster, or academic,

---

[8] See above, ch.1, §1.4.

and respect him for his disinterested concern with us and for values we share; and then the provision of services free with no question of paying the professional man for what he does seems entirely appropriate. But occasions arise when we, either individually or collectively, are not content with what is being offered, and want to have things our own way, and are willing to accept a connexion between paying the piper and calling the tune. It is implausible to make out, as some free-marketeers have done in recent years, that this should be the norm; but implausible, too, to hold, as socialists have done in recent years and Establishmentarians in time past, that it is inherently wicked to allow money to buy such services. In fact, Dissenting Sects and private health schemes not only act as a safety valve, but provide the free services with healthy competition and a valuable stimulus to innovate.

§8.10 Taking on the Professions

In recent years the British Government has been "taking on the professions", regarding them as white-collar equivalents of trade unions, running a cosy cartel to restrict competition, keep up prices, and retain feather-bedding practices, against the public interest. It is difficult to deny these charges completely. Any visit to a court of law conveys a strong impression of overmanning. But it is important to recognise the value of the professional *ethos*, and unwise to suppose that opening up professional life to the rigours of competition and the bracing breezes of the market place will prove uniformly beneficial.

We need disinterested advice. We value disinterested concern. In the admass society our individuality is in danger of being swamped by the unindividualised concerns of market managers, interested in us only as units, and not a persons. The non-tuistic approach of commercial life cannot answer all our needs. Life would be poorer— and shorter—if we could not turn with confidence to a doctor, a priest, or an academic, in the knowledge that he would accept a fiduciary role, and give us not only standard good advice, but advice tailored to the best of his ability to our own, highly specific individual needs. The market cannot give grounds for justified confidence. As consumers, we lack the *expertise* to make a rational choice, or to think that others are able to. When buying a car, we know that each salesman is concerned to sell his wares, but we can consult *Which?* and the specialist magazines, ask friends, and, if the car proves unsatisfactory, not go to that showroom again. We have only one life, only one soul, and cannot afford to learn by trial and error. We need guidance in fields where knowledge is beyond us, and not being able to attain it ourselves, need to know whom we can trust, so that we do not fall into the hands of charlatans.

The professions are not perfect. They have the opportunity of feathering their own nests, and feather-bedding their own members, and it is right to look for institutional checks to safeguard the interests of the public. But it is perverse not to recognise much high-mindedness in the professional *ethos*, and much devoted service to valuable ideals and the public good on the part of many professional people. And it would be short-sighted and a dereliction of public duty to destroy the professional *ethos* out of mistaken zeal for the competitive activities of the market place.

Chapter 9
Codes, Sanctions and the State

Contents

Abstract

Codes and sanctions are sometimes needed, but there are limits to what they can achieve, and they cannot replace individual responsibility for deciding each case in the light of the various obligations that obtain. Although the State alone controls the ultimate sanction of coercion, and has the function of providing the legal framework on which business depends, it does not have unfettered power, and there are limits to the laws it can expect individuals to obey. The laws have to be reasonable, and strike an acceptable balance between the parties affected, or they will be ineffective and counter-productive. The State's right to be obeyed has to be earned, and can be lost if it exercises its authority unreasonably. Democratic institutions enhance a State's legitimacy, but are not necessary, nor by themselves sufficient in cases of abuse.

§9.1 Codes

An underlying argument of this book is that the obligations a responsible agent should recognise cannot be fully articulated in a formal code or set of rules. Their generality precludes their taking into account all the relevant considerations, so that they are liable, on the one hand, to rule out perfectly reasonable practices and, on the other, to permit unfair or dishonest ones. Some codes of business practice waffle in a high-sounding way without giving guidance on the decisions where guidance is needed. They may encourage hypocrisy, with lip-service being given to unexceptionable precepts which are largely ignored in practice. Codes are external, and in danger of remaining so. Often the mere fact of there being a code will lead people to abrogate responsibility, and instead of trying to take the right decision, reckon that it is enough to take one that accords with the code: instead of asking themselves the question 'Is it right?', they may ask 'Can we make out that it is allowed by the rules?'. In many cases codes are not called for, and do no good. Even where they are called for, there are stringent limits on what they may enjoin. They are no substitute for responsible decision-making. The law in particular is an inadequate specification of the constraints within which businessmen ought to operate, and in taking decisions they have to consider a variety of factors, and strike a balance between them.[1]

Nevertheless, codes have their place. They are more determinate. Justice, being indeterminate,[2] needs to be filled out in particular contexts, with particular understandings, particular expectations, particular conventions. We need to know what the Romans do, if we are to act justly in Rome; and if different Romans do differently, we may be at a loss, until some definitive statement of practice has been made, so that everybody knows where he stands.

Codes, also, are more communicable. A manager's practice may be excellent, but the people he deals with and his successors may not fully understand it or know the principles on which it is based. Many modern firms now make a statement of their principles (a "mission statement"), and though such statements are often unclear or platitudinous, they do give employees and others something to base their argument on if they disagree with a management decision.[3] The first legal code in ancient Athens was demanded not only so that citizens could know where they stood, but so that they had some basis on which to argue with the magistrates and contest their decisions.

Codes, again, are more open to criticism. A code can be criticized on general grounds, whereas the particular decisions taken in practical situations often involve too many factors for trenchant criticism to be feasible. It is difficult to characterize a particular decision correctly. Is it a case of hauling a slacker over the coals and telling him to pull his socks up, or is it a case of victimising a person with problems who is trying his best and who needs encouragement, not criticism? A code is explicit in what it lays down, and it is clear what is to be criticized or defended.

And, finally, codes are more open to collective alteration. Where individual firms are often unable to bring about a needed change

---

[1] See above, ch.4, §4.7, and ch.1, §1.2.

[2] See above, ch.2, §2.5.

[3] See above, ch.6, §6.6.

of practice by their individual example, because they are in a Prisoners' Dilemma,[4] an industry-wide or nation-wide change of code may be effective in instituting a better practice. Many employers in the nineteenth century found their own employment practices repugnant, but could not afford to pay better wages, or not to send women down mines or boys up chimneys, so long as their competitors were doing so. They were glad to be compelled to do what they knew to be right. Quite often a code, whether enforced by law or by public opinion, can alter a widespread practice where individual initiatives would be ineffective, and might be financially disastrous.

For these reasons, in spite of their defects, codes are helpful, and sometimes necessary. They can crystallize the best practice and encourage people to follow it, and in that sense they can contribute to defining what kind of considerations should be brought into play when we try to decide what our obligations should be.

§9.2 Sanctions

Codes may be promulgated but not obeyed. In some cases it may be because the code did not articulate adequately existing practice, and it is simply a matter of articulating more adequately the approved practice. But businessmen, like other men, sometimes depart from good practice, contravene the code, or break the law. And if they can continue to do this with impunity, they establish a new practice, and the code falls into disrepute and the law becomes a dead letter.

If an action contravenes a code, what reason is there for not doing it? In many cases the knowledge that it would contravene the code is a sufficient dissuasive. Many businesses promulgate their own codes and would not wish to appear hypocritical. Even when the code is not one of their own devising, but has been formulated by the trade or industry as a whole, businesses have voluntarily adhered to it, and accept its recommendations, or at least do not want to appear not to. Images and reputations are important. Many businessmen have an image of themselves as responsible members of society, and if a code highlights some action as one difficult to justify, they will focus attention on it, and not do it by inadvertence; and even if they are not themselves imbued with a sense of responsibility, they remain uneasily aware that a bad reputation is bad for business.

The line between morality and prudence is blurred,[5] and, con-

---

[4] See Appendix A, p.226.

[5] See further below, ch.13, §13.3.

trary to Kant's teaching,[6] it is good that the still small voice of conscience should be reinforced by the louder precepts of social and commercial prudence. At one time the City of London was dominated by wearers of old-school ties. It was much condemned by egalitarians, but it had one great advantage, that each man's behaviour was subject to long-term and inescapable scrutiny by his social peers. A man who was dishonest in his youth would be known to be untrustworthy; and if anyone in later life were tempted to engage in sharp practice, he would know that all his friends and acquaintances would get to know of it, and would adjust their view of him accordingly. With these considerations taken into account, the game was not worth the candle, and the City's reputation for integrity was high. There was, admittedly, an element of exclusiveness, and it may well have been the case that some people in the City were not as bright as those who have since been able to gain admittance. But, now that this social sanction no longer operates so strongly, there is widespread concern in the City that its reputation for straight dealing has suffered; and it is far from clear that the country has benefited from the change.

More generally, we need to set against Adam Smith's observation that, when members of a trade gather together, they conspire against the public interest,[7] the countervailing consideration that their informal judgements and exchanges of information constitute a powerful sanction against wrong-doing. Tried in the law courts or the popular press, I may well get away with it, because not enough is known, not enough is understood, and attention is too fleeting. Tried by the opinion of my peers, I cannot expect to be able to throw wool in their eyes, nor to escape the adverse effects of their censure. We may need to counter collective selfishness and rigid exclusiveness, but should not lightly dispense with the collective scrutiny of individual actions and social sanctions against misbehaviour.

In many cases a guild system is inappropriate. Other means may be devised to publicise breaches of a code, and to bring pressure to bear on those who flout its provisions. The Consumers Association's publication *Which?* has been influential. Few manufacturers like to be Not Recommended, and few can be sure that

---

[6] See Glossary

[7] Adam Smith, *The Wealth of Nations*, Bk I, ch.10, Everyman ed., vol.1, p.117; quoted in §7.4.

their sales would not suffer in consequence. *Which?* has always excluded advertisements. Journals that take advertisements, as trade journals invariably do, have a powerful financial incentive not to publish unsavoury truths about their advertisers' wares. Until readers are prepared to pay more to secure unfiltered information and unbiased judgements, the press is an inadequate guardian of good business behaviour, though the BBC has a good record in fearlessly exposing business rackets and abuses, and the occasional programme on Channel 4 and ITV, and articles in newspapers like the *Guardian* and the *Independent* have done something to alert the public to what is going on.

Government agencies can bring pressure to bear. In some cases they may be entrusted with inquisitorial powers to discover abuses, and can always publish their findings in official reports.[8] But that may not be enough. Some governments use government contracts to bring additional pressure to bear, but there are costs in restricting the number of firms to whom contracts may be awarded, and where a bad practice is pervasive, there might be no takers for the contract at all.

The difficulty with all these sanctions is that they are resistible, and some firms might find it profitable to resist them, and then others would follow suit. If I am to forbear from employing boys as chimney sweeps, I must be reasonably sure that others will forbear too, and I cannot be sure that they will, unless I know that they cannot get away with it if they do. And for that, there must be some sanctions that are irresistible, sanctions backed up ultimately by coercive force, that is, sanctions involving the power of the State.

§9.3 The State and the Limits of State Power

We find it difficult to think clearly about the State. At times it seems an alien, even a hostile, power, which makes us obey its laws, pay its taxes, and fight its wars: but then, especially at times of national crisis, we—the businessmen among us very prominently—identify strongly with our country, and reckon its failures our failures, its successes our successes, and its values constitutive of our own individual identities. But although often we identify with the State, and accept its demands as entirely legitimate, we do not regard every demand of every State as one that ought unquestioningly to be obeyed. Even in Britain and the United States where

---

[8] See above, ch.7, §7.3.

it is taken for granted that the law of the land should be obeyed without question, businessmen try to find "tax-efficient" ways of paying their employees so as to avoid paying to the State the taxes it is seeking to raise. Many other regimes are much less respected, or worthy of respect. In determining what our responsibilities to the State are, we need to have a clearer idea of what the rationale of the State is, and why its edicts should be obeyed.

There are many different reasons, some purely external, some internal, no single one by itself sufficient. For many people, and for many thinkers in the Anglo-Saxon tradition, the obvious and conclusive reason is that one will be punished if not. The State has a monopoly of coercive power, and can enforce its edicts on the recalcitrant. Since there are recalcitrant men around, it is necessary that the State should be able to enforce its laws, since otherwise they would be flouted by some, and soon ignored by all. The coercive power of the State gives us an assurance that our obedience to its edicts will not be in vain, but that others will obey too; I am not being a mug if I refrain from stealing, because if anyone else were to steal, he would not get away with it.[9] And if any authority is possessed of coercive power, it must have a monopoly in its area if there is not to be a state of war there. From this necessary aspect of State power Hobbes[10] argued that the State is to be understood in terms of coercive power alone. Laws are the commands of the sovereign backed by force, and that is all there is to it.

But it is difficult to sit on bayonets. The sovereign needs to be strong enough to coerce the evil-doer, but neither needs to be, nor can be, all-powerful: he needs the help of auxiliaries to man the police force, administer justice, staff the gaols, and some of them at least must be giving their help uncoerced. They at least must be cooperating freely, to some extent identifying with the State, sharing its values and accepting its ideals. And some lesser degree of cooperation is needed even outside the ranks of the *apparatchiks*: the sovereign is not omniscient, and cannot know things unless people tell, and people will not tell the truth if they cannot trust the State to respect their integrity—it was the need for *glasnost* that led Gorbychev to dismantle the Soviet system. Without witnesses and

---

[9]　See further below, Appendix A, p.227, and §10.3.

[10]　See Glossary

plaintiffs the administration of justice cannot take place. A regime need not be liked or loved, but unless it is trusted to deal fairly with those who offer it testimony or seek its aid, people will not bring their disputes to it at all, and will have some other system of their own,[11] leaving the regime to exercise a distant suzerainty, but not real government. Such were the origins of the Sicilian Mafia.

The big stick theory of the State is inadequate. Government does not just impose itself on the populace by force; the law is not the irresistible command of an unfettered State, but is a function of society, and hence under pressure to conform to the requirements of its social function. It follows, first, that there is a much more internal, rational and moral aspect to the law than Hobbes allowed, and, secondly, that there are limits to the State's right to legislate and tax.

The *rationale* of law derives from the unselective nature of the State, which does not choose its citizens, but has to deal with all those who happen—typically by accident of birth—to live within a certain area. Since they are unselected, some may be—almost always are—recalcitrant, not minded to abide by the customs and practices of their society. In the absence of sure-fire sanctions they would flout the law, and if they got away with it, others would follow suit, since sometimes it is burdensome to keep the law, and the law would fall into disuse. The law must, therefore, be enforced, if necessary by force, or it will cease to be in force; and the State must be able to muster irresistible coercive power against actual or would-be law-breakers. But because coercion *is* irresistible, great caution is needed in its exercise. There have to be many safeguards against the full force of the law being exercised improperly. Although we often feel, and sometimes rightly, of some misdoing, that there "ought to be a law against it", there are often sound prudential arguments against actually enacting such a law: it may be difficult to detect breaches, costly to enforce, give rise to blackmail. And even if there is a law, we need due process and a high standard of proof before transgressors can be punished. We cannot

---

[11] An interesting recent example was quoted by Ziad Aba Amr, professor at Bir-Zeit University in Ramullah in the Wall Street Journal 15/9/95: "Clan loyalty also acted as a deterrent against the total collapse of the social order during Israeli occupation. There was no real court system or law enforcement, but you knew that if you impinged on property or rights of others, their clan would avenge them."

enshrine the whole of morality in law, but only a somewhat minimal
standard of conduct, conduct we cannot allow to continue uncor-
rected. The criminal law is thus an inadequate guide to reasonable
practice. Similarly in the civil law we need elaborate procedures
to ensure that both sides of the case are heard and heeded: and
often legal contracts do not, on account of the cumbersomeness
of legal procedures, state the real understanding between the parties. Law provides only the skeleton, not the living flesh, of social
life. Although it needs to be internalised by some members of the
community, it is viewed by others entirely externally, and has to
be reasonably predictable and hence relatively rigid. Sometimes it
is governed by the rule of precedents, often it is formulated in a
code, and has the demerits, as well as the merits, of codes generally.
It was for these reasons, among others, that it was an inadequate
specification of the businessman's duties that he should simply keep
the law.[12]

§9.4 Reason and Balance

Although the law needs to be enforceable, it cannot be enforced by
force alone, but needs the uncoerced support of some. It must com-
mend itself to most of those affected as being reasonable and even-
handed. Many laws and regulations fail on these counts, thereby
impairing the legitimacy of the civil authority that promulgates
them. Where the legitimacy of the government is unquestioned,
the regulations are obeyed, though complainingly. In many countries, however, regulations are seen as obstacles to be circumvented
as much as taxes are impositions to be avoided. Even where they
are obeyed, there is a strain. Just as legitimacy can be earned, so
it can be lost, and the more unreasonable the demands of government, the less ready are we to conform.

Laws and regulations are like codes, and many err in not taking
account of particular circumstances. It may be sensible to lay down
standards for new buildings to ensure that they have adequate
light, ventilation, damp-proofing, *etc.* But sometimes people have
special requirements—do I really need a window in a dark room?—
or are adapting old buildings, and cannot apply the regulations
in any sensible way. They are being prevented from satisfying
perfectly reasonable wants for no good reason. We need procedures

---

[12] See above, ch.4, §4.7.

for adapting regulations to particular circumstances not foreseen by the regulators. Equally we need common sense in interpreting them. In 1980 the University of Oxford was fined for breach of the fire regulations in the St Cross Library. The St Cross Library had been built of highly incombustible brick a few years earlier with the advice and approval of the then fire officer. After his retirement his successor deemed the building unsatisfactory because there was not, as required by the latest fire regulations, a separate exit for the staff to leave by in case of fire. The staff occupied an open chamber situated between two large doors, so that they could see everyone coming in and out, and make sure that nobody took library books out. But it was true that both doors were available for readers to use, and so did not count as being separate. Useless to protest that the point of the regulations was to ensure that the staff could escape in case of fire, and that with two large doors at hand they were as well placed as anyone could be. The fire officer was adamant: 'separate' meant 'separate'. The University was taken to court. The magistrates dismissed the case, but the fire officer was upheld in the Divisional Court on appeal and leave to appeal to the House of Lords was refused. The University has complied with the fire regulations by blocking access for readers to one of the doors, so that it can be used only by the staff. In the unlikely event of the brick catching fire, it will be marginally more difficult for the readers to escape. But the regulations will have been complied with.

Fire regulations are difficult to criticize because they are intended to protect against unlikely events, and fire officers have a better appreciation of the hazards than arm-chair critics. But there are dangers and there are costs. Just as doctors are wooed by pharmaceutical companies, so it is worth bringing to the attention of those who enforce regulations the latest state-of-the-art products that could be said to enhance safety. Compliance with the regulations has clearly brought a lot of business to the manufacturers of fire doors and sprinkler valves, and it is difficult not to wonder sometimes, wandering down corridors through fire-doors propped open with fire extinguishers, whether the increased degree of safety is worth the great cost involved. In some cases it is not. It was quite common for women widowed while still in vigorous middle age to think of keeping the family house and having some old people as residents, but after the fire officer had told them what would be necessary to bring their house into conformity with the regulations, to think of it no longer. Old people are a fire hazard. They smoke in bed and fall asleep. There is a real risk of fire, and of being burnt alive. But old age is dangerous anyhow, and commonly fatal. Hypothermia is a bad way to go. Many old people have died in Britain in recent years, cold, alone, unfed, unwashed, uncared for. Against the real risk of being burnt alive must be set other risks, equally real, equally unpleasant. We needed to strike a balance, and the right balance was not struck.

The difficulty is that the costs imposed by regulations are not borne by those who make them. The fire officer is not held responsible for deaths caused by hypothermia: he would have to carry the can if some resident of an old people's home he had passed died in a fire. So he plays safe. To be absolutely above criticism he specifies the most modern equipment. Great costs are borne by others, but they are concealed from him. And so with other regulators too. Unless determined action is taken, costs will not be properly borne in mind. And unless costs are reasonable, the temptation to evade the regulations will be great, just as it is when the regulations themselves are not reasonable.

Regulations make room for corruption. There is a public interest in hygiene, and we need to have inspectors going round the kitchens of hotels and restaurants looking out for cockroaches, mouse-droppings and general slovenliness. But considerable power is placed in their hands, and power tends to corrupt. It would be easy to overlook the tell-tale mouse-droppings in the restaurant where one had been stood a superlative dinner, and to come down heavily on the restaurateur who had not evinced sufficient friendliness. These dangers can be overcome, by judicial appeal, by rotation of inspectors, double-checking, and the like. But in many countries the dangers are great, and in all we need to be on our guard.

There can be impropriety in the making of regulations as well as in their enforcement. Soon after the collapse of communism a Polish factory secured an order for 7,000 shovels. But the European Union banned their import on the grounds that they were strategic implements. Once there is reasonable suspicion that a regulation has been promulgated at the behest of some lobby with clout in Brussels, it ceases to command respect. Just as legitimacy can be earned, so it can be also lost. In countries like Italy, where the government is known to be corrupt, regulations are seen as a challenge, to see how best to evade them, not as an obligation to the wider community which ought to be carried out even though awkward or costly. Regulations have to be seen to be legitimate; when they are formulated and imposed by bureaucracies, unanswerable to the people whom they seek to regulate, or by politicians susceptible to the blandishments of well-heeled lobbies, they may be seen as illegitimate interference.[13]

These edicts of the State forfeit respect because they are unreasonable, either because they are too rigid, or because they are too costly to comply with, or because they invite or involve corruption. Others fail because they are not even-handed, and do not strike a fair balance between the parties involved. Because of the indeterminacy of justice[14] there is some latitude in choosing where to draw the line between the opposed rights and interests of different groups, but not an indefinitely wide one. Law is a function of society; it develops as a means whereby different members of society can coordinate their actions and adjust their behaviour the one towards the other; it is, therefore, essentially two-sided, one man's rights being correlative with another's duties, and for this reason subject to the constraints of justice in much the same way as economic transactions. And if justice is not observed, people will take steps not to put themselves in a position where they will be unjustly treated. As the consumer movement grew more powerful, there were calls for further legislation to give consumers an even better deal. In some cases this was reasonable—the extension of the Sale of Goods Act to cover services as well as goods. But it became clear that putting the consumer in too favourable a position would not be to his advantage; for if the contract were so weighted in his favour as to be unfair to the vendor, vendors would cease to sell. This has happened with medical services in the USA, where patients sue their doctors if anything goes wrong. In some cases, sadly, there has been negligence, but in the nature of the case doctors cannot, however great their care and skill, always make their patients better. In order, therefore, to avoid malpractice suits, American doctors regularly subject their patients to a whole battery of expensive and sometimes painful tests, and in some fields refuse to take patients altogether. Although current

---

[13] See Samuel Brittan, *Capitalism with a Human Face*, Aldershot, 1995. p.270, for "rent seeking", *i.e.* lobbying for unfair favours.

[14] See above, ch.2, §2.5.

practice or explicit convention can up to a point determine what is the just apportionment of rights and responsibilities, costs, and rewards, it can do so only within limits; and attempts to go beyond these limits are counter-productive.

Much modern legislation is flawed on this count. The Protection of Employment Acts[15] make it very difficult to sack employees once they have been in a job for more than a short time. It is right that employers should be required to act justly, and not use the power they have over other men's livelihoods arbitrarily and capriciously. But it is difficult for outsiders to have a proper appreciation of what a particular job demands and how well a particular employee is doing. Tribunals tend to be soft. Unless an employer has fulfilled all the requirements of the Act to the letter, and can prove to their satisfaction that the employee was drunk, disobedient, or inattentive, they award large sums in compensation. But the right to a job is not inherently like the right to life, liberty and property, and it is in nobody's interest that engine drivers should retain their jobs because the proof that they were drunk was not beyond all reasonable doubt, or that bad teachers should not be sacked, or that homosexual wardens of children's homes should be able to go on abusing children, because the evidence against them was only hearsay.

It may be a good thing that mothers should have maternity leave. It stems from a vision of society that rejects the traditional picture of home life and the family, and sees the work-place as the centre of value, and the single mother as the standard breadwinner. If this be our vision of society, then maternity leave with pay and the right to return to her previous job is a good thing, but in that case it is incumbent on society as a whole to pay for it, and to provide replacements who will not themselves have acquired a right to permanent employment. If the employer has to pay for it, or if, every time a female employee has a baby he is obliged to take on a new permanent employee, then he will tend to avoid employing potential mothers. Firms which in the normal course of events would be large employers, install labour-saving machinery, or contract out work to smaller firms or single operators, like Benetton

---

[15] Employment Protection Act, 1975; Employment Protection (Consolidated) Act, 1978. Some provisions of these Acts have been repealed; see 1980 c.42 and 1982 c.46.

in Italy, in order to avoid falling foul of complicated legislation and increased labour costs.

These arguments do not show that legislation in economic matters is always wrong. Although there is a presumption against legislating, because codes are rigid and laws are heavy-handed, the presumption can be rebutted. Sometimes we need to lay down the law in order to clarify it, and to enable people to know where they stand: sometimes legislation is needed to escape from the Prisoners' Dilemma, as it was in the last century when it enabled employers not to be pressured into sending women down mines or boys up chimneys.[16] But the pendulum has swung too far. Employees, like customers, are one side of a two-sided transaction, and the other side needs to be taken into consideration too, on grounds not only of justice but of expediency also. There is a parallel with the Rent Acts. They were so heavily weighted in favour of the tenant and against the landlord, that nobody would be a landlord, and rented accommodation disappeared from the market. Although the Rent Acts were intended to protect tenants and help the homeless, they had the effect of making it impossible to obtain tenancies and greatly increasing the number of homeless.

In modern times enthusiastic social engineers, unable to persuade people at large of the rightness of their ideals, have resorted to legislation to bend society to the shape they think it ought to have. Where the legislation is promulgating some convention to fill out and make determinate our mutual rights and obligations, there are inherent limits on how the balance may be struck, since if it is too adverse to manufacturers, doctors, employers, or landlords, people will cease to occupy those roles, and we shall be left without goods, doctors, employment, or rented accommodation. In other cases legislation is intended to provide an escape from the Prisoners' Dilemma, or to forbid, or to insist upon, some pattern of behaviour. But again, there are stringent limits, not sufficiently observed, to what may be accomplished by legislation. The law is a blunt instrument. Like all codes, it is general, and fails to discriminate finely between relevantly different cases; and just because it involves the potential use of coercion, it has to be subject to careful safeguards. Reformers are often impatient, seeking to by-pass the courts and to put the burden of proof on the accused rather than the prosecution. It is a dangerous expedient; it only needs one or

---

[16] See above, §1 of this chapter.

two people to be condemned who are evidently guiltless for the law to be brought into profound disrepute.[17] But if we take steps to avoid condemning the innocent, we let many of the guilty get away. The law, with all its proper safeguards, cannot discriminate finely enough to delimit exactly the boundary between what is acceptable and what is not. It is essentially a long-stop—necessary to provide other sanctions with purchase, and to prevent the brazen from being able to flout all sanctions with impunity, but unable by itself to draw the line precisely where it should be drawn, or to prevent some buccaneers from sailing close to the wind.

§9.5 Political Legitimacy

The arguments against a purely external view of the State tell also against the purely internal one that holds that we are totally identified with the State, which can therefore command our total allegiance in doing whatever it sees fit. By a curious quirk of history the fight against the totalitarian regimes in the Second World War led to an intellectual acceptance of totalitarianism on the part of the victors. The total mobilisation of Britain in order to defeat Hitler encouraged people to think that a similar all-out drive should be continued in peace-time in order to achieve democratically approved objectives. The difference between the Axis powers and the West was seen to reside in the fact that the governments in the West were democratically elected rather than in the limitation of the powers of government by the rule of law. The rhetoric of the twentieth century has proclaimed that democracy is a good thing, but without any clear idea of what democracy is.[18] Not that the Western powers abandoned their constitutions

---

[17] In November 1972 Admiral of the Fleet Lord Mountbatten of Burma and his grandson were fined £20 each as owners of Broadlands Farm, Romsey, Hampshire, on two summonses of being in possession of milk for sale for human consumption to which water had been added. They were also ordered to pay £20 costs each. They were not actually concerned with the running of the dairy units, which were under the control of the farm manager and the estate manager. *The Times*, Friday, November 17, 1972, p.2, col.5. Few people thought worse of Lord Mountbatten in consequence, but the reputation of English justice took a further knock. The law's asinine aspects are not confined to England: in Italy a seven-year-old boy was fined for not having a receipt after buying chewing gum in a bar.

[18] See, more fully, J.R.Lucas, *Democracy and Participation*, Penguin, 1976.

or seriously compromised fundamental liberties—when in 1947 the Labour Government promulgated its Control of Engagements Order, there were great protests by the trade unions, and it was soon scrapped. But there was a background assumption that We, the People, were entitled to choose how we were governed, and it was up to us to decide whether to direct people into suitable jobs or leave them free to choose for themselves. The last resort of legitimacy has been seen as the sovereign voice of the people, taken to the extreme in the idea that the voice of the people is the voice of God—the ultimate authority to which all must give way.

But the voice of the people is not the voice of God. The issue came to a head in ancient Athens, when after the battle of Arginusae, those in command were accused of not exerting themselves enough to pick up the survivors of the ships sunk by the Spartans. Rather than bring them to trial, where they would have been able to answer the accusation and bring forward evidence in their defence, the demagogues proposed a decree that they be executed forthwith. It so happened that Socrates was the chairman of the Assembly that day, and he refused to put the motion to the vote, as being illegal; whereupon there was a great uproar with people saying that it was a terrible thing not to let the *demos* (people) do what it wanted.[19] But Socrates was right. And if, perhaps under the influence of some future Committee for Public Safety, an Act of Parliament were validly enacted in Britain decreeing that all Marquesses—or all Marxists—were to be hanged, we might, reluctantly, be forced to concede that this really was the people's will, but would still insist that it was wrong, not only immoral but legally wrong as well. Not everything is lawful for a government, not even if it is what the people want. Since the Treaty of Versailles the right of national self-determination has been thought to override all other considerations, and as the British Empire was dissolved, it was often said that self-government was more important than good government. Fifty years and many millions of deaths later, we are beginning to have doubts.

Democracy does not of itself confer legitimacy, but it can enhance it. Democratic regimes can fail to be legitimate—often do, when there are minorities whose rights the majority is not sensitive to—and many benevolent monarchs have enjoyed the well merited

---

[19] See Xenophon, *Hellenica*, I, vii, 1-16; and *Memorabilia*, i, 18; Aristotle, *Ath.Resp.* 34, and Plato, *Apology*, 32b; see also *Politics*, III, 10.

esteem of their subjects without the trappings of modern representational government. Nevertheless, a democratic element in the political system of a State enhances its authority and legitimacy, giving dissenters an opportunity to state their case and have it heard, and assuring everyone that the decisions of the government enjoy a considerable measure of popular support.

Legitimacy is a complicated concept. The mere fact that a government exists and is able to maintain itself confers on it some right to be obeyed, but many governments that exist *de facto*, and are recognised internationally as the *de jure* governments of their territories, none the less lack full recognition on the part of their subjects. Legitimacy is conditional—this is not to say that it is up to each individual to decide whether or not to obey the government (that would be to deny the need for political obedience altogether, and would entirely subvert all forms of government)— and cannot be claimed independently of what the regime does. It needs to be earned, and it takes a long time to earn it. Historical memories are potent, and the successful violence of yester-century is still remembered, and not acquiesced in, by the vanquished. The scars of the French Revolution still leave the French *psyche* divided; Italians still think of their government as alien, imposed by the outsider, whether Spaniard, Austrian, the monarch of Piedmont and Savoy, or even, after the advent of the Italian Republic in 1948, by a party system taken over by the party boss rather than the party leader.

The governments of Britain and the United States are exceptional in enjoying largely unquestioned legitimacy, largely on account of their having continued uninterruptedly for many centuries: few Saxons now resent the alien Norman yoke; few Jacobites still drink to the King Over The Water; and even fewer Yorkists still lament the outcome of the battle of Bosworth field. Legitimacy has been reinforced by a political system which allows change and avoids the dangers of a permanent *staus quo*—"things have to change so that they can stay for ever as they are".[20]

---

[20] Giuseppe de Lampedusa, *The Leopard*, (*Il Gattopardi*, Milan, 1959.)

Chapter 10
Fiscal and Distributive Justice

Contents

Abstract

Many States in the Twentieth Century have sought to redistribute the national wealth according to some principle of distributive justice, usually an egalitarian one. They have failed. Wealth is not a material substance that can be completely controlled or manipulated, and the attempt to control its distribution requires great concentrations of power, which themselves generate inequalities far worse than the ones they were supposed to remedy.

Equality is not only an impracticable, but an incoherent, ideal. It only makes sense when the respect is specified in which people are, or should be, equal; and however many the respects in which people are equal, there are others in which they are, and should be, different. The arguments for egalitarianism are fallacious, although in some situations distributive justice requires limited equalities. In most business contexts, however, distributive justice requires that regard be paid to the contribution made by each individual, and hence favours differentials, though often practical difficulties, and sometimes ideological principles, may argue against. Even if distributive justice, rather than equality, is the aim, the State cannot distribute national wealth fairly, or adopt an overall incomes policy that is just, because the State does not exist for an agreed, overriding aim (though there is enough agreement on values to enable the State, in those few cases where such decisions have to be made, to make them on the basis of distributive justice).

Because the State cannot be based on distributive justice, no satisfactory justification of the economic set-up can be given. There always will be grounds for legitimate complaint, based on the irrationalities and injustices that emerge when many people are making free decisions. Businessmen and others who make decisions should do what they can to be humane and to mitigate the misfortunes of the unlucky.

§10.1 Politics and Economics

Businessmen are usually unenthusiastic about politics, and like to keep out of politics as much as they can: and politicians are uncomfortably aware that though they can say what is to happen, it very often does not happen as they say, whereas businessmen have a knack of actually making things happen as intended. But no divorce of politics and economics is possible. Quite apart from macro-economic questions, which have to be decided politically, micro-economic transactions can take place only within a framework of rules, and it is a political decision what these rules shall be. Whatever decisions are reached, they affect business. Businessmen not only have an interest in being able to participate in making those decisions, but need to consider the demands of the State—for compliance with regulations and legislative enactments, and, most obviously, for taxes—in taking their own decisions.

§10.2 Limits of the Market Economy

Although the advocates of the social market believe that most economic ills can be cured by sufficiently well-thought-out regulation, their track record has not been good, and the right of the State to dispose of its subjects' time and property is, as we argued in the previous chapter, greatly restricted, far more than was recognised after the Second World War. Even if the social marketeers are careful to respect the rights of the individual, and not to overreach themselves in the exercise of State power, they still cannot order our affairs aright, because every market needs the freedom to adapt to changing conditions without being constrained by regulations which impede flexibility and transformation.

Modern businessmen are far more likely to side with the freemarketeers who see the disadvantages of regulation, and think that the market should be left to sort itself out without any legislation or interference. But the free-marketeers are wrong too. Every market needs some regulation—about the making and enforcing of contracts, for example—and different regulations have different effects, not all of them equally good. As we saw in Chapter 7, the simple principle of *caveat emptor* weighted the scales against the buyer in the modern world, and needed to be supplemented by the Sale of Goods Act, 1893, the Unfair Contract Terms Act, 1977, and the Supply of Goods and Services Act, 1982.[1] A law determining

---

[1] Ch.7, §7.1.

what was to count as a contract altered the working of the free market so as to make the purchase of motor cars a much fairer deal for the purchaser. Once we recognise that we cannot give an adequate account of economics in terms of freedom alone,[2] we need to consider what would constitute a just bargain, and once we realise that justice itself is indeterminate, we need to promulgate some code to specify what each party is entitled to expect of the other. And it matters very much to businessmen, as well as to other citizens, what the exact details are.

Besides taking the framework of rules too much for granted, the free-marketeers err also in not recognising the imperfections of the market. Most obviously, the market provides no escape from the Prisoners' Dilemma. If each individual agent seeks to maximise his own pay-off, then in certain situations all will fare worse than if everyone forbore from that course of action which would be most to his own individual advantage. The only way we can avoid pollution and traffic congestion is to interfere with the individual's freedom to drive as he pleases, and either by heavy taxes or by direct prohibitions deprive each individual of the option of taking his car into town. In a somewhat similar way, many public goods cannot be financed through the market, since once they are provided, people can enjoy them whether or not they pay for them. If they are to be available at all, it must be either through private charity or public taxation. If it is left to the market to provide them, nobody will produce them, because no one need pay for them. Even where payment could be exacted for some service or the use of some good, the cost of collecting the fee might be too great, and make the whole exercise uneconomic. Much of the money collected on toll-roads in America and Europe goes on the cost of collection (though electronic devices may reduce the cost in the future). It is neither economic nor medically desirable for victims of road accidents to have to produce their credit card or insurance certificate before the ambulance will give emergency treatment. Services free at the point of delivery save much hassle and book-keeping.

The very existence of firms witnesses to the limits of the market. Firms are single economic units. The employees are paid wages, but do not trade with one another. I do not send you a bill for having a telephone conversation with you, as a solicitor does, nor

---

[2] See ch.3, §3.2.

does my secretary invoice me for each letter she types. If everything should be left to the market, firms should be broken up into separate units, each sending out bills and receiving payments for services rendered. But that would be a very inefficient way of doing business, wasting much time and causing much hassle. Where there is sufficient community of values, it is much more efficient to cooperate in order to achieve common objectives without any money changing hands. It is only where such community of values does not obtain that we need money to enable us to cooperate none the less. Monetary transactions enable us to cooperate when otherwise we could not, but do not improve cooperative activity that can take place anyhow.[3]

Admittedly, there are disadvantages too. As we saw in Chapter 8, if the consumer does not have to pay, he has less clout, and cannot exert pressure against those who fail to deliver satisfactory service, and may not find it easy to have everything to suit his convenience.[4] But it does not have to happen like that. Many public services are provided adequately. Although the consumer cannot vote with his money, he can use his voice, and a public authority that persistently ignores the voter's voice is likely to incur an authoritative re-ordering of priorities. Sometimes both market and non-market provision of services is expedient. In any case, the argument is not that the non-market provision is always better, only that the market provision is not always adequate. And since we sometimes need services which the market cannot provide and which cannot be provided without cost, we have to pay for them from public funds raised by some form of taxation.

§10.3 Fiscal Justice

Taxes are burdensome. We do not naturally want to pay taxes, though we may be prepared to, in order that the State may realise certain values we share or provide us with services we want. But if it were possible to realise those values and provide those services without our having to pay we should not object.[5] It follows that, contrary to our usual way of speaking, the apportionment of burdens raises issues of justice very different from those relevant to the allocation of benefits. We do not naturally wish to miss out on

---

[3] See above, ch.2, §2.1.

[4] In §8.9.

[5] But see the Bishop of Oxford, *The Times*, October 15th, 1994, p.13, 'Praise be to taxes, the sign of a truly civilised society'

benefits, but we are not naturally inclined to shoulder burdens, and there is a problem in ensuring that we do not shirk them. Instead, therefore of talking of the distribution of benefits and burdens in a single breath as one single aspect of justice, we should distinguish from the aspect of justice concerned with the distribution of benefits the markedly different aspect concerned with the contributions that may be fairly demanded.

The dominant problem in contributive, or fiscal, justice, as we may call it, is the Prisoners' Dilemma, that it is the interests of each one of us to avoid contributing, but if we all do, we shall all be worse off. The Americans call it the "Free-rider" problem. If I can dodge paying my fare, I can ride free on the train, and be better off in consequence. And as long as I alone am free-riding, the revenue will be diminished by an insignificant amount, and the trains will continue to run. So it would seem like a good idea for me to dodge paying the fare whenever I can. But that line of reasoning appeals to other people too. If we all adopt it, the trains will not run. But even if I decide to pay my way, I can see the attractiveness of the reasoning to other people, and am rationally afraid that I may be paying to no avail, since others are dodging their fares, and my paying will not secure for me a future train service.

It becomes rational for me to pay if I can be sure that others will pay too: in this respect the case is the same as with obedience to the law.[6] I will pay my share if I can be sure that others will pay their share too. But what is my share? I can think of all sorts of reasons why it should not be as much as might at first be supposed: I have a blind relative to look after, a mortgage to pay, a daughter to marry off. But while I am making these points, with some show of justice, others are looking over their shoulders to see what is being demanded of me, each ready to ask 'Why should I be so heavily taxed when he is getting off so lightly?'. Although justice always addresses itself to the individual, seeking to justify to him the adverse decision being reached, contributive justice has to take seriously the assurance problem, and the fact that others too are needing to be addressed and assured that the individual in question is not getting away with an unduly light burden. It follows that contributive justice has to be rough justice. It cannot be as individualised as the individual might reasonably expect, but must be based on crude categorizations whose relevance is evident

---

[6] See above, ch.9, §9.3, and Appendix A, p.223.(Dec 95)

to all. It is for this reason that a poll tax is often adopted as the
fairest available. It is manifestly simple, and any other would raise
more problems than it would solve. But though a flat subscription
is acceptable for many clubs and voluntary associations, yet where
the tax levied is heavy, as it usually is with modern States, a poll
tax seems disproportionately more burdensome for the poor to pay
than the rich.

It is difficult to measure equality of burden. Each is conscious of
the burdensomeness of his own tax, but tends to make light of the
taxes others have to pay. The poor man observes that the rich is
richer than he, and concludes that the marginal £ extracted from
the rich is less of a sacrifice than if it were extracted from him.
The rich observes that he is paying more, and is being left with
proportionately less. It did not seem fair to him in Britain after
the Second World War that out of an extra £ he should be left
with only 2p, when the standard rate is leaving most of his fellow
countrymen with 67p in the £. Many people agree. Although
there is an argument for progressive taxation, steeply progressive
taxation is unjust.

Steeply progressive taxation is often defended on the principle
"From Each According To His Ability". But that is a communist
principle, which denies altogether individual rights. Once we acknowledge the individuality of individuals, we need to consider not
only the community's point of view, looking round to see who can
bear the marginal increment of taxation best, but from the tax-
payer's point of view, who may feel he is being unjustly mulcted.
If we consider only the question of ability, then it will always be the
case that however much has already been taken, the shoulders of
the rich are broader than those of the poor: even after he has paid
98p in the £ the rich man has more left than the poor, and so, if
ability to pay be the only criterion, he should pay a further impost.
Only when he has paid 100p in the £ are the rich man's shoulders
no longer broader, and no longer to be singled out as worthy to
bear a further burden. But that is to discount his point of view
altogether. When more is called for, he can legitimately argue that
he has already paid more, and that this should be counted unto
him for righteousness. To ignore the past, and the contribution he
has already made, is to ignore him. It cost him a lot, in choices
foreclosed and pleasures forgone, to write the previous cheque to
the Inland Revenue. If that is not taken into account, justice is
not being done. And quite apart from tax already paid, the State

ought not to ignore the antecedent position. If the rich man was rich before the tax was levied, that too was part of his situation which ought not to be obliterated by the activities of the tax man. He may have earned his riches, he may have been given them by the choice of other men. In either case, the State should show some respect for his efforts or other men's choices. Once we abandon the totalitarian view that the State has a *carte blanche* to do what it likes with its subjects' possessions, it takes on a duty to have some regard for what they do and who they are independently of its own plans and dispositions.

These counter-considerations are pertinent. They are too often disregarded in the modern world. An unfortunate practice has grown up whereby the Chancellor of the Exchequer in presenting his budget talks of "giving away" tax concessions. But when he reduces the standard rate of income tax from 27 to 25p in the £, he is not giving anything away, but merely refraining from taking other people's money. If he were giving money away, very different principles of distributive justice would come into play, and it might well be right to give a bonanza to the poorest in the land. But when contributions are being asked for, the antecedent situation of, and contributions already made by, the contributors become relevant. Not that they rule out progressive taxation altogether. Ability to pay is relevant; also—a point insufficiently attended to—the fact that those who pay more to the State are typically those who gain more from it.

We need to distinguish two different bases on which a tax may be demanded. It may be a contribution as a member of an association for the furtherance of its shared values: or it may be a *quid pro quo*, a payment in return for the benefits made available. I pay a subscription to the National Trust, and might do so even if I was living abroad or bed-ridden, because I wanted to preserve England from speculative builders. But I might pay because I was in the habit of entertaining Americans by taking them to view stately homes, and it was cheaper to be a member and go in free. Similarly with the State. Americans wanted America to be the first country to put a man on the moon, and could be asked accordingly to contribute to NASA's costs: but also the State provides many services—protection from external enemies, the maintenance of law and order, the fire brigade and National Health Service—and can ask each of us to fork out. In the former case the relation is internal: it is as members of a community, and sharing its common

values that we are being called on to contribute: in the latter case
the relation is more external, with each being asked to consider his
own interest, and recognise that the tax asked for is a reasonable
bargain from his point of view.

Historically it was the latter view that predominated. The king
bargained with parliament, asking for money so that he could do
things they wanted. Vestiges of this view still remain, in the formula used to give the royal assent to fiscal measures, and, more
importantly, in the wrong-headed doctrine that there is no equity
in taxation. If I, through my representatives, have struck a bargain
with the crown in return for things being done that I want, then I
am committed to the letter of the contract, and cannot appeal to
equity to soften its hard edges. But that is not how things really
are. All that we can say is that some of the services rendered by the
State can be assigned to individuals as benefiting them, and consideration of the sort of bargain it would have been reasonable for
them to strike in order to obtain these services may be relevant to
justifying the tax actually levied. Thus the State provides consular
services, and tries to protect its nationals in foreign lands; this is
a benefit to those who travel abroad, and those who travel abroad
tend to be rather rich—the very poor cannot afford the fare. So
the rather rich can be asked to foot the bill, and are thus justly
called on to pay more in taxes than the poor. In the same way, although we all benefit from there being prisons in which thieves can
be incarcerated and prevented from thieving, the rich have more
goods at risk than the poor, and thus, in this sense, benefit more
and should contribute more.

These arguments carry weight, but need careful handling. Hy-
pothecated taxes (taxes raised specifically for stated purposes) may
be more acceptable to tax-payers, but make little sense economically, because, among other things, of the difficulty of allocating
costs clearly. Moreover, imagined bargains are indeterminate as to
their terms, and do not commit the parties in the way real ones
do. In order to make the argument stick, two things need to be
shown: that no alternative provision was available at anything like
the same cost, and that the State was exercising due care and economy in giving good value for money. State-run services tend to be
inefficient; "If you want a thing done badly, get the government to
do it", as the saying goes. In many countries State-employees are
appointed on grounds other than competence or merit—because

they voted the right way in an election, or because they are members of some group it is desired to favour. The tax-payer then has reason to be resentful, and to wonder whether he could not do better on the open market. Sometimes he can. In recent years public opinion has swung round in favour of private provision. But private provision has its drawbacks. It necessitates charging, which is itself costly, and does not provide universal access, often excluding the poor. Public provision, free at the point of delivery, can be more cost-effective. It depends. In Britain it is being questioned whether the National Health Service is efficient: in America it is being realised that private provision is not. In Britain the Royal Mail has given, since it was instituted in Victorian times, with its employees appointed without political interference, good service: in America the post office has not.

Where taxes are being justified on account of the benefits given in return, there is need for consultation, to bring out into the open whether the benefits are really wanted and whether they are commensurate with the tax. This was more recognised in time past than now, when democratic theory has militated against particular groups having a special say in how they are taxed. But it remains important, particularly for businesses which, as such, have no vote. Businesses do benefit from consular services and from the incarceration of criminals, and often much more so than individual persons. They should pay. But in so far as the grounds on which they are being asked to pay is the supposedly greater benefits they are receiving, some attempt should be made to evaluate these benefits, and to compare those that the businesses receive with those given to others. Precision is impossible, but discussion is not. Although each firm separately has an interest in paying as little as possible, letting others bear the burden, collectively a more reasonable approach is natural, and the wisdom of paying to ensure that the work-force is properly educated may be apparent.

The *quid pro quo* argument goes some way to answering the tax-payer's question, but only some way. Much more weight is put on the internal argument that as a member of the community he should share the burden of promoting its values. Where the shared values are many, the argument will go a considerable way, and when sufficiently strong, will quell almost all objection; in the Second World War extremely high tax rates were not objected to, because however burdensome, they were better than Hitler. Even if I do not share some particular value, I may be carried along by the others I do share. I am not much of a sportsman, and it does not make me happy if a fellow-countryman wins a bronze medal at the Olympics; but it makes others feel proud, and so I do not grudge a corporate decision to devote public money to training our Olympic team. Much individual dissent is overridden by the communal decision-procedure, itself grounded in the large number of values we do share. But though individual protests may be overridden, the argument remains, and it does not follow from the fact that a particular tax has been levied, that it is therefore fair. If a poll tax can be criticized on the grounds that it is unduly burdensome to the poor, other taxes can be criticized on the grounds that they bear too heavily on others. Why should tobacco, alcohol and petrol be taxed, and not sweets, milk and coal?

Exact arguments cannot be given. Fiscal justice is rough justice. Revenue has to be raised, and considerations of expediency very largely, and quite properly, determine how it is done. Taxes need to be simple—a point on which some British taxes fail badly—easy to collect, difficult to evade. Tobacco and petrol, being mostly imported or landed through a small number of large installations, are suitable under this head; with alcohol there is always the consideration that if the tax be too high, people will start making their own hooch. Arguments of public policy are pertinent: tobacco is bad for health, and so is alcohol if taken too freely; petrol-users damage the environment and make life more difficult and dangerous and much less pleasant for others. Indirect taxes have the merit of simplicity, and being to a large extent voluntary—I do not have to buy tobacco (the salt tax, levied in many countries was properly criticized for being charged on a necessity, and one consumed as much by the poor as the rich). But though grounds of public policy afford some reason for choosing one form of tax rather than another, we need to be wary of social engineering. The function of taxes is to raise revenue, not to reshape society according to the predilections of those possessed of political power. They need always to remember, in this century perhaps more than in any previous one, that political power can do much damage but little good.

§10.4 Redistribution

States redistribute economic resources. Policemen would not be paid, drains mended, patents protected, unless money was raised to meet these expenses. By levying taxes the State redistributes money from tax-payers generally to its employees and beneficiaries, in order that the various purposes it has may be achieved.

In the twentieth century the principle has often been extended to claim that the State should take it upon itself to redistribute, by means of taxation, the national wealth in accordance with the principles of distributive justice. And if, indeed, the State had unfettered power, it would seem that it could allocate economic resources as it thought best. The communists tried, and failed. They failed because wealth is not something material, like steel, which can be manipulated and pushed around at will, but much more slippery and intangible, depending ultimately on the ability to choose, itself something inherently not subject to dictation from outside. The communists were able to make people make steel, but could not make them want it. The command economy ground slowly to a halt, and only the black economy flourished in the closing years of the Soviet era. Money is valuable as a lubricant, facilitating cooperation that enables different people to get what they want, but of little use if people cannot get what they want: you cannot run a car on engine oil.

Communism is ostensibly an egalitarian creed, and it was large-ly in the name of equality that the communists and others have sought complete control of the national economy. But complete control requires great concentration of power in relatively few hands, and, as we have seen,[7] power is closely allied with wealth. In most countries in most ages those possessed of great power enrich themselves, sometimes by fair means, more often by corruption. The second half of the twentieth century has been no exception. Rather few egalitarians have practised what they preached when they had the opportunity to do otherwise. The purity of motive that fired the young man with a righteous zeal to make the world a better place by abolishing riches tends to evaporate when he is a Member of Parliament with a nice loss-making farm in the Home Counties. But even the many Members of Parliament who pass by the opportunity to make a tidy pile are not really on an economic equality with their fellow citizens. They get sent on fact-finding missions at the public expense; when they arrive in a foreign capi-tal, they are put up by the ambassador in the embassy, rather than in a bed-and-breakfast near the station. It would not be sensible

---

[7] Ch.3, §3.1.

to have it otherwise. But life is not the same for those in power as for the general public. The food in the embassy is nicer.

Economic equality is undermined by the political inequality needed to enforce it. But even if power were in the hands of dedicated public servants who sought nothing for themselves and were scrupulous in never enjoying any good thing not available to all their fellow-citizens, economic equality would still be unattainable. Wealth is too slippery for the State to be able to control it completely. Maybe I am not allowed to have more money than anybody else. But I am still in a position to do others a good turn, and they may well reciprocate. Doors open for the doctor which otherwise remain tightly shut.[8] In Great Britain very heavy taxes have been levied on inherited estates. But although at first it had the effect of eliminating the class of people who thought that taxes ought to be paid, it has not diminished the number of the very rich. The very rich take expensive advice on how to avoid inheritance tax. The Inland Revenue used to spend much time and money trying to stop up loopholes, but as fast as they legislated against one, ingenious minds found another. It could not be otherwise. For if I am in a position to confer on others greater power of making choices, I can persuade them to make the choices I want made, even after I am dead in favour of my heirs. The effect of the legislation has not been to stop the Duke of Westminster being very rich, but to provide many lawyers and accountants with a profitable line of business.

In other countries, too, egalitarian measures have had inegalitarian results. India, on the face of it, has been a socialist country since independence, but the effect of socialism was to create a maze of directives and regulations which only people with know-how could thread their way through. Those within the charmed circle were in a privileged position, able to enjoy the good things of life, and safe from competition. Although money, left to itself, tends to be unequally distributed, it is in one respect more equal than any form of allocation. The poor man's penny is as good as the rich man's, and he does not have to have any special contacts or esoteric know-how to be able to spend it. States that take unto themselves great powers to regulate the economy disfranchise the poor and uneducated, making it more difficult for them to grow

---

[8] See, for example, A.Solzhenitsyn, *Cancer Ward*, tr. N.Bethel and David Burg, Penguin, 1971.

rich, or even to use the little they have to get what they want. Not only is it contrary to fiscal justice for the State to undertake a general redistribution of wealth, but it is counter-productive too, creating greater, and unfairer, inequalities than those it was supposed to eliminate.

§10.5 Equality and Difference

Equality is a treacherous concept. It seems very simple, and is in fact rather complicated. We readily suppose that it is a simple matter whether two persons are, or ought to be, equal: but until we are clear in what respect the judgement is to be made, the question is empty, and no answer can be given.

Equality has the internal logic of equivalence relations, such as 'same', 'similar' and 'like'. We need, first, to specify the respect in which things are said to be equal—same age, same weight, same income, same religion, same nationality—and then, almost unconsciously, see that the relation is transitive—if I am the same age as you, and you are the same age as Peter, then I am the same age as Peter—and symmetric—if I am the same age as you, then you are the same age as me; and that equivalence relations divide up a group into mutually exclusive "equivalence classes"—cohorts, those in the same income bracket, co-religionists, compatriots. These equivalence classes are of great importance in society; they are often bonded together by powerful ties of shared experience—old comrades associations—or common interest—trades unionists—and fraternal fellow feeling is an important ingredient of social solidarity. But the fellow feeling is often accompanied by, and reinforced by, feelings of hostility towards those in another class: the different generations are conscious of the generation gap, the rich and the poor feel threatened by each other, Rumanians hate Hungarians, and *vice versa*. Society would fall apart, were it not for the fact that there are many different respects in which each of us can be the same as somebody else, and we may be cricketers together even though of different ages, and rich and poor alike assemble to share their wartime experiences and remember their fallen comrades.

There are many different respects in which we are the same, and therefore many different respects in which we are different. We are all the same in respect of being human, and each one of us is different in being the unique individual that he is. Because we are all human, we all have rights, the right not to be killed, not to be injured, not to be imprisoned. Because we are all different, each one of us is to be treated as an individual, and not a mere unit, and addressed individually about any adverse decision that may be in prospect or may have been taken. Sometimes samenesses dominate our thinking, sometimes differences: we are all equal before the law, and every man should be tried fairly, and according to laws that apply generally; but the courts are there to differentiate between cases, and even the most ardent egalitarian does not believe that innocent and guilty should be treated alike. Justice demands that like cases be treated alike, but reminds us also that circumstances alter cases. What circumstances are relevant, and what not, is often a matter of dispute. Sometimes circumstances, in themselves naturally relevant, are deemed irrelevant. There may be good reasons for this—ease of administration, or uniformity of practice—but to set against them there may be some sense of justice not having been done, since justice bids us take all relevant factors into consideration.

§10.6 Egalitarianism

Equality has been an emotive slogan in the twentieth century. It has aroused very strong emotions, usually of hostility towards existing institutions, and usually accompanied by great cloudiness of thinking. People, realising that they are different from other people, some of them better off than they are, conclude that they are being discriminated against, and that the difference between them must, at all costs, be abolished. And the costs have been heavy. In the name of equality *kulaks* have been liquidated, nobles humbled, great houses razed, the heritage of history destroyed, freedom fettered, economies hamstrung, nations impoverished. Sometimes some sort of equality is a good thing. But it is well to be discriminating in its application, and think through its implications before hitting out at existing inequalities.

In economic affairs the main thrust of egalitarian sentiment has been in favour of equality of income and against differentials. People do not see why one person should be paid more than another. The fact that he works harder, or is more skilled, or is more in demand, is held to be irrelevant. The man who sweeps the floor in a factory has just as large a mouth, just as great a thirst for beer, as the man who operates the lathe, the foreman, or the designer, and so should have as much money to spend. They may not agree, but he is not persuaded by the force of their arguments, and continues unconvinced that they should have more.

Like all forms of scepticism, it is, within its own terms, impregnable. If a man does not want to see the force of an argument, he cannot be made to. But others can be equally sceptical, and not see why he should be paid the same, or indeed anything at all. Some positive argument for equality is needed if the dialogue is not to end in mutual incomprehension. Positive arguments can be adduced: arguments from need, arguments from status. These are arguments of distributive justice, and will be considered in the next section. But often no specific argument is put forward, only a vague sentiment that equality is good thing. Against such sentiments we can only invoke other sentiments, that liberty is a good thing, or justice, or prosperity, and then rub the egalitarian's nose in the fact that equality is incompatible with these. The clearest case is liberty. If we value liberty at all, we must let people dispose of some things as they please. We may not like the taste of teenagers, but if they like giving money to pop stars, we ought not to try to prevent them or to nullify their choice. They might just want their favourite pop star to be rich, not as a consequence of their purchasing his hits, but just because they liked the idea of his having gold-plated taps in his bathroom. Their individually small contributions to his benefit fund could total many millions. What then would the egalitarian do? He could confiscate the money— some egalitarians have argued for marginal tax rates of more than 100%—but then he is denying freedom of donation to his fellow country-youngpersons, or he may compromise his egalitarian principles enough to allow people to give presents, but then cannot object to fathers enriching their children, and cannot justify confiscatory death duties. There is no escaping this dilemma. If we have liberty we allow people to make choices as they think best, and they may dispose their worldly wealth so as to make one person better off than another. Either we insist on equality, and deny people that liberty, and hence every non-trivial freedom, or we respect the choices of others and must therefore accept the differences and inequalities they may choose to create. It is a dilemma that most political thinkers of our age resolutely refuse to face. But however much the issue is fudged, it remains the case that we cannot have equality and liberty, and that if we set any store by liberty, we must abandon all thought of equality being in itself a good thing, and seek only those more limited forms of equality that can be argued for on other grounds.

§10.7   Distributive Justice

Equality can be argued for on grounds of distributive justice. When
giving out food in a refugee camp, we may give everyone equal
rations because their need is the same. The purpose of distributing
food was to meet the needs of the refugees, and their needs are
substantially the same. Or the basis of distribution may be status:
in the regimental mess, the school, the monastery, everyone has
the same food because they are all comrades, and it would indicate
a lack of togetherness if they ate differently. In these cases the
purpose of the distribution is given by the context or the nature of
the association. The nature of a business enterprise is different. It
exists to provide goods or services for sale, and can only do so on the
basis of the efforts contributed by its employees. In its contracts of
employment with each employee, the employee agrees to cooperate
in certain ways so as to enable the firm to benefit from the fruits of
cooperation. Because the fruits of cooperation naturally accrue to
the firm alone, pecuniary adjustment is called for. In determining
what this should be, it is relevant to consider how great the fruits
of cooperation are. If one employee, the lathe operator say, makes
a larger contribution than another, the sweeper, say, then he would
be unjustly treated if he were not paid more. Differentials of pay
are justified by differentials of contribution.

The egalitarian will have none of that. He does not see why
a difference of contribution should be relevant. But in refusing to
acknowledge the relevance of what the employee contributes, he is
refusing to recognise that he is an individual with a point of view
of his own, who could have chosen not to make the contribution
that he did. It was up to the lathe operator whether he would or
would not operate the lathe, and his decision actually to operate it
should not be taken for granted. To brush aside his point of view
and ignore the fact that he has made a greater contribution is to
treat him not as an individual but as a unit, a pair of hands but
not a person. It is line with the egalitarian's general preference for
a homogenized admass society, and his dislike of differences and
individual variation. And it is profoundly wrong.

The general argument against differentials is flawed, but differentials are often exceedingly difficult to assess. Many people
make a contribution that is vital, if lowly: the night watchman
who prevents a break-in or calls the fire brigade in time to avert
serious damage saves the firm thousands of pounds; is he to be
paid less than the skilled designer? In large organizations it is

exceedingly difficult to make any estimate of what each employee contributes, and instead of trying to do so, some conventional measure is adopted, and written into the terms of employment. Up to a point the market provides an impartial and usable yardstick. If other firms find it worthwhile to pay skilled workmen more, then that is an indication that their contribution is worth more. But the market is highly imperfect. Many employees are rationally reluctant to switch employers, and, furthermore, skills take a long time to learn, and changes of technology may put a premium on some while making others less in demand. Paper qualifications are highly regarded, perhaps too much so. Age and experience are often cited, but this is often taken to mean mere seniority. Social convention plays a large part. None of these are satisfactory as indicators, but are adopted for want of anything better. Different grades of employment are established with recognised differentials between them, and the employee is paid according to the appropriate scale. Essentially, distributive justice is codified and replaced by a series of different entitlements, which do not claim to correspond exactly to distributive justice, but are evidence that it is not being entirely ignored.

The approximation to distributive justice is crude, and open to criticism. The differentials can be criticized as being too finicky, or as not being fine enough, and correspondingly it may be urged that they should be smaller and fewer in number, or that they should be refined to take individual differences of desert into consideration. Either move may be appropriate in some circumstances, neither is a panacea. It is right to reduce differentials, and even to abolish them altogether, when there is a strong sense of community fostered by a strong sense of common purpose, as in a monastery or a nation in time of war. Where we have a sense of being all in it together, we may be ready to forgo the differentials which are or due. Some egalitarians, to their honour, have been happy to work for the same wage as those who were evidently not making as large a contribution as they themselves were, just because they believed in equality, and wanted to practise what they preached. On a quite different tack, it may be generally recognised that though different individuals do contribute in different degrees, it would be so difficult to try to determine what different individuals had in fact contributed, that it would be expedient not to try, but pay everyone the same, recognising that it was, indeed, rough justice, but that any alternative would be impracticable. On a different tack again, equality of remuneration may be appropriate in the professions, where the identity of purpose of the individual and his profession is so great that the contribution he is making to the profession is equally a contribution he is making towards fulfilling his own aspirations. Some preachers are more eloquent than others, some pastors more effective than others, some priests more devoted than others: but no injustice is done in paying them all the same stipend, because those who have done better by the profession's standards have done better by their own, and seek no further reward. The same is true in the academic world, as is shown by the old practice of Cambridge colleges to pay each fellow an equal dividend. We readily agree the principle that some academics make a greater contribution than others, but know we will not be able to make an accurate assessment until a hundred years have passed, and in any case reckon that those who have been able to make the greater contribution are happy to have done so, and were not doing it for the money.

In recent years, partly as a reaction against egalitarian practices, the argument has been the other way. Piece work rather than hourly wage rates are in vogue, and job descriptions are refined and awarded more finely differentiated rates of pay, and wherever possible, salaries are performance-related. It is appropriate where there is no vocational commitment, the job can be precisely specified, and the performance accurately assessed. What is reasonable to ask of clergymen or academics is not reasonable to ask of salesmen. They have no antecedent commitment to selling soap. They may take a pride in doing their job well, but their job is essentially determined externally. They do it for money, and if they do it well, they should have more money, and not be told that they should be so much identified with the firm that having done well by the firm should be satisfaction enough. In such cases, distributive justice is clearly served, and each employee has a strong incentive to get the best job he can, and to do it well. By tying its costs closely to its inputs, a firm can maximise efficiency, and ensure that its resources are being used to the greatest possible effect. Under suitable conditions more finely tuned differentials are fairer and enhance efficiency. But often these conditions do not obtain. Differential stipends, except by way of recompense for extra expenses, are inappropriate for the clergy and for academic work. Performance-related pay is not only inappropriate but counter-productive in many walks of life. Often it is difficult and costly to assess performance. And often also the method of assessment and the criteria used will send the wrong signals to those being assessed.[9]

Questions of distributive justice arise within a business enterprise or a profession, where there is some common objective to which individuals make a contribution by cooperating. But in times of peace there is no overriding common objective underlying the existence of the State. The State is an unselective community to which people belong willy-nilly merely by the accident of geographical location: that is why the laws have to be enforced, if necessary by coercion. But without a common set of values, the basis for distributive justice is lacking.[10] We cannot have an incomes policy that is fair. Many people think we should, and are affronted at a pop star's earning more money than a nurse. It is defensible to think the nurse more deserving, and if the State were a business enterprise, it ought to pay the nurse more. But the State is not a business enterprise, and exists primarily not to carry shared objectives into effect but to provide the framework in which many different people and organizations with different aims can live together in peace. This is not to say that there are no shared values underlying the State. There are: but they do not constitute a single system of objectives that can be realised in a coherent set of activities. And therefore we cannot establish an overall incomes policy based on principles of distributive justice. Pop stars will always get more than they deserve, and nurses, sadly, less.

The impossibility of there being an incomes policy based on principles of distributive justice has been taken by many thinkers to show that appeals to principles are always out of place, and the market alone can determine what people are to be paid. But that does not follow. We cannot have an overall incomes policy, but sometimes we have to make collective decisions about incomes and cannot leave it to the market. How much should the Queen be paid? There is no market in queens. Lots of people would be prepared to be Head of State, Prime Minister, Member of Parliament, Admiral of the Fleet for no pay at all, and we have no means of determining what the going rate for the right sort of person would be. We have

---

[9] See further below, ch.12, §12.4.

[10] See Aristotle, *Politics*, III,9; III, 12, 1283a10-12; V, 1, 1302a3-5. See, contemporarily, Samuel Brittan, *Capitalism with a Human Face*, Aldershot, 1995, pp.236ff.

to decide. We base our decision in part on the expenses of office, and the compensation we should give people who have abandoned more lucrative occupations in order to serve their country in public office, but we are often also guided by some idea of the contribution made by the office holder to the safety or well-being of the realm, that is, by some canon of distributive justice.

§10.8 Economic Legitimacy

The impossibility of there being an incomes policy based on principles of distributive justice means that incomes, and the possession of wealth generally, is unfair. People do not always get what they deserve; nor, it should be added, what they need. Perhaps they ought to get what they need. Many people, thinking so, argue for a minimum wage, to ensure that those at the bottom of the pile do not lose out altogether. Against this it is argued that a minimum wage would increase unemployment. It is not a straightforward matter. Since the market is not in perfect equilibrium, many of the conclusions of school-book economics do not apply. We can, up to a point, change what is taken to be the going rate, and might be able to raise the level of the lowest paid. But only up to a point. Labour can be priced out of the market,[11] and as a general rule it is better to be employed, even at a low wage, than to be on the dole. If we want to ensure that people get what they need, we should supplement their incomes at the general expense, not try to make employers foot the bill. But even if we do so, the minimum level will be low indeed, and although they will not starve, those at the bottom of the pile will feel disadvantaged. There is not a simple argument that can be addressed to them to show them why they should get less than everybody else. The justifications we can give are complicated and tenuous, and may well fail to carry conviction. But justifications are called for. People do lose out: we owe them some explanation, some attempt to reconcile them, some attempt to make things easier to be reconciled to.

Much of the explanation is the old one, that the alternative is worse. At present in the aftermath of the communist experiment, it is easy to mount that argument, and be believed. But just as the memories of the Civil War and of the French Revolution faded, and ceased to reconcile the poor to their lot, so in time to come the

---

[11] See ch.6, §6.10.

horrors of communism will be forgotten, and the manifest defects of the economies then in operation will provoke serious questioning. And it will be seen that theoretically a better arrangement would be possible: what is less easily seen is that in practice most changes will be for the worse. Revolutions have a natural tendency to go sour. Those who get into power to overthrow the established order become corrupted by the power they have seized, and use it for their own aggrandisement rather than for improving the lot of the underdog.

We need to dispel false images. As long as people think of money in quasi-material terms, it will seem evident that the way to make the poor richer is to make the rich poorer, and greed will reinforce envy to destabilise society. As long as the theory of business is that of the Economic Man out solely for himself, others will feel entirely alienated from him. We need also to point out evident truths. The stable framework of law that enables the rich man to be rich secures also the life, liberty and possessions of the poor. Although the "trickle-down effect" has been derided, it remains true that the poor in rich countries benefit enormously from the productivity of the economy and the wealth of the rich: slum-dwellers in the United States who riot would not have TV sets at all if there had not been rich people who could afford to buy the first, pricey, models.

The arguments, though tenuous, are valid. But where emotions are concerned, attitudes are more telling than arguments. The attitudes of Economic Man are uncaring. The admass society conveys the impression for caring only for the customer's dollar, not for the customer himself. In part, as we have seen,[12] it is the other side of the coin from freedom; but it is greatly reinforced by the adversarial aspect of economic transactions, untempered by considerations of justice. The emphasis of much contemporary thought about how business should be conducted is not only wrong, but wrong-headed. By concentrating on profit-maximisation alone, to the exclusion of all other considerations, a businessman portrays himself as essentially external to everyone else, alien and hostile. If only the emphasis were on dealing with each case fairly, and acknowledging the importance of the other party's values, the sense of alienation would be greatly assuaged. We need an "other-directed" style of management, and not one focused exclusively on the self.

---

[12] See above, ch.3, §3.2.

A sense of togetherness is the strongest antidote to alienation. A society in which there are many different associations sharing common interests and objectives is one in which everyone can find a *niche* where he belongs and is valued for himself and not his money. Many of these associations will not be business ones, although, as will be argued in Chapter 12, it is perfectly proper for businesses to make donations to them. But businesses, too, can share objectives with the rest of society, and the more they are seen to be doing this, the greater will be the identification with them, and the greater the legitimacy of the economy in which they operate. The legitimacy of the economy, like the legitimacy of the State, is always under strain: things are often not what we should wish them to be, often not what we think they ought to be, but we are required to put up with them none the less. The mere fact of being the established order confers some measure of legitimacy, but is not conclusive. Beyond that, economic and management legitimacy can, like political legitimacy, be earned, but can also be lost. The underlying thrust of economic transactions is cooperation, but there is an inevitable adversarial aspect also. By stressing cooperative concerns and being guided by clearly communicated canons of justice businessmen can enhance the legitimacy of the economy, and make it more acceptable even to those who benefit least.

Chapter 11
The Third World, Growth and Resources

Contents

Abstract

Businessmen are often castigated for being too little concerned about the Third World, and for being committed to unsustainable growth at the cost of the environment, and missing out on the great goods of life. These criticisms are often captious, and therefore ignored. But businessmen do have to deal with the Third World on occasion, and as citizens may have to vote; and although often there is not much to be done, it is important to have a clear mind about the implications of economic activity, if only to avoid being made to feel guilty, and to prevent potential recruits being put off from business life.

§11.1 Guilt

We are made to feel guilty about the Third World. It is our fault that rain forests are being cut down, indigenous peoples chased out of their primitive simplicity and herded into shanty towns, millions of children left living off garbage bins on the streets of Rio. Compassion fatigue at length sets in, and we are glad to be told by others that the Third World is none of our business, and that each country should look after its own, and that it is morally wrong to raise taxes to be spent on international aid. All these views are wrong, though some contain some kernel of truth. In spite of there not being much that any of us can do about the Third World, there is something, and we should think carefully about what we can and should do, all of us in our capacity as private citizens, some of us also in some business capacity.

We also feel uncomfortable about growth. On the one hand, growth is thought to be a good thing. Politicians boast that the

Gross National Product has increased during their term of office, and they therefore should be re-elected. We are bemused. We are not convinced that things are better than they used to be in the good old days, but cannot contest the figures. And we are obscurely worried. Environmentalists point out that the world is finite, and there must be a limit to the growth that can be sustained. They tell us we should be more economical, and we agree, and they go on to say that unless we are really uncomfortable there is no hope for us. We shiver, and turn up the central heating.

We would like to be friends with the Environment, but do not know how to evaluate the issues collectively, or deal with them individually. Man's intervention in the world has not always been for the worse, but clearly he has been a great polluter, and the world would be a better place if we all exercised restraint. It is an instance of the Prisoners' Dilemma, and the responsible businessman is torn between particular imperatives of competitive survival and general obligations to the wider world.

§11.2 Transferability

Guilt and compassion fatigue are enhanced by some of the arguments addressed to us. "Do you need £10 more than this starving child does?" It is clear, on the one hand, that we could make an extra donation, but on the other, if we did so, the same argument could be adduced again and again and again. But then we begin to sense something wrong. Although any unit of money is highly transferable, it does not follow that the same holds good for very large sums. I can give £1 to War on Want; I can give £1,000; but to give £1,000,000,000 would disrupt the economies of both donor and recipient: for, as we have seen,[1] money is not a quasi-material object that can be shunted around, but something that obtains its value by being used to facilitate cooperation. The pound sterling gets its value from the cooperative activities of the British, and cannot be drawn off from the British economy in indefinitely large amounts. I can donate an ounce of blood, a half-pint of blood, or a pint, but not seven pints. The gift relationship is not indefinitely expandable. Although more needs to be done, and more can be done, yet there are limits, and it is well to be aware of these, so that what can be done is done to the best advantage.

---

[1] See above, ch.3, §3.4. and ch.10, §10.4.

§11.3 Education and Trade

Aid does not have to be ineffective. Many charities and private
ventures show that. Those who administer it are dedicated volunteers, whose fingers are not sticky, who are content to do undra-
matic good, and are receptive to the suggestions of those they are
trying to help, and sensitive to the needs and possibilities of the
areas where they work. Much can be done, much has been done,
often by helping the recipients to help themselves.

One of the services the West can render to other countries is
in education, particularly in educating future governments. There
are difficulties. Hitherto when we have had students from poor
countries they have often not wanted to return. More important
than technical skills are general attitudes. After the collapse of
the Berlin Wall, the West German Government was able to second many deputy burgomasters to East Germany to set their local
government on the right lines. Perhaps the greatest service Britain
could offer would be to take on foreign students after their gradu-
ation in central and local government offices for a number of years,
so that they could learn how to run things competently and imbibe
the public sector *ethos* of public service.

Perhaps the most effective way of helping others to help themselves is to join with them in cooperative exercises. By trading
with the Third World we enable them to stand on their own feet,
learning in the process the skills and attitudes that have made
the West rich. Substantial progress has been made in the liber-
alisation of world trade, but restrictions and barriers still remain.
The 1994 Uruguay round should result in a 40 percent cut in developed countries' tariffs on industrial products, and an increase
in the value of those imports that receive duty-free treatment in
developed countries from 20 to 44 percent.[2] Furthermore, the restrictions imposed by the Multifibre Arrangement (MFA) will also
be relaxed and phased out over a period to 2005, although there will
be a mechanism in place (the Textile Monitoring Body), which will
adjudicate in cases where the importing country can demonstrate
that imports have been arriving in such quantities as to damage
seriously the domestic industry. Such measures are welcome, but
not enough. The developed countries are still protectionist—the
market for agricultural products in the European Union is a case

---

[2] *Trading into the Future*, World Trade Organization, 1994.

in point—and Third-World countries may argue that the rich countries of the West are using their political power to keep the poor countries poor. Protectionist policies prevent poor countries being able to sell the things they are capable of producing, while leaving them eager to import the highly sophisticated products of the West which they cannot produce for themselves.

There is a real dilemma. Is it right for British clothing manufacturers to be put out of business as a result of cheaper imports from the Far East? The British consumer and the Far East worker say Yes: the unemployed textile worker says No. A balance has to be found between their claims. Workers in Britain, though for the most part not as poor as those in the Third World, are none the less deserving of consideration, and unemployment is a great evil. But the poverty of the Third World is a great evil too, and it is hypocrisy to give small amounts in direct aid, while shutting the door against the far more important trade and the benefits which the elimination of barriers can bring.[3]

§11.4 Globalisation

The globalisation of business is a major development over the last forty years, and raises new questions for the legitimacy and practices of international business both as regards the civil authorities and the local culture in the countries in which they operate.

Big business operates in many countries, and is no longer subject to any one sovereign State. It can choose where to conduct business, and if a regime is unreasonable, it can move elsewhere.[4] This greatly increases its bargaining power. Multinational firms are like barons in middle ages, and able to stand up to the crown. In part this is good. Just as the crown needed curbing in the middle ages, so the State needs to be stood up to now. It is a salutary experience for a finance minister to find that if he decides to appropriate all the golden eggs, the goose flies away. But multinationals

---

[3] See D.A. Hay, *Economics today*, Leicester, 1989, ch.7, §3, esp. p.260 and sources cited in fn.31. For a different form of protectionism, see above, ch.9, §9.4. For protectionism under guise of high-mindedness, see Samuel Brittan, *Capitalism with a Human Face*, Aldershot, 1995, p.222.

[4] Not that tax should be the chief factor. Many multinational firms reckon that if they let tax dominate their commercial decisions, their business would deteriorate.

may abuse their power, and not pay their fair share of the costs of running the societies they operate in. Companies registered in the Cayman Islands, like tankers registered in Liberia, do not inspire confidence that they will be mindful of their obligations generally.

A study conducted by Fiat[5] revealed that 40% of the managerial jobs in the company dealt with international matters, and as a result identified the need to redefine management responsibilities in the context of international operations. To find out more about the competencies of multi-country managers, the Ashridge Management Research Group interviewed managers from a diverse group of multinational companies.[6] The study identified new competencies for "doing", such as acting as an inter-cultural mediator and change agent, and for "being", such as cognitive complexity, which is the ability to see several dimensions in a situation rather than only one, and to identify relationships and patterns between different dimensions. These new management competencies are required for operating effectively in different cultural environments. For example, Japanese and Western styles of management differ.

> The first important characteristic of Japanese management is the strong emphasis on people, which paves the way to different patterns among the Japanese, Europeans or Americans in response to a given set of similar circumstances. Whereas the systems-type of management found in the US and Europe emphasises the decision maker, the professional, the individual's creativity and responsibility, the functional relationship and management by objectives, the organic-type found in Japan makes the boss a facilitator, a social leader and emphasises group strength, free-form command and management by consensus.[7]

This kind of debate about how multinational companies are to be managed takes business into new areas of ethical behaviour. No longer is it sufficient to do business on the basis of a "colonialist" approach whereby the local nationals should be grateful to

[5] E.Auterio and V.Tesio, "The Internationalisation of management in Fiat", *The Journal of Management Development*, vol.9 no.6, 1980.

[6] K.A.Barham and S.Wills, "Management across Frontiers", *Ashridge Research Group*, 1992.

[7] J.Graverau, "Japanese Management", *The Financial Times Handbook of Management*, ed. Stuart Crainer, 1995. See further an Indian example from F.G.Bailey's *Stratagems and Spoils*, quoted in ch.12, §12.3.(p.194 of Dec 95)

receive the advantages of superior management techniques. Economic behaviour in international business now calls for a much more cooperative and inter-active approach, and represents a major opportunity for *alteritas*, recognising and corresponding to what is different from "my way".[8]

The potential for conflict exists, particularly if one culture, or system, believes its existence to be under threat, giving rise to "fundamental" defences of the local culture, as happened at the end of the Shah's reign in Iran. There is an alternative, however, in which a positive cultural exchange through business activity breaks down nationalist barriers. Montesquieu spoke of his "being first a man, then a Frenchman; or rather, being of necessity a man, and only a Frenchman by chance." In such a way multinationalism can put economic activity in a new light, placing new emphasis on its original meaning of 'household organization',[9] where a sharing, rather than a conflict, of interests is the motivating force.

§11.5 Corruption

If we trade with the Third World, we face problems of employment policies, of environmental issues, and of corruption. Of these corruption is the most perplexing. If a firm refuses on principle to bribe government officials, business becomes impossible; if, however, it goes along with the prevailing practice, it is reinforcing it, and making it more difficult for the country ever to have an honest and competent government. And corruption spreads. Those who are instructed to give bribes may see nothing wrong in taking them.

Some firms maintain a strict clean-hands policy and survive. That is, undoubtedly, the best course, and one found, if it were tried, to be more possible than is commonly supposed.[10] Some firms keep their own hands apparently clean by getting others to

---

[8] For a practical instance, see Appendix B.

[9] see Glossary

[10] The United States Foreign Corrupt Practices Act of 1977 makes it a criminal offence for American persons to offer or provide payments to officials of foreign governments in order to obtain or retain business, even if doing so is not unlawful in the foreign country concerned. (cited by Elaine Sternberg, *Just Business*, London, 1994, p.276, n.20.) The costs and non-costs of high-mindedness are discussed by Samuel Brittan, *Capitalism with a Human Face*, Aldershot, 1995, p.33.

do the dirty work. Some British firms pay a 10% commission on all their sales in India to an Indian agent who has an incentive to lay out considerable sums to secure that orders come their way. Some simply pay what is demanded as and when they need something from officialdom. It is difficult to blame them, difficult to feel quite happy about it. "When in Rome, do as the Romans do . . . " but. At least one would like to be taking such steps as were possible to rid the country of the scourge, perhaps only by keeping records for future use, possibly by moving away from areas where bribes were necessary to those where it was possible to be honest.

A similar problem arises with organized crime. In Eastern Europe, especially in Russia itself, protection money is regularly demanded. It would be irresponsible for a firm simply to ignore threats, and expose its employees to kidnap or murder, but equally every extorted payment reinforces the extortioner's power. Some firms simply refuse to do business in any country that cannot or will not maintain law and order and give effective protection to law-abiding residents going peaceably about their own business. Large firms which do not wish to, or cannot afford to, pull out, can provide their own protection, housing their employees in fortified camps, and conveying them in armoured vehicles, with the same degree of armed protection accorded to diplomats in unsafe countries. It is an expensive policy, but a good one, not only because it provides effective security, but also in showing up the limits of the Mafia's might. Every demand for protection money not acceded to weakens the credibility of further demands; the mere existence of a safe area encourages the formation of other safe areas and strengthens the will to resist.[11]

§11.6 Foreign Aid

Corruption is the chief argument against governments' undertaking foreign aid. Much of it is wasted. It goes from government to government, and governments are corrupt. In the Third World they are openly and blatantly corrupt, and much of the poverty of those living in the Third World is due to the vanity and incompetence of those of their fellow-countrymen they have the misfortune to have as rulers. But even among the relatively respectable governments

[11] See, for example, Geoff Winestock, "Strong Arms and the Law", *Business Russia*, Economist Intelligence Unit, London, July 1995, vol.1, no.4, p.1.

of the West, there is a deep tendency to turn idealistic initiatives to self-interested ends. Money is given to the impoverished country, but is tied to its being spent in the donor country not on what is actually needed but on buying something the donor country has to spare, something it cannot sell anywhere else. Under the guise of foreign aid it is really a form of outdoor relief for ailing industries.

After the collapse of communism the countries of Eastern Europe needed help. Many experts were sent out by their governments, giving a lot of advice, much of it of a somewhat obvious kind—'That reactor is dangerous; you ought to replace it'. Much money was spent on five-star hotels that could have been better spent on providing the wherewithal to carry out some of the suggestions made. There is an inherent tendency for government money to stick to the fingers of government officials handling it.

Governments tend to suffer from megalomania. Big projects get into the newspapers and make ministers look good. Sometimes big projects are needed: perhaps only some colossal endeavour could turn back the encroachment of the Sahara desert. But the track record has been bad. Not only has much money been wasted by big projects funded by governments and the World Bank, but often they have done damage. Irrigation has not made deserts more fertile but saltier, dams had been better not built, cattle not raised.

Often the argument against governments' undertaking foreign aid is based not on what actually happens, but high principle. It is held that it is morally wrong to raise taxes to be spent on international aid. The State's right to raise taxes rests, it is argued, on an implied contract, which authorises the State to legislate and raise revenues for the benefit for its citizens but for no other purpose. But, with the possible exception of the United States of America, States do not owe their existence to any actual contract, and non-actual contracts suffer from the grave defect of being indeterminate. Who is to say what terms I might have agreed to, had I been drawing up an agreement with a future sovereign? I might have stipulated that he was to act only in my interests, narrowly defined, but I might equally have required him to be faithful to the tenets of Islam, and act always in accordance with the teachings of the Prophet. Not every State has been founded on the principles of a public utility company. Many have shared values of a more idealistic kind, and nations have often striven collectively to achieve national ideals.

The contract theory of the State, apart from its other defects, suffers from the same inadequacy as the classical view of the public limited company, in imposing too strict a limitation of authority.[12] Citizens cannot exclude moral considerations from those their government may take cognizance of, any more than shareholders can with their directors. If governments have authority to make any decisions at all, they must have discretion to take account of moral considerations as well as others. And in fact they must take up some moral standpoint, situated as they are in a wicked world in which other powers are minded to displace them by force. In order to survive, States have to be able to fight, and if they are to be able to fight, people must be prepared to die for them, and nobody is prepared to die for reasons of self-interest alone. States must stand for something people are prepared to give their lives for, values that go beyond the limited concerns of a public utility company.

It does not follow that a State must devote some of its revenues to foreign aid. But it may. It is a corporate decision that may be legitimately made without contravening the fundamental principles that form the *raison d'être* of the State. A nation may think it part of its national mission to help other nations, and may decide to devote revenues to this purpose. But there are difficulties in ensuring that they are well spent. Foreign aid is not in principle wrong, but often in practice ineffective.

§11.7 Beware of Numbers

Malthus[13] haunts our subconscious. The spectre of uncontrolled population increase seems realised in the Third World, and we often feel responsible in as much our humane efforts to improve health have only removed the natural curbs without replacing them by artificial ones. Although it is often argued that increased prosperity is the only way to limit population increase, there is much doubt whether it actually works—or at least whether it will work in time. Government initiatives have been helpful, though not, as yet, effective enough. There is not much individuals can do, except not to use Malthusian nightmares as an excuse for not doing anything about the Third World, or even not thinking about it. We need to think, partly in order that when we have to take decisions, we

---

[12] See above, ch.4, §4.6.

[13] See Glossary.

reach them in the right way, partly because we are liable otherwise
to be paralysed by bogeymen we have not dared contemplate, and
therefore have not seen through.

Collective action is often called for. But strategies for taking
decisions are not well understood. We mostly think in terms of sur-
veying available alternatives, and attempting a cost-benefit analysis for the more promising ones. But that is unrealistic. The
reliability of the conclusions drawn is no greater than that of the
numbers fed in; and although numbers have an inherent appearance of precision and reliability, the ways in which quantitative
assessments are actually made are often imprecise and unreliable.

It is quite difficult to attach numbers to magnitudes. In the
physical sciences after centuries of thought and experiment we can
measure temperature, electric current and atomic weight, but in
economics we have no theory to help us, and few facts on which to
base a quantitative measure. We can count population, number of
telephones, number of bankruptcies; where there is a large market
with many transactions, we can record the price at which shares
or currencies were bought and sold. A firm can have reasonably
reliable knowledge of its stocks, the number of employees, its takings, the bills it has to pay, and the money it has in the bank; but
beyond that figures are often only guesstimates, and sometimes
worse. The rate of inflation over the next twelve months, the pre-
Christmas sales, the incidence of VAT—only time will tell. Worse
than that, many figures are deliberately falsified. With sufficient
effort, I might get to know the income tax returns for Italy: but
I should be a fool to infer from them what incomes in Italy actually were. Throughout Eastern Europe figures have been falsified
for decades. Yet so great is the worship of numbers that in 1994
the Czech Gross Domestic Product was being calculated using a
deflator based on 1984 prices, which had been heavily manipulated by the authorities.[14] Often it is admitted that the figures
are based on unreliable foundations, but then argued that since
they are the only figures available we must do the best we can
with them. That is a mistake. Unreliable figures are unreliable
figures. Calculations with unreliable figures are unreliable calculations. Conclusions drawn from unreliable figures are unreliable
conclusions. Instead of being mesmerised by figures, businessmen
should simply say that they do not know, use their eyes, back their

---

[14] *Business Eastern Europe*, XXIII, no.44, October 31, 1994, p.1.

hunches, knowing that they do not know, and accepting the standing condition of all decision-making that it is done with imperfect
information. If we do not know, we do not know, and it is much
better to know that we do not know than to have a barrage of
figures to conceal from us the fact that we do not know.

Not all figures are totally unreliable. Although we need to be
aware of the reasons people may have for falsifying their returns,
some statistics are reasonably reliable, though not absolutely accurate. It is a useful exercise then not simply to adopt the best
figures we can get, but to note what effect a somewhat different
figure would have on the final calculation. Some systems are relatively insensitive to variations of some parameters: others much
more so—ice-cream sales to day-time temperatures. If we have a
reliable but imprecise figure for a magnitude, it is good to know
the corresponding range of variability for the final figure.

But we cannot quantify probabilities at all accurately, and such
guesstimates as we make are subject to imponderable chances.
What is the probability of the yen rising against the peseta next
year? It all depends. If the King of Spain were assassinated by a
Basque terrorist, then the peseta would fall: if yet another Prime
Minister of Japan is bowled out for corruption, the yen might. Or,
again, it might not, being buoyed up by the US deficit and distrust
of the dollar, or by Japan's success in keeping out imports. We
cannot enter even imprecise probabilities for such events, and all
analyses based on such figures bear little relation to fact.

In any case cost-benefit analyses are largely beside the point,
because they fail to focus on the key question a decision-maker
should always be asking himself: 'What if I am wrong?' Instead
of COBA (COst-Benefit Analysis) we need ACE, Assess Cost of
Error. There is a new venture suggested for the firm. It might
prove very profitable. But what if not? If, should it fail to come
off, the firm will go bankrupt, we should look on it quite differently
from the way we should if the starting-up costs could easily be
written off. In the latter case, if I wrongly decide not to go ahead,
I forgo great profits, whereas if I wrongly decide to have a try, my
losses are limited; and this presents an entirely different choice for
me from the one I face if a wrong decision to go ahead will end
in bankruptcy.[15] The same approach is needed in deciding public

---

[15] On one occasion in Singapore four investors were wondering whether to
build a $10,000,000 steel mill, and the senior investor asked "Can we afford
to lose $10,000,000?", and the answer being Yes, they went ahead with the
project.

policy. At present we are much exercised about the greenhouse
effect, which may be due to our great consumption of fossil fuel.
The causal connexion is unproved. We may be witnessing only a
random fluctuation. The ocean may be able to absorb a very large
amount more of carbon dioxide. There may be some homeostatic
mechanism at work. We do not know. We cannot sensibly quantify the probabilities of any of these hypotheses being true. The
assumptions we put into our models are so arbitrary as to make the
models almost valueless. But what we can do is to work out what
will happen either way if we are wrong. If we are wrong in supposing that there is a simple causal connexion between burning fossil
fuel and global warming, we shall restrict fuel consumption and
spend money on developing alternatives needlessly; we shall end
up with expensive nuclear power stations and a shivering house-
bound population denied oil-fired central heating and easy motor
transport. But we shall survive. If, however, we decide the other
way and are wrong, we shall discover our error too late to put it
right, and global temperatures will rise, deserts will expand, the
ice caps will melt, and most of the big cities of the world will be
under water.

In the face of uncertainty we have to act on imperfect information, and have to take risks. But in deciding what to do, we need
to consider not just alternative courses of action, but alternative
assessments of future course of events, taking seriously the imperfection of our information, and our inadequate powers of assessing
it. We need a policy of safety first. But in discerning the dangers to be avoided, we need to scrutinise them carefully, to make
sure that they are real dangers, and not just figments generated
by misuse of figures, and inadequate grasp of the issues involved,
leading us to suppose that the whole purpose of economic activity
is to increase, without limit, some spurious index, such as the Gross
National Product.

§11.8   Gross National Product

The Gross National Product (GNP) is a measure of economic activity. It is based on the amount of money changing hands over
a particular interval in payment for goods and services. If more
money changed hands, then more goods were purchased, and more
services rendered. And that, it is supposed, is a good thing.

In fact, very much more is supposed. It is taken for granted that the Gross National Product is a measure of wealth generally, and that the greater the Gross National Product, the greater our wealth, and that the whole object of business activity is to increase the Gross National Product. But that is absurd. The Gross National Product leaves out many factors. It has difficulty in accounting for public goods that are unpriced. It takes no account of cooperative activities in which no money changes hands.

Housewives work; mothers work; volunteers work. Their labour makes an enormous difference to the well-being of society, but is ignored in calculations of the Gross National Product. Defenders of the Gross National Product argue that we can still use changes of the Gross National Product in one country to measure increases of wealth, because these factors are unlikely to change much from year to year, But we do not know that. Technological improvements and alterations in social patterns have greatly affected work in the home and in voluntary pursuits—smoke control and central heating have lightened housework, baby alarms between houses have liberated mothers. Over longer intervals of time, and between different societies, comparisons of Gross National Product are even less meaningful. And whenever they are made, they have the insidious effect of denigrating the worth of all those who work for free, and making out that whatever is priceless is valueless.

Public goods are difficult to account for. Some, defence for example, are entered at cost. In the years since the Second World War Britain has spent a much smaller proportion of its Gross National Product on the armed services than Germany did in Hitler's time: but for Britain the money spent secured the blessings of peace, for Germany disaster and defeat. Environmental goods are enormously important. Life in Los Angeles is insupportable, however many dollars each wage-earner brings home each week. "Where there is muck, there is brass" it used to be said; and in recent years, multinational businesses, criticized for locating in India hazardous processes which were not allowed in the West, have claimed in defence that the Indians needed the money, and the choice was between hazardous industries and no industry at all.[16] These are possible defences. But the fact that they can be put forward at all shows that there is some trade-off between environmental goods

---

[16] For a different concern, where the criticism was not that the industry was hazardous, but that its products were not needed, see Appendix B.

and monetary ones, and hence that a monetary measure alone cannot be an accurate measure of the good life.

Many cooperative activities do not involve money but do make us better off. Consider two National Health Service doctors, one good, one bad. The good one takes a lot of trouble with his patients, listening carefully to what they say, exercising considerable skill in diagnosing their complaints, often reassuring them that nothing much is wrong. The bad doctor pays no attention to what the patient says, and prescribes barbiturates for everyone. All in all more money changes hands as his prescriptions are paid for by the National Health Service, while the treatments prescribed by the other average out cheaper. The bad doctor increases the Gross National Product, the good doctor the national well-being.

We can multiply instances. In the one case two academics who never cooperate, each giving the same boring lectures year in and year out: in the other they spend a lot of time reading and discussing each other's work, write interesting articles in consequence, and collaborate in giving lively and stimulating seminars. Or we can imagine two towns, one in Italy where there has always been a municipal opera house paid for out of local taxes, the other in America where it is supported entirely by the tickets it sells. And it could be that the revenue raised in each case was the same. But in the Italian town the opera is played each night to full houses, with poor as well as rich flocking to hear their favourite Verdi, while in America only the select few can afford to pay what it costs to hear *La Traviata*. Or, to take an example characteristic of the late twentieth century, a bus service is withdrawn because it is losing money. Most of those who were accustomed to use it stay at home because they cannot afford to do anything else: but occasionally they have to go to the doctor or the chemist, and then take a taxi. The taxi, let us suppose, is run by the former bus-driver, who was made redundant; and let us suppose further, what he takes in fares from his bus-less customers is the same as what was paid to him and was spent on maintaining and fuelling the bus previously. The Gross National Product is the same, but many people are much worse off.

The motor industry has been a great beneficiary of the obsession with the Gross National Product. More money spent on cars was registered as an increase of the Gross National Product, and so thought to be a good thing. Undoubtedly it brought great benefits to some, which should not be ignored. But it imposed great costs on others, which also ought not to be ignored. Many people were killed,[17] many injured, some children stunted by lead poisoning, many more confined to home and denied the freedom to roam, on account of the danger from motor traffic. These were real costs, inadequately registered in calculations of the Gross National Product.[18]

The fundamental flaw in the Gross National Product is that it takes account only of those transactions in which money changes hands, that is, those cooperative activities where there is not sufficient community of values to achieve common objectives without any money changing hands. Monetary transactions enable us to cooperate when otherwise we could not, but do not improve cooperative activity that can take place anyhow.[19] Great care is needed in interpreting the Gross National Product; it is not to be worshipped; nor should we suppose that business is committed to its limitless increase.

§11.9 Is Economic Activity A Good Thing?

What the Gross National Product does measure is economic activity, and it might seem that economic activity was inherently a good thing. If there was no economic activity we should all be much worse off, and the effect of each transaction that takes place is to leave the parties better off than if it had not taken place. To some extent, then, it must be a good thing. But before we generalise, we need to consider alternative activities it might displace. They might be a good thing too, and might, indeed, be better. One man likes skiing. He works overtime to get the extra money to fly to Austria for a skiing holiday; his mate likes fishing, and rather than work overtime, occupies his leisure hours patiently and inexpensively, at the riverside. It is clear that the former is better off as a result of his economic transactions than if he had neither

---

[17] In one Cost-Benefit assessment to determine whether a pedestrian crossing should be made in Woodstock Road, Oxford, the deaths of old-age pensioners were entered as a benefit, since it would save their pensions having to be paid.

[18] See more fully, E.J.Mishan, *The Costs of Economic Growth*, Staples Press, 1967; F.J. Hirsch, *Social Limits to Growth*, London, 1970; and D.A. Hay, *Economics today*, Leicester, 1989, ch.8, §2.

[19] See above, ch.2, §2.1.

earned nor spent the extra money: but it does not follow that he is better off than his mate. In some cases, indeed, we should be strongly inclined to think the reverse. Two sisters are married and have children. One works in an insurance office, earning good money which she spends on a baby-minder and on convenience foods. The other is domestically inclined, and spends her time at home, feeding the children on home cooked food and dressing them in clothes she has made herself. Many would say that her children were better looked after, though her sister had engaged in many more economic transactions.

Money confers freedom, though only of a certain sort.[20] The man who works overtime could choose to go to the Carpathians instead of the Alps, or to go water-skiing in the Mediterranean, or pot-holing in the Pyrenees, whereas the fisherman has a much narrower range of options. The sister who sells insurance can buy angel's whip or hamburgers or potato crisps for her children, whereas her sister can only re-heat the shepherd's pie. To that extent economic activities are good, enhancing choice. But other activities are good, too. Cooperative activities within associations holding many values in common are inherently good, realising shared values at the same time as engaging with other people over a wide range of concerns. Although the choice is more limited, the engagement is greater, and more fulfilling. The check-out girl at the supermarket does not get into a deep personal relationship with the sister buying the fish fingers, whereas conversations over the garden fence about different ways of making turnip soup can be part of a continuing and deeply satisfying relationship. Hirsch makes the further criticism that we often earn money in order to be better off *than other people*. But we cannot all be better off than everybody else. Many of the goods sought are "positional goods", which cannot, in the nature of the case, be available to all. In so far as we engage in economic activity in pursuit of these goods, we are bound, most of us, to be disappointed.[21]

No simple answer can be given to the question whether economic activity is a good thing. Sometimes it is, sometimes it is undertaken at the cost of something better. It is good that people

---

[20] See above, ch.3, §3.1 *ad fin.*

[21] F.J.Hirsch, *Social Limits to Growth*, London, 1970; see also D.A. Hay, *Economics today*, Leicester, 1989, pp.289-293.

should have a wide range of choice. Many of the goods and services made available by modern economies make life far healthier, more varied and more interesting than in times past. But it does not follow, and is entirely false, that we ought to increase economic activity regardless of other considerations. Sometimes there are more efficient ways of obtaining what we want, and often there are better things to be doing with our time.[22]

§11.10 Limited Resources

The prophets of the present age fear for the future of mankind if economic growth continues unabated. Some of their fears are, as we have seen, rational. The world is finite, and could not continue for ever to sustain an exponentially increasing population. Even if the population is stabilised, many resources are non-renewable, and must be exhausted some time, and will be exhausted soon if consumed at the prodigal and increasing rate of the present age. We need to conserve energy, fossil fuels, and scarce minerals, and must stop polluting earth, sea and sky.

Many thinkers, however, go further, and claim that economic activity is itself inherently unsustainable. We must, they say, abandon altogether the idea of economic growth, and adopt entirely new economic objectives. What in fact we need to abandon is a false image of economic activity. If we think of the manufacture and exchange of goods as the paradigm economic activity, then we readily assume that making material goods is the basis of wealth. If this assumption were true, then the mining of iron ore and coal and the dumping of derelict cars would be a real indicator of national wealth, and it would follow that in the fulness of time the mines would be exhausted and the dumps occupying all the available land. But the assumption is wrong. We do not create wealth by manufacturing material objects, but by satisfying people's wants and needs. They need food, water, medicines, clothes. They want cars, transistors, compact disks. In as much as they want material things, economic activity will be geared to making what they want, and it is a proper criticism of some Western economies that they stimulate wants for material goods by advertising. But that need not be so. As real wants change, so it will become more difficult to stimulate artificial ones greatly at variance with them. The bigger car gives way to the faster computer, the voluminous bathing costume of the last century to the scant bikini of today. In the eighteenth century the Physiocrats[23] argued that since we all had

---

[22] See D.A. Hay, *Economics today*, Leicester, 1989, ch.8, §2.

[23] See Glossary.

to eat, agriculture was the only activity that really created wealth, and all non-agricultural labourers were parasites living on the backs of the peasants. We laugh at such simplicity today, thinking of the green revolution and the effectiveness of combine harvesters, but make the same mistake about manufacturing generally. The doctor who persuades the worker on an assembly line to stop smoking is improving things quite as much as the worker who screws on carburettors; writing software is not parasitic on making hardware: rather, the relation is one of symbiosis, and this is true of the economy as a whole.

It follows that economic growth is not inherently prodigal of natural resources. It has thus far been associated with increased consumption of material goods, and a good deal of waste; but waste diminishes as technology improves, and as people become richer they may become more discriminating in their tastes. We cannot be sure of this, and may anyhow need to take collective action to conserve resources and reduce pollution. But once we rid ourselves of these false images, we see that we do not have to despair.

Chapter 12
Towards a Non-Privative View of Business

Contents

Abstract

Because the two parties to a business transaction have significantly different priorities, business has been thought of in terms of confrontation. But the cooperative aspect of business association is equally important, and in many institutions, whose significance has not been recognised, predominant. The confrontational aspect, however, cannot be eliminated. Both individuals and firms may need to be subjected to a searching hard look, to see if they measure up to external standards. Nevertheless, though sometimes necessary, it is always costly, and can be counter-productive. The chief emphasis is on co-operation, especially as business becomes more concerned with ideas and less with things; and the more this is realised, the readier businessmen should be to respond to a wider range of obligations, often being able to obtain, by virtues of the resources they have at their disposal, desirable results which would not otherwise be forthcoming, and which, at least in indirect ways, benefit both the firm and its shareholders.

§12.1 The Spectrum

The two paradigm associations that emerged in Chapter 1[1] were paradigms only, We are never perfectly of one mind with one another, even in a monastery, even in the most united of families, and equally in commercial life one party is never in complete disagreement with another it is doing business with. Just as it is a mistake to think in politics that a General Will always exists and can easily be discovered, so it is wrong to assume in economics that the interests of the two parties are completely opposed, and no basis for mutual give-and-take can exist. But paradigms, just because they are paradigms, exercise a magnetic distortion on our thinking. We

---

[1] In ch.1, §1.5.

too readily think in terms of the two extreme forms of association: those in which we have all values in common, and those in which we have none. George Richardson recounts how, when he began to teach, he told pupils that "firms were islands of central planning in a sea of market transaction", and only gradually came to realise first that the sea was not a sea, and latterly that the islands were not islands either.[2] We never have all values in common, we never have none. And correspondingly, many of the decisions we reach are neither the result of a centralised decision-procedure nor the outcome of tough bargaining. We often compromise, and instead of insisting on the course of action we believe to be really the best one, agree to a less good one that others are prepared to agree to, reckoning general acceptability more important than doing what actually is best: and likewise we often do not hold out for the best bargain we could obtain, setting greater store by the association's general cooperative purpose being achieved than maximising our own particular pay-off. The stark alternative of either a command economy with a centralised system of decision-taking, or a market economy with a completely decentralised one in which the parties are completely external to each other, is a false alternative. Not only is neither paradigm instantiated as a pure case, but there is a wide spectrum of cases in between; and there are pervasive pressures, both within the internal organization of the firm, and in their external relations to one another, towards the middle ground. We can see why. The same considerations that make firms efficient economic units, make other, more limited, forms of give-and-take efficient too: and the arguments for decentralisation, which lead us to replace votes by vetoes,[3] and authoritative allocation by separate bargaining, are arguments also for devolving decision-making within the firm to the lowest feasible level.

---

[2] G.B.Richardson, "The Organisation of Industry", *The Economic Journal*, Vol 82, September 1972, pp.883-896; reprinted in G.B.Richardson, *Information and Investment*, Oxford, 1990; and G.B.Richardson, "Some Principles of Economic Organisation", forthcoming, to which we are greatly indebted.

[3] See, above, ch.1, §1.5.

§12.2 Shared Values

Complete separation does not work. Although some economists regret the existence of families, and think it would be better if each member—or at least, each adult member—were a separate economic unit, trading with the others, setting a monetary value on goods and services supplied and received, and keeping proper accounts, families none the less exist, and so do firms—artificial families[4]—and for good reason.

Most obviously, there are great costs in keeping proper accounts. Although sometimes necessary, either as a safeguard against misappropriation or as a tool of analysis to ensure solvency or enhance profitability, keeping accounts takes up much time and effort that could be better spent elsewhere. It often clogs decision-making, and is likely to involve decision-makers in considerable hassle in agreeing a monetary value for their transactions. Often also the overhead costs are high and the running costs are low. The House of Commons and the BBC each have a library service, to enable MPs and producers to find out and verify the facts they need for their speeches and programmes. If a charge were made, not only would much money be wasted in keeping track of the money, but there would be a standing temptation to economize on use, which would leave the overheads the same, but the value obtained from them much diminished. Many universities have medical departments which cooperate with hospitals run by the National Health Service. If a professor treats a patient and then writes up the case to publish in a medical journal, he is promoting the aims of both the National Health Service and the university; it does not make sense to make some division of the costs. Sometimes he will use university paper and a university xerox machine to do clinical work, and sometimes a secretary funded by the National Health Service will type references for an academic appointment. And often the give-and-take will go much further. A doctor entirely funded by the National Health Service will give seminars, and university lab assistants will analyse patients' specimens. Or again, to take another medical example, if I am a surgeon operating on a patient and I discover a carcinoma whose excision necessitates a lengthy further procedure, I take it for granted that the anaesthetist and nurses are as anxious to cure the patient as I am, and will not

---

[4] See above, ch.2, §2.2.

grudge the extra time and effort required for the longer operation. If the parson asks you to read a lesson in church, the exercise of working out how much more it will benefit him than you, so as to set a suitable price on it, is fatuous. Within the world of shared values, setting a price on cooperation is not only time-consuming and difficult, but altogether without sense.

Transaction costs are the most obvious, but not the most fundamental, reason for having organizations, rather than always trading with one another as separate individuals. More important is the need for reliability.

Serious economic activity cannot be conducted on the basis of *ad hoc*, one-off transactions, but requires some assurance that supplies will continue to be available and demand will keep up. I need friends who will be friends in need. Instead of having always to shop around, I enter into long-term contracts, and go regularly to the place where I am accustomed to be treated well; and often, in the same spirit and for the same reasons, enter into much closer partnerships, where each can rely on the other to do what is needed. In the open market everything is up for grabs, and, for all I know, others may grab tomorrow what I shall desperately need. The open sea is too mobile, too uncertain, for me to launch out on it with my whole being. I seek some security for the future in the *terra firma* of reliable expectations.

§12.3 Delegation

It is often assumed that the only way of achieving un-paid-for co-operation is to establish an umbrella authority which can tell the different bodies to cooperate without sending in a bill. This is the converse view to that which would have everyone a separate economic unit. But unitary command systems are expensive to maintain, and often do more damage by issuing ill-informed directives than good by coordinating effort and facilitating cooperation. Many conglomerate companies have been formed in which a "parent company" takes over other companies, and runs them all, providing centralised direction and some common service. Most have been failures, with the parent company not enhancing the performance of the companies it owns sufficiently to off-set its own costs. Often the interventions of the parent company have actually detracted from the performance of the companies taken over. Only under rather special conditions does the centralised ownership and control of different firms prove economically efficient.[5] Decision-taking needs information, and information is often more available locally than at the centre. Separate centres of decision-taking are likely, therefore to take better decisions, arranging between themselves those forms of cooperation which, in the light of the aims they have in common, make good sense.

The same holds good on a smaller scale within the individual firm. We think too much in terms of hierarchy and chains of command: even when subordinates are responsible to a superior, they still have some discretion as to how they carry out their commission, and the boss who is always telling his subordinates how to do their jobs is wasting his time as well as theirs.[6] He needs to be able to tell them what their jobs are, and to specify further in case of doubt, and adjudicate in case of conflict, but in general he should be ready to delegate all that can be delegated, and to facilitate discussion and agreement between subordinates without reference to him.

The appropriate degree of devolvement depends not only on the people involved but on the sort of decisions being made. An example from the way the men of Bisipara in India take decisions is illuminating:

> In a day's hunting there were three kinds of decision to be observed. The headman would talk over with other experienced men where the animal could have gone and what stand should be taken next: he would then say where they would go next and, this decision taken, the discussion would give way to idle chatter until the time came to make a move. The move from a rest position towards a new beat seemed to be spontaneous. Someone would get up and stretch and say 'Let's go. Let's go.' Some time later someone else would do the same until most of the party were on their feet and stubbing out their leaf cigarettes, and all saying, to no-one in particular: 'Let's go. Let's go.' Then they would go, setting off in single file through the trees, led by no-one in particular; everyone knew the way. The third type of decision was quite different: it arose in response to an emergency. Occasionally the beaters would raise a leopard or a bear, which would cut out sideways

---

[5] See Michael Goold, Andrew Campbell, and Marcus Alexander, *Corporate-Level Strategy*, Wiley, New York, 1994.

[6] See above, ch.4, §4.1, and ch.6, §6.2. See also, G.B.Richardson, "Some Principles of Economic Organisation", forthcoming

between the guns and the beaters. At once the operation would change
from being a sport to a military operation: the headman took charge
and directed both guns and beaters where to go with swift laconic
commands, which were instantly obeyed.

This vignette illustrates three kinds of situations in which decisions
are taken and three kinds of decisions. First there are commands which
arise as instant responses to an emergency, in which it is important
for the leader to ensure that action is initiated quickly. Whether the
members of the team understand and agree with what they are being
told to do, is less important than that they should do what they are
told. This, as everyone knows, is the situation in wartime in our own
countries. Secondly, there are decisions in which speed of action is
not so important that it leaves no time for debate about what is the
best action to take. This is the situation in which the hunters debate
about which stretch of jungle should next be drawn. Then it is much
more important that both guns and beaters should understand what is
proposed, and the reasons for it, and should go along with the decision
and cooperate with it. In the third situation, that of moving off after
rest, the decision is of quite a different kind. It is entirely consensual:
it does not matter whether the rest is of five or ten or fifteen minutes
duration. One feels almost that the occasion is taken to emphasize
that they are all hunters together, relaxing as equals, and that no-one
is in command. It is, indeed, difficult to think of the move after a rest
as being the occasion for a decision at all.[7]

In a business enterprise the variables are different. There is
no question of danger: compliance is secured in return for payment. Much depends on the nature of the jobs undertaken, and
the value of feed-back from those undertaking them. Where the
jobs are simple and do not greatly depend on the performance of
others, coordination of effort by simple instructions from a boss
is feasible: where the jobs are complex, those carrying them out
know better than their superiors the problems involved, and had
better be consulted about future plans; and where the performance
of each depends on that of others, all need to be in on decision-
making so as to know what has been decided and why, and how
each particular job fits into the whole plan.[8] Beyond these specific
considerations is a general one: just because the organization of

---

[7] F.G.Bailey, *Stratagems and Spoils*, Oxford, 1969, pp.67-68.

[8] See above, ch.6, §6.2.

business enterprises is usually hierarchical, and prevailing thought denies employees any real responsibility, regarding them merely as "hands", it is valuable to have some measures to convey the opposite impression and indicate that they are all real people, able to make up their own minds for themselves, whose opinions are valued, and whose autonomy is genuinely respected.

§12.4 Accountability

As we revise our notion of responsibility in business enterprises, so we must alter our application of the concept of accountability. Accountability is a concomitant of responsibility. In giving an answer to the question 'Why did you do it?', we are giving an account of our actions. In recent years accountability has been much in vogue, and many people are being required to account for themselves, filling in forms to record their activities and achievements. But although there is an underlying truth in the concept of general accountability, its actual application needs careful qualification.

For one thing, time taken on accounts is time not spent on other activities, and it is other activities that bring in the takings; more important, however, is the fact that too much accountability not only wastes time, but can be counter-productive, because it is implicitly adversarial. In being asked to give an account of my activities I am being challenged to justify them. Maybe I can: but I am being put on the defensive, and defensiveness is not the attitude that engenders positive initiatives or flights of creativity. Instead of being myself trusted to get on with the job and do the best I can, my actions are being weighed, and may be found wanting. Maybe I shall not get promoted; maybe, even, I shall get the sack. I must make my dispositions accordingly. Instead of doing what is best for the firm, I must see to it that my actions, when scrutinised, will appear in such a light as to work out best for me. I shall economize with the truth where it might redound to my discredit, and shall embroider a little where it might embellish my image. And in my future actions, I shall always be looking over my shoulder to see how they will appear to the efficiency auditors. As soon as I can figure out what yard-stick they are going to use, I shall put my best foot forward along that yard. And that well may be not the best way for the firm to go. In the 1980s, when accountability and performance-related pay were in fashion, many banks and financial companies paid executives according to the loans they had made.[9] Loans were accordingly made: and provision is still being made for the bad debts. Similarly in the civil service the introduction of performance-related pay has not only wasted a lot of time, but undermined the public service *ethos*. Civil servants had been imbued with a sense of public service which led them to take decisions in the public interest, without regard to their own.[10] Introducing performance-related pay signalled that it would be wise to take not the steps thought to be most in the public interest, but those that were likely to be approved by the assessors. The adversarial edge of accountability cut against complete identification with the values of the civil service.

Accountability may be counter-productive in another way too. It is often difficult to explain oneself. Reasons are hard to articulate. In practical affairs we have to size up a situation quickly, and often have a clear sense of what to do, but only a hazy one of the exact balance of reasoning that justified it. Even where we have deliberated long, we may end up much clearer about which way to go than the precise reasons for doing so. Many men are not nimble in their use of words, and cannot express themselves well, if called to account. But their judgement is good none the less: the decisions they take turn out to be the right ones; things go well when they are in charge. Instead of asking them to justify their decisions in detail, we need simply note the overall picture, and applaud.

Although we can always ask the question 'Why did you do it?', filling in the *it* in any way we please, we cannot be always asking the question 'Why did you do it?', with respect to different *its*. As we have seen,[11] if the boss commissions his secretary to get some paper-clips, he implicitly leaves it to her discretion which way she goes and to which shop, and if he details exactly the shop she should go to and way she should go, he cannot complain if, the shop being out of paper-clips, she does not go to another to buy them. So, too, on a larger scale, the more we limit discretion, the less we can look for in the way of actual achievement or new initiatives. We have to choose. We may decide to back people, reckoning that a good

---

[9] See above, ch.5, §5.5.

[10] See above, ch.1, §1.4, p.15.

[11] In ch.4, §4.1.

man is his own severest critic, and that if we trust him to follow his hunches, they will, by and large, prove profitable. Or we may keep a tight rein on them, being well safe-guarded against severe dereliction of duty or gross incompetence, but forgoing the chance of their doing unexpectedly well. Which course to take depends partly on the calibre of the people concerned, partly on the nature of the risks and rewards. Where mistake can be fatal, we impose strict guide-lines: doctors, naval officers, judges and civil servants can wreak havoc if they do not conform to precise procedures; poets, producers, playwrights, scientists, academics and artists are usually in no position to do much harm, but might, if encouraged to follow their own star, achieve great things. Most businessmen are in between, depending on the actual decisions they are called upon to take, and the adverse consequences of decisions taken wrongly.

Sometimes the businessman needs to take a long hard look at his operations, and see whether they make economic sense. But he will not be doing this all the time, any more than he would be seeing his solicitor all the time. The law sets the bounds within which we operate, and sometimes we need to take stock of our legal position, and make sure that under the most adverse conditions we shall still be all right. Similarly the businessman needs to look to his accounts, and keep a careful eye on his costs, and make sure they are covered by his takings. Sometimes a businessman needs to go over the past with his subordinates in order to anticipate the future, as when they are drawing up a budget for next year in the light of what actually has happened this year. Occasionally a careful review of a whole organization is called for, and each part subjected to a searching scrutiny—though contrary to an oft-expressed opinion a thorough shake-up is not always good for an organization: after all, though occasionally shock therapy is called for, it is not in general beneficial for human health. More often, sadly, a businessman may have to keep an employee up to the mark, reprimand him, or even sack him. But these occasions, though important, are not typical. The adversarial element is a subordinate one, taking its place only within a wider, cooperative, framework. Although discipline is essential in the armed forces, the wise commanding officer inspires his men with a sense of shared purpose, so that each identifies with the regiment or the ship, and feels on his mettle to do his best. So too in a firm. Employees are accountable for what they do and fail to do, and sometimes it is necessary to call them to account, and if the account is unsatisfactory, to haul them over the coals. But that should not be necessary often, and should not be done unless necessary; for the cost is considerable, not only in the obvious way of the time and money spent on the exercise, but, more insidiously, in the loss of cooperativeness and the falsification of facts and figures engendered. In many institutions efficiency audits have been highly destructive of efficiency. Often it is wise to limit the extent to which people are obliged to answer—respond to—the question 'Why did you do it?' or 'Why did you not do something to prevent it?', in order not to inhibit or antagonize them. But this is a tactic of expediency and human psychology,. It may be wise not to ask me 'Why did you do it?', in order not to seem to be accusing me of anything, but that does not mean that I am not responsible. Even if I am not responsible *to* anyone, I am still responsible: even if I am not pressed to answer another's questioning, I still must answer my own.

§12.5 Common Ground

It might seem that even if the paradigm models of association, in which the members had either all, or else no, values in common, were never perfectly exemplified, there was nevertheless a substantial separation between associations with a definite decision-procedure, which could act as a single unit, and those without, where agreements were bound to reflect the different values of the parties to it. But even this distinction is blurred in practice.

Although decision-procedures are characteristic of modern business enterprises and nation states, they evolved gradually, and still are subject to implicit restrictions. They enable all the questions that are likely to come up to be decided, but not all those that could conceivably come up or could be devised by a clever logician. Could the United States of America pass a constitutional amendment deleting the provision of Article V protecting the right of every State not to be deprived, without its own consent, of its territory or its two members of the Senate? Article V was intended to entrench these State rights beyond the power of amendment; but if it could itself be amended, the entrenchment was nugatory, as the entrenchment of coloured voting rights in South Africa proved to be, while if it could not be amended, then Article V appeared not to mean what it said. Decision-procedures are never completely clear-cut, and depend for their acceptance on their being operated reasonably within the general understandings on which they are based. Often they are crystallizations of practices which led to agreement on the questions that actually had to be decided. They evolved thus in the churches of the ancient world and in the universities of the middle ages; in the modern world there are many bodies—the scientists, the academics, the medical profession—that can come to be of one mind on questions that concern them, without their being formally organized with a centralised authority. Such bodies, of course, are slow to make up their minds, and cannot decide many questions quickly. None the less, decisions are reached, and we can know where the doctors, the academics, or the scientists, stand on certain issues.

Equally from the other end of the spectrum, where the parties are external to each other, there is no sharp cut-off point where bargains cease to be bargains and become compromises. We often cooperate with friends, neighbours and colleagues, as well as with members of the family, without bothering about how the cooperators' surplus should be divided, largely because we have so many values in common that we both benefit anyhow.

There are many cases of autonomous or quasi-autonomous bodies cooperating within the context of shared aims: the colleges of Oxford and Cambridge; universities generally; government departments;[12] local government authorities; trade unions; churches. Many businesses are in the same case, remaining entirely independent of one another, yet frequently cooperating, sometimes on a give-and-take basis, sometimes with money changing hands, but without bargaining.

Monetary payment is appropriate when, despite the many values held in common, there is, perhaps as the result of the way institutions are set up, a significant divergence of interests. But it is not toughly bargained over—some standard fee is agreed for giving a seminar, some standard charge for analysing a specimen. Since the two parties are not external to each other, and the fruits of cooperation are beneficial to both, no real bargaining can take place; the basis for determining what the standard price should be is, rather, that of ensuring that neither party is out of pocket as a result of the cooperation.[13]

---

[12] Although government departments are all nominally Departments of State under the ultimate control of the Cabinet, they are in practice quite largely independent organizations, yet freely cooperating to serve the public interest.

[13] Compare ch.8, §8.4.

The common meeting point is important, and in practice exercises an attractionon the way we do things in the opposite direction to the way the paradigms affect the way we think about them. Consensual decisions are better than those relying on the authority of a decision-procedure: agreements negotiated on the basis of mutual understanding and give-and-take are better than those reached by tough confrontational bargaining which coerces unwilling cooperation. For, the more willing all parties are, the more likely they are to carry out the decision effectively, and the more the agreement is felt to be in both parties' interests, the more likely it is to be the basis of further business. This willingness is also based on the degree to which people are able to trust each other and form associations in which they have confidence.[14]

These are pervasive pressures, often overridden by considerations of practicality, but pervasive none the less. Often a decision must be reached, sometimes quickly; we cannot afford to do nothing unless and until a consensus is formed. Often also the divergence of interests is too great for cooperation to be feasible or fair without some monetary payment. Being human and having different values, we cannot live in an ideal consensual and cashless society, and need the different modes of decision outlined in Chapter 1,[15] and their appropriate forms of association. We need bracing competition as well as cosy cooperativeness.[16] But the pressure towards common ground remains, and should be taken into account in our thinking, both political and economic, as well as in our doing.

§12.6 The Wider View

The predominance of cooperativeness in the underlying rationale of their business practice justifies the wider view of their responsibilities taken by some big firms. Some firms sponsor concerts, some patronise the arts, some support training schemes for disadvantaged youths.

---

[14] See Francis Fukuyama, *Trust: The Social Virtues and the Creation of Prosperity*, London, 1995.

[15] §1.5.

[16] This is the element of truth in Adam Smith's strictures (quoted in §7.4 above) on traders getting together.

Such use of company funds has been criticized, somewhat sur-
prisingly, from the left, as well as from the libertarian right. Sorell
and Hendry endorse the view they find implied in the remarks of
Mary Rimmer, a local councillor, and Gordon Brown, a Labour
Member of Parliament, that it is morally wrong, because

> By taking on obligations that are properly those of government, it
> could be argued, businesses discourage governments from discharging
> its obligations itself.[17]

It is a surprising view. No government discharges all its obligations.
There are too many calls on its limited resources. Sometimes, perhaps, a government could be criticized for supinely relying on businesses to do what it ought to be exerting itself to provide, but
to criticize businesses for doing what ought to be done but is not
being done by the existing government seems perverse.

Apart from the purely stipulative definition of Elaine Sternberg,[18] the main objection on individualist grounds is that it is
none of the directors' business to decide what the shareholders
want: only the individual shareholder can decide how his money
should be spent, and the directors should channel as much money
as possible into the shareholders' pockets.[19] But that does not
follow from the nature of a public limited company. Although the
directors have a fiduciary duty towards the shareholders, they can
take a wider view of their interests than an exclusively pecuniary
one, and have an ineliminable discretion in how they carry out their
commission, which entitles them to take into account other factors
and obligations arising from the nature of the business they carry
on and the position their enterprise occupies in the general scene.

It would be possible for the shareholders to direct their directors not to make any, or some particular, donation, and insist on
all profits being distributed as dividends; and it might be reasonable, if the enterprise were a small, short-term one, having fairly
few values in common with the rest of society. But they do not
have to make that decision, nor would it be reasonable in most
cases. Most business enterprises are not located at the end of the

---

[17] Tom Sorell and John Hendry, *Business Ethics*, Butterworth Heinemann,
Oxford, 1994, p.161.

[18] Elaine Sternberg, *Just Business*, London, 1994, ch.2, quoted in ch.5, §5.2.

[19] See, for example, Samuel Brittan, *Capitalism with a Human Face*, Aldershot, 1995, pp.45-46.

spectrum, and it is natural for some, especially the larger ones, to share quite a number of aims with the rest of society. "What is good for the United States is good for General Motors" is not just pious rhetoric, but an obvious platitude. If the shareholders decide to—or more realistically, acquiesce in the directors deciding to—devote some corporate revenue to achieving collectively what they could not individually bring about, they are being entirely rational. Devoting some corporate revenue to promoting common aims makes corporate sense. If ICI sponsors concerts, Shell patronises artists, NatWest subsidises cricket, their shareholders benefit. They live in a society in which concerts happen, artists paint, cricket matches occur. If no such expenditures were made, and dividends increased by less than 1%,[20] few shareholders would be able to achieve a comparable effect with their increased dividends. The concerts and cricket matches would not take place, my buying just one picture would not keep the artist in business. I should be able to buy a few extra packets of cigarettes, but other good things I might reasonably desire would be simply not available.

It is much the same as with taxes.[21] I cannot as an individual secure the services of a policeman, fireman, ambulance man, and I may not in fact, if I am lucky, ever need their services; but I am better off if they are there, and am foolish to begrudge my contribution to their being available in case of need. Similarly I may not go to concerts or cricket matches, or care about pictures, but overall am likely to benefit from some of the charitable donations made by some of the companies in which I have shares, and even if I obtain no personal benefit, these are aims valued by many, including many of my fellow shareholders, which it would be reasonable for me to endorse.

Big may not be beautiful, but it has reason to be bountiful. In time past rich individuals would be municipally munificent. Often it was pure benevolence, but it was not always only that. They stood to gain by having a better city, a better country. Whereas the contributions of the poor were individually too insignificant to

---

[20] Pilkington, an exceptionally generous and community-minded firm gave just over 0.4% of its profits in charitable donations in 1984 (Tom Sorell and John Hendry, *Business Ethics*, Butterworth Heinemann, Oxford, 1994, p.160).

[21] See above, ch.10, §10.3.

establish a municipal art gallery, and any individual contributor would have a Prisoners' Dilemma incentive to leave it to others to pay; a single rich man, or a few of them clubbed together, could actually make an effective difference and bring about a better state of affairs. And a better state of affairs municipally was a better state of affairs for each of them individually. The city fathers, by very reason of their wealth, are identified with the city, and feel its benefits as their own. The same logic applies to big corporations. They are located towards the centre of the spectrum. By reason of their size they have much in common with society generally; its aims are largely their aims, and its prosperity part of their own. So that although the typical public limited company has as its prime purpose the making of money to be distributed among its shareholders, it can quite properly spend a small portion of its profits on aims it has in common with much of the rest of society.

We can view these non-profit-maximising expenditures as a form of cooperation. In the typical case other people are contributing time, effort and initiative. But in our moneyed economy almost every activity involves some expense, and many people are in a position where it is difficult for them to foot the bill—the local choir will give up much time practising and rehearsing, but cannot afford the hire of the Town Hall. A firm can provide the money, which will enable the choir to give its time to the benefit of all who care to listen. These cooperative voluntary ventures seem much more deserving of support than purely commercial ones. They fit the role of the businessman as a cooperator and enabler, operating in a context of give-and-take, where he is putting up some money, enabling the efforts of others to result in an outcome that realises aims that the firm has in common with many others.

§12.7 The Non-Privative World

Our economic concepts have been formed under conditions of scarcity in which goods were typically material objects, which could be given to others only at the cost of thereby forgoing them ourselves. I can share the cake with you, but what you eat I cannot have. Money has been fashioned to be similarly privative. But many of the things we want are not like that. I can give you information and still have it myself. Perhaps this is why telling strangers the way has been the practice of almost all societies.[22] Now, with the development of information technology, far more good things are non-privative. Information, ideas, musical recording, television plays, software, all are essentially non-privative. Some of them we copyright, in order to fit them into our existing economic framework, but cyberspace is a world of sharing, not a world of trading, in which give-and-take rather than bargaining is the rule. It is difficult to foresee how this will affect business, but we may conjecture that cooperation will become more dominant, and adversarial bargaining over the division of the cooperators' surplus increasingly pointless. There will, of course, still be those who want to take without being willing ever to give; it will still be necessary, on occasion, to refuse to cooperate; but the rational strategy will be to start by being cooperative, and only refuse those who have been persistent non-givers.

The conclusion is important. We have been used to seeing business in a privative sense—"it's mine"—rather than a non-privative one—"it's ours". In terms of responsibility and the role of the businessman this is a fundamental change, because it can take business out of what seem to be the narrow confines of self-interest into the wider world of social purpose and contribution. Business becomes a contributor, a giver, rather than a maximising taker with little regard for the other's needs and interests.

[22] See ch.1, §1.1.

Chapter 13
Can a Businessman be Moral?

Contents

Abstract

Morality seems opposed to making a success of business, but it is not really so. There *are* moral arguments against worshipping money, and for some people it *is* right to give up riches, as it is for others to forgo other forms of worldly success, but, special cases and special considerations apart, it is better that people should flourish than that they should do without the good things of life. Arguments of morality are difficult to disentangle from arguments of enlightened self-interest, and seem even easier to ignore. They differ in not being limited in scope, and those who ignore them limit themselves in consequence.

§13.1 Survival

Businesses can fail. It is a *sine qua non* of economic activity that businesses will fail, and failure means the destruction of all the business set out to do both in financial and in human terms. It is the business equivalent to death.

Machiavelli worked out the implications of the imperative to survive. Although the morality of *The Prince* has been widely condemned, the problems of political survival are directly relevant to business. Machiavelli rejected Christian virtues as enfeebling the State, and putting its survival at risk. Strong leadership and the civic virtues of Ancient Rome were what was needed to ensure survival, which must have priority over all other claims: *salus populi suprema lex*, the safety of the people was the supreme law, as Cicero once said.[1] So too in business. Morality is one thing when the enterprise is flourishing and profitable; another when it

---

[1] Cicero, *De Legibus*, III,iii,8.

is fighting for survival, either in terms of bankruptcy or in fending off a hostile take-over bid. Businessmen then can be put under extreme pressure to bend the rules, default on payments or resort to measures which break the law or contravene accepted codes of conduct. The directors of Guinness sailed too close to the wind in a time of stress.

Moral appeals to abide by fair and honest business practices appear unrealistic to a businessman who is about to go under and face the loss of all his capital through bankruptcy. Its implications are harder than many suppose, and constitute critical occasions of moral choice. Although we no longer put bankrupts in the debtors' prison, the moral stigma remains, and the pressures to avoid financial disaster in business make morality a difficult ideal to realise in practice. Do I come clean with my creditors that I cannot meet my obligations? or do I place another order hoping that it will help me turn the corner? There is a Machiavellian adage in Italian business: *Promettere e mantenere è da paurosi*, "to promise and maintain one's promise is for the timorous". There is a positive side to this apparent repudiation of honest dealing: do I have the courage to come clean when my back is against the wall? Or, again, do I in a hostile takeover bid, prop up my share price by persuading friends to buy a substantial *tranche* of shares? These are moral questions that no businessman can avoid, and create situations where the temptation to do the wrong thing for understandable reasons is very great. In the end codes of practice may help him to decide but they can never relieve him of his ultimate responsibility. The possibility of business failure cannot be eliminated altogether, and, though we may criticize the businessman for not assessing or managing his risks correctly (as happened in the *post mortem* on the Barings' crash) we cannot judge him too harshly—to err is human.

In the end the choice depends on the moral calibre of the individual. Neither legislation nor sanctions can determine his choice, only the business acumen which knows when to call it a day, and the honesty to say "I have failed", or "I have been unable to fight off the bid". The moral dilemma is acute, as it is in comparable dilemmas in ordinary life. Am I entitled to kill and eat the cabin boy if stranded on a desert island, and he is the only alternative to starving? Was the mother right to give up her child to the other woman instead of having her offspring cut in half by Solomon? Or Antigone to sacrifice herself in order to give her brother a decent burial. Or Captain Oates to walk out into the blizzard?

§13.2 False Alternatives

The moral dilemmas faced by businessmen are not easily resolved. He cannot simply follow Machiavelli and justify every action by saying "I did it so that the business could survive", but faced with the apparently insatiable demands of morality, he may feel impelled to relegate morality to a private world, as not being applicable to the world of business. In each case, however, he is misidentifying the dilemma he has to face, and instead of making difficult decisons between real alternatives, he impales himself on the even sharper horns of imaginary dilemmas. The conflict between morality on the one hand, and survival, and more generally self-interest on the other, is less absolute than Machiavelli made out, because our very notions of self-interest and success are themselves not absolute, but coloured by evaluations of what we are and aim to be: and the morality that bears upon business decisions is not the all-encompassing personal morality of individual vocation and commitment, but the public, universal morality that stems from each of us recognising others as autonomous agents with minds of their own, and hence a point of view that ought to be taken into account, as we each decide what to do.

Although in particular cases, survival, self-interest and success, seem fairly definite, the general policy of pursuing them is indeterminate. Economic Man was a maximiser. Economists defined rationality in terms of maximising one's pay-off. Although they were wrong,[2] they are widely believed. And though there are natural limits to the amount of food I can eat, or the number of cars I can drive, there is no natural limit to the amount of money I can own. Money, having been fashioned as a transferable uniform token of value can go on being transferred to me without regard to how much I already have. When wealth took material form I might have some problem pulling down my barns and building bigger ones, but with bank accounts there is no difficulty in adding an extra million to my account. And why not? Money is what we can all do with more of. And if at all times it is reasonable to reckon more money acceptable, it seems to follow that it is reasonable to be always wanting more. Avarice appears as articulating the natural ambition of maximising man.

Ambition is not inherently bad. Although we are not sure we like the ambitious thruster, we condemn the unambitious man, who

---

[2] See above, ch.3, §3.5.

fails to make good use of his talents. It is up to each one of us to make the most of his opportunities, and to wait for others to take the initiative is a dereliction of one's obligations as a rational agent. One ought to aim high. And in trying to do the best one can, it is natural to compare oneself with others, and to try to do better than they. And making money is one outlet for the competitive spirit. Some seek to climb the highest mountain in the world, to run a mile faster than anyone else, to be the most famous film star, to win the men's open singles at Wimbledon, to get to the top of the tree in their particular walk of life. Others set their sights on money and strive to amass more than their rivals. In itself it need be no worse than other competitive exercises. But competition, though not in itself bad, is highly damaging when carried to extremes. Many tennis stars have ruined their lives by concentrating on acquiring skills bound to deteriorate rapidly with age. The personal lives of film stars are notoriously unhappy. Idolatry is spiritually unsatisfying and psychologically damaging. In the case of money it is much worse because avarice is not only addictive but destroys personal relations. People get hooked on money. The very words 'substance', 'property' express unhealthy psychological attitudes, making it appear to be that which constitutes our being, that which makes us the persons we are, distinct from everyone else, as is shown by the old question 'Is he a man of substance?' Those who are addicted find it difficult not to make a quick buck, even at the cost of losing friends or reputation; misers are not given to generous hospitality, and have few friends. Even if there is no addiction, the possession of great wealth, like that of great power, is a barrier to easy social intercourse. If people know that I am very rich, they may butter me up in the hope of securing some crumbs falling from my table, and even if they do not, I cannot be sure that they do not. That is why rich men only feel at ease in the company of others as rich as themselves; and the richer I become, the fewer there are for me to consort with; and if I reach the summit of my maximising ambition, I shall occupy my lonely eminence bereft of the companionship of my peers.

§13.3 Enlightened Self-Interest

Arguments of enlightened self-interest are often adduced in favour of acting morally. Honesty is the best policy; you do well to do good. Often the moral sceptic is argued with on the basis of his own self-interest. Often the arguments are not bad.   The young man who has liberated himself from the shackles of morality is on the way to losing out generally in life's race, and a timely word of warning may save him from self-destruction. And yet we feel uncomfortable.

Our discomfort is partly logical. We feel that we are being conned into buying morality on spurious grounds. As Elaine Sternberg works out the implications of her definition of business as seeking to maximise owner value over the long term by selling goods or services,[3] we sense difficulties in the phrase 'long-term': not only is it unclear as to when the long term is concluded—Keynes' adage "in the long term we are all dead" applies—but it suffers from elasticity. If we make the term long enough, almost all morality can be subsumed under enlightened self-interest; but in the here and now there is a conflict between my duty not to pollute and the profitability of so doing. In the long term it is good to be loyal to employees, but it would pay me over the next five years to sack old Bill, who has served us well, but is now less good than a younger replacement would be. In the long term it is good to be honest with customers, but in the short term, before the end of the accounting year, it will cost a lot to replace some defective goods, and there is no hope of those customers coming back for many a year. It does not help clarity to give the time of accounting so much elasticity that every conflict between morality and self-interest is smoothed away. On the day of judgement all immoral acts will appear as having been contrary to self-interest. But meanwhile there seem to be real conflicts.

Our discomfort is also moral. Morality is not the same as self-interest. To base morality on self-interest is to miss its main thrust, and to make it out as something much less than it really is. Morality involves a disinterested concern for others; not a cupboard love based on an expectation of favours returned, but a genuine regard, based on rational concepts of freedom and justice, and a recognition of the autonomy of the individual as a person in his own right.

Although the actions recommended by enlightened self-interest largely coincide with those enjoined by morality, the reasons for doing them are different. The arguments from self-interest tend to be tenuous and convoluted, and depend on taking a long view, making various assumptions about the way of the world, and having certain

---

[3] Elaine Sternberg, *Just Business*, London, 1994, p.32.

wants. The arguments of morality, by contrast, are peremptory—
categorical in Kant's terminology—and cannot be evaded by making different assumptions about the world or adopting different
wants. Honesty may be the best policy for most people, who are
always in danger of being found out, but what if I have Gyges'
ring?[4] or a very good public relations man? or Goebbels to run
my propaganda? Or what if I am not concerned to get on in the
world, marry a nice wife and have a Volvo and 2.8 children, but
want to make a name for myself as someone who was his own man,
and acted really authentically by blowing up an air liner and slash-
ing the Mona Lisa? Arguments from self-interest can be countered
by a host of objections which have no force where moral arguments
are being adduced. In particular cases it may be sensible to do the
right thing, but the reasons are different, and only coincide sometimes, and not always or necessarily.

Moral sceptics deny the validity of moral arguments, while allowing the expediency of moral behaviour on prudential grounds.
They advise a general observance of moral precepts, but only pro-
visionally and conditionally. John Mackie expresses it incisively in
his *Ethics: Inventing Right and Wrong*, when he advises his readers
to tell the truth usually, but when it is necessary to tell a lie, to tell
a whopper.[5] But it is advice difficult to follow. Mackie himself did
not practise what he preached, but lived a life of scrupulous moral
rectitude. Although in theory we can agree that occasions might
arise when we should abandon morality and pursue self-interest
alone, it is difficult in practice to be sure that the occasion has
arisen. I may need to tell a lie to get out of a scrape. But if I
do, I am not just saving my skin, but am also by that very action
abandoning morality. I am no longer a man of integrity, no longer
to be trusted, no longer someone people can rely on. No doubt
on future occasions enlightened self-interest will lead me to behave
in an apparently honest way, but others will be able to trust me
only so far as they can see. All this I shall know. And what I can
know others may be able to know also. In constructing imaginary
situations I can specify that I shall not be found out, but in real
life I cannot rule out that possibility by *fiat*. I may be found out.
I may not be punished, but I shall lose my good name, and any

---

[4] see Glossary.

[5] *Ethics: Inventing Right and Wrong*, Penguin, 1977, p.183.

further prospect of being trusted absolutely. I may get away with it, like the princes Machiavelli admired, who knew when to break their word and when to keep it. But their narrowly conceived *vertu* limited the scope of their actions—Machiavelli himself laments that there was no leader capable of uniting Italy, without realising that it was because they followed his precepts that they were unable to transcend the pettiness of their ambitions, and could not inspire the trust and devotion that a national leader would need.

Even if I am not found out, I shall know I may be. I shall have to live with that possibility, and it may be uncomfortable to live with. And so at the moment of decision I may rationally decide not to take on that incubus. Even if the fear of punishment does not deter me, the fear of the fear of punishment should. It may be the perfect crime, and yet I may draw back, rationally avoiding the fate of Raskolnikov in Dostoievsky's *Crime and Punishment*.

These are arguments of self-interest. But they are not just counsels of prudence. Rather they establish the limitations of limited self-interest. Although self-interest is not the same as morality, we cannot set actual limits beyond which it is inexpedient to go. Wherever we set the limits, further reflection shows that they are set too narrowly. The more enlightened self-interest becomes, the closer it approximates to simple morality.

Morality can thus be seen as the limiting case of enlightened self-interest, but that is to misrepresent it. Although, in the limit, arguments of self-interest will recommend just the same actions as morality enjoins, the force of the arguments here adduced is not to show that morality is nothing but enlightened self-interest, but that the concept of self-interest is too narrow to provide a basis for rational action. We can form the concept all right, and use it within limited contexts, but when we try to generalise it, we find we are constantly needing to amend it, if it is to prove adequate to the tasks now imposed on it. There is an analogy with the games-theoretical definition of rationality in terms of maximising one's pay-off. It is adequate for some simple, single-shot discussions, but needs to be expanded over times and persons if it is to prove adequate generally.[6] The Prisoners' Dilemma shows the irrationality of a strictly defined maximising strategy: and a similar dialectical argument here shows why Mackie was wise never actually to tell a lie.

---

[6] See above, ch.3, §3.5, and Appendix A.

§13.4   Renunciation

We are confused about morality. Sometimes it is seen simply as enlightened self-interest, sometimes as essentially opposed to self-interest. Sometimes it is thought of as essentially rational, at other times as a matter for the emotions, or some existentialist leap of faith. Businessmen and economists generally are wary of morality. They do not know what they are letting themselves in for, and fear that if once they start down the morality path they may end up selling the factory plant and distributing the proceeds to the inhabitants of the Third World or the local one-parent families.

They are right to be wary. Often morality is defined entirely negatively, in total opposition to self-interest, prescribing a policy of complete self-abnegation. Often also there is a confusion between the universal morality incumbent on us all, and the particular ideals particular people are called on to embrace. There *are* moral arguments against making too much of money; there *are* moral arguments in favour of renunciation; there *are* moral arguments for some vocations of poverty: but these are all particular arguments addressed to particular classes of people in particular circumstances, and should not be generalised beyond their conditions of applicability. In either case the remedy is to think the arguments through, not to ignore them completely; to recognise their cogency, but also their limited applicability. And then to recognise how moral considerations, properly understood, are ego-enhancing rather than simply set to deny the self altogether; and the range of moral considerations relevant to the necessarily external field of business transactions.

Money is what we can all do with more of. But then we have qualms. Is it really a good idea to be always wanting more? If money is addictive, as it surely is, the only cure is to give it up absolutely. In any case, the world is finite, with only limited resources: continuous economic growth must be unsustainable. Morality, it seems, demands that we abandon the will-o'-the-wisp of always having more, and should embrace sister poverty, renouncing the riches of the world along with the sins of the flesh and the promptings of the devil.

Renunciation is a first-personal concept. I can renounce riches for myself, but not for you. Whatever the merits of my embracing poverty for myself, there are none in my imposing it on you. There is a realm of personal morality in which some may be called to follow the example of St Francis, and although their motives need to be subjected to close scrutiny, it may be the right thing for them. But it does not at all follow, as has been supposed by many twentieth-century egalitarians, that it is wrong to be rich, and that we should therefore tax the rich into godly poverty for the good of their souls. Although there are many spiritual and psychological dangers associated with the riches, as there are with power, riches are not morally bad *per se*, but on the contrary good, expanding the range of human choice and the possibilities of human achievement.

We should be wary of renunciation. It may be done for good motives, but is not always. We sometimes fall in love with the dramatic gesture, and see ourselves as a latter-day St Francis or Albert Schweizer, and want others to see us so. But the image is not the reality, and our protestations prove phoney as we publicise our self-sacrifice while privately yearning for the flesh-pots. Even when our commitment is genuine, it needs scrutiny. It is one thing to give up something good for the sake of a greater good, quite another to give it up just for the sake of giving up. The clergyman, the writer and the artist may be poor, because they want to devote all their time and energy to their calling, and not to the business of earning money. That makes sense. But the poverty is inessential, and when his pictures begin to sell, the artist quits his garret and has a good meal at the bistro. Others, slum priests, social workers and volunteers in the Third World are poor in order to be on a level with the people they seek to help, to identify with them and share their sufferings. That, too, is a proper motive, though it cannot operate over a lifetime and is best deliberately limited in time. Others again are disciplining themselves, curing themselves from avarice, or seeking to empty their minds of all worldly concerns in order to concentrate on the things of the spirit. That may be right, too, for some. But all too often renunciation is a form of self-hate, a sickness of soul, masquerading as morality but really an exercise in self-flagellation, spilling over, in many cases, into wanting to cut other people down to size too. It may be all right sometimes to deny oneself in order to procure a greater good, but mere negativity for its own sake is not life-enhancing in the end.

§13.5 Vocations

The morality of omni-temporal, omni-personal rationality is not the only one, and many businessmen fight shy of admitting any moral considerations to their decision-making, because they feel they will then be called upon to adopt some idealistic ideals that are completely unrealistic in the context of the real world in which ordinary business life is lived. We need to distinguish first-personal moral intimations adopted by individuals for themselves from omni-personal moral precepts which we urge on everyone.[6] The distinction parallels that already drawn between first- and third-personal interests, and between the second person singular and the second person plural.[7] In addressing *thee*, the unique individual that thou art, I recognise that thou hast a mind of thine own, and it is for thee to decide ultimately what thou wantest. But I reckon that *you*, a typical person, are a rational being, swayed by many of the same reasons as we all are, and while I can never really get inside thy skin, which is necessarily unlike anybody else's, I can imagine myself in your shoes, or at least in your position which could be occupied by anyone else suitably circumstanced, and I ought to consider things from your point of view.

Many people have intimations of how they ought to lead their lives, as a matter of personal vocation, without any suggestion that others should do likewise. I may have a vocation to be a poet, a painter, a missionary, to manufacture washing machines or to write software; but in adopting that way of life I do not hold that

---

[6] These moral principles are sometimes termed E-type (from Existentialist) and U-type (from Universalisable) respectively. See E.Gellner, "Ethics and Logic", *Proceedings of the Aristotelian Society*, **55**, 1954-5, pp.157-178; reprinted in Ernest Gellner, *The Devil in Modern Philosophy*, London, 1974, ch.7, pp.78-93. See also P.F.Strawson, "Social Morality and Individual Ideal", *Philosophy*, **36**, 1961, pp.1-17, esp. p.4; J.R.Lucas, *Responsibility*, Oxford, 1993, §4.6, pp.65-69.

[7] In §1.4, §2.4 and §8.9. In order to stress the point made in §2.4, that business, although non-*tu*-istic, is not non-*vous*-istic, we shall, at the cost of seeming quaintly archaic, use the second-person singular for discussing the morality of "I-Thou", personal relations, and the standard 'you' for the public morality that should guide the "I-You" business dealings that I have with You. See, further, J.R.Lucas, *On Justice*, Oxford, 1980, ch.16, pp.261-263.

it should be a universal precept. If we all were missionaries, to whom would we missionise? Commitments of this sort, whether to a particular walk, or to a particular way, of life, are necessarily not universal, not omni-personal. The morality of business ethics, by contrast, is omni-personal, the same for everybody, being *vous*-istic, though not *tu*istic, concerned with the interests that can be imputed to you, not the ideals that thou alone canst avow. It is a morality stemming from the shared values of the business firm and from the requirements of justice. The claims of justice are omni-personal. In justifying my actions, I need to address myself to you, *vos, vous*, the typical person in your position, but I am not obliged to address myself to thee, *tibi, toi*, the unique individual with ideals, aspirations, desires and wants, not necessarily or generally shared by others; and hence I must justify it according to the canons of the basic morality recognised by almost all mankind, not of some high-flown morality, which thou holdest to but one could reasonably reject. The business firm is, typically, a corporation, a public limited company. Corporations, we conceded, have no souls.[8] They are not open to the call of heroic self-sacrifice, the search for absolute purity, for artistic integrity, intellectual creativeness, or the many other ideals that have won the allegiance of the human spirit. They are not called to manifest in their actions some ideal, or some vision of the world. Theirs is a down-to-earth morality, characteristically evaluating actions by their impact on other people, not a personal morality concerned as much with witnessing to an ideal, and expressing the mind of the agent, as with the general effect of their consequences on others.

§13.6 The Moral Businessman

In the course of this book many different considerations have been put forward which ought to weigh with a businessman in making decisions and deciding what his obligations are. In large part we have been concerned to free contemporary thought from false images that distort our understanding of business activity and prevent us from recognising the applicability of ordinary moral arguments. But even if false images are removed, businessmen may still resist the arguments of this book and remain unconvinced of their cogency.   Three different sorts of reason may be adduced. In the

---

[8] Ch.4, §4.6.

first place they may feel that they have no room for manoeuvre, no freedom to do anything other than what the market dictates. And they may be right. All we have shown is that perfect competition, which effectively eliminates any room for manoeuvre, does not generally obtain. Admittedly, there are cases—currency markets, for example—that approximate to it, in which traders can only do their best to guess which way the market is going to go, and adjust their prices accordingly. But many markets are not like that, and though it is seldom possible—and even more seldom sensible—to buck the market, there is in very many cases some room for manoeuvre, some latitude within which different decisions may be made. The responsible businessman cannot alter the world, but he may be able to make his own corner of it a little better than if he had never tried.

In the second place many businessmen shy away from acknowledging any ethical dimension to their decision-making for fear of being landed with impossible obligations and insupportable responsibilities. They can be re-assured. The morality of the market place is like the morality of ordinary life. It does not demand self-denying altruism, only a reasonable regard for the rights and interests of others. Our duties towards others, though real, are limited, and do not demand some total abandonment of all our own projects, interests and rights. On the contrary, they legitimate them. It is only because each of us is a centre of concern that others have a claim on us. We accord validity to their points of view because their points of view are like our own, and our own are valid. Moreover, the reflection is filtered. I deal with you non-tuistically, as a general *vos* or *vous*, whose interests I can vicariously impute to you by analogy with my own, not as a particular *tu*, with all the actual concerns thou actually hast. Thus it was that the employer should extend only limited latitude to his inadequate employee. All of us have lapses, and it may be reasonable not to fire at once a secretary who fails to enter a booking. But it is not the employer's business to temper the cold blasts of reality to the shorn lamb. To carry the can for the sins of the whole world is an exercise of grace, not of the moral law. Some businessmen, after they have made their fortune, have devoted it to charitable purposes. But that is a work of supererogation, not something called for by ordinary morality, in the way that truthfulness, the keeping of contracts, and fair dealing are. I have a duty not to deceive or defraud those I have dealings with, but not to give up my life to making a success of theirs.

In the third place, even if a businessman agrees that he has some freedom of manoeuvre, and is assured that in admitting moral considerations he is not starting down a slippery slope, he may still regard the arguments adduced for his having duties towards his customers, his employees, his suppliers, and even his competitors, as too fine-spun to weigh with a hard-nosed man who has to make his own way in a tough competitive world. And indeed, the arguments are fine-spun: arguments about what we ought to do mostly are. And it could be that the ones actually adduced here lack cogency, and that others would be better. Moral arguments are inherently fallible, and often can be improved. But if a reader is inclined to dismiss all such arguments *tout court*, he should consider how others might be equally dismissive of arguments he would like to regard as valid. It may seem pusillanimous not to blacken the name of his competitors, or not to steal his trade secrets: but cowboy operators regard it as equally pusillanimous to carry out their side of a contract and do a workmanlike job. A sufficiently hard-nosed businessman may be dealing with cowboy suppliers, dishonest employees, and customers who do not pay, but will he be happy when the Mafia come and demand protection money if he is not to have his office vandalised or his children kidnapped? The normal response is to regard *mafiose* activities as outside the pale; but why? Moral arguments are inherently resistible, and if we are prepared to resist those that press on us the duty of fair dealing, we must not be surprised if others find the obligations of honesty equally avoidable, or if yet others see no reason why they should not resort to intimidation and violence in order to make their way in a tough competitive world. It is easy to be sceptical of the arguments of others, difficult to accept that others may be sceptical of arguments one accepts oneself. Many modern-minded thinkers have adopted a policy of selective scepticism to rubbish the bearing of moral considerations on business decisions, forgetting how much they take for granted as regards honesty and the avoidance of violence. They should remember the Mafia.

The argument goes deeper. If I disregard the claims of *alteritas*, I diminish myself, because in refusing to recognise the validity of the other person's interests, I am downgrading the status of human beings, and thus also devaluing myself. Our values are highly constitutive of our identity. The sort of arguments I accept determine the sort of things I do, and the sort of things I do determine the sort of person I am. I can be a cowboy: but if I am, I diminish myself. I cannot be proud of my work, or stand in my own eyes as a good workman who gives good value for money. Even more if I am a thief, even more so if I am a hit man. The less I identify with my fellow men, refraining from taking their possessions or doing them harm, the less identity I have. False, fleeting, perjured and violent, I may well drown a sense of my own unbeing in a drunken haze, being unable to give an account I can live with of who I am. And the same if I am a Gadgrind. It is not so bad to be a ruthless man of business as it is to be a thief, but better to be fair as well as honest, and better still to be humane as well as fair, being able then to think of oneself as being, because one is, a man of good standing with all those he has done business with. If such qualities are characteristic of a rational agent engaged in business activity, then he will face difficult questions on occasions when the demands of self-interest run counter to those of honesty, fairness and humanity. Moral considerations thus inevitably enter in to making business decisions. Even if there is not always a simple answer, the question still has to be asked, and answered as best he can, if the businessman is to be considered a rational moral being, and not just an economic manipulator.

SO WHAT?

1. The iron laws of economics are not iron laws. We do have some freedom of manoeuvre. We are responsible for our choices. When a businessman says he had no alternative, what he really means is that he reckoned the arguments against the alternatives were overwhelming. He may be right, but needs, at least occasionally, to think them through, and make sure that the reasons really were compelling, and that he is not making a stock response on unwarranted assumptions.

2. Economics exists on account of the fact that each of us is, and should be allowed to be, partial to himself. In reaching business decisions we are not required to be altruistic or selfless, and are entitled to be primarily concerned with our own interest or the interest we are representing. BUT

3. It does not follow from this that we should consider *only* our own interest, or should seek to maximise profits at all costs. Our own interests cannot be adequately expressed in monetary terms alone, and often involve considerations of long-term security, as well as the respect in which we are held by others. In the short term there is often a real conflict between our own interests and those of others, but a general policy of not taking any account of the latter is irrational, and in the long term unsustainable.

4. Although a businessman is rightly concerned to make a profit, he does so by cooperating with others to their mutual benefit, and his activities only make sense if they are to the benefit of those he deals with as well as to himself. Even when there is no question of a customer coming back, it is a good test to ask whether he would be well advised to do so.

5. In considering others, a businessman, unlike the professional man, is not obliged to enter into all their concerns, but only to provide goods or services which would be a reasonable bargain for the generality of those he deals with. The morality of business is the public morality of universal application, not the personal morality of individual commitment.

6. The complex structure of modern business enterprises produces a complex structure of responsibilities. That of employer and employee is the closest and has the most fine structure, but other responsibilities are also important. In evaluating these, the businessman is properly partial to his own concerns, but should consider also how his actions impinge on other people and other interests, and the part he should play in the cooperative framework within which he works.

7. In business we are not just competing, but cooperating as well. It follows that:
   (a) a businessman should not be concerned solely with maximising profits, but should consider also the interests of customers, employees, suppliers, the trade, the locality, and the wider communities within which he operates.
   (b) a businessman should not be trained exclusively in the mastery of specialised skills in his particular field (although technical competence is necessary), but should also acquire skills in solving conflicts of interest between the people with whom he deals and in responding to moral issues.
   (c) a businessman should see himself not as motivated by mercenary considerations alone, but as a facilitator who enables people to benefit from the goods or services he provides, and to do better with his aid than they would have done without.

8. Although the demands of justice are real, there is no absolute just price or just wage that can be discovered by all men of good will. In particular, we should not regard the market as necessarily giving the right answers nor suppose that a socialist State could do so either. Codes can sometimes be useful, but again are of limited value. Again and again a businessman will have to decide for himself what the right course is, balancing the relevant considerations as best he can. He cannot be provided with an exhaustive list of *dos* and *don'ts*. In the end, he is his own moral adviser, and must himself take the decisions he can live with.

APPENDIX A

The Theory of Games

The Theory of Games helps us understand our reasoning when we make decisions involving more than one person. It shows why I need to take account of other people's decision-making as well as my own, why what has happened in the past is relevant as well as what may happen in the future, and why my values need to develop to encompass our common good and not just my own individual good.

In the Theory of Games each decision-maker, or "player", has a number of choices, yielding a large number of "outcomes" according to the choices made by himself and other players. Thus if there are four players each with three possible courses of action, there will be 81 (*i.e.* 3x3x3x3) possible outcomes. Each outcome is evaluated by each player according to his system of values, and the value he assigns to it is called his "pay-off". The pay-off is normally expressed in numerical terms, with the suggestion that we are dealing with the cardinal, interpersonal utilities that utilitarians believe in, but there is no need to assume that they are always cardinal and interpersonal; for most purposes it is enough that each player can decide his order of priorities as between the various outcomes that may result from his and others' choices. The outcomes are evaluated differently by the different players whose actions brought them about.

The Theory of Games enables us to characterize cooperative activities as opposed to purely competitive ones. In a competition there are necessarily losers as well as winners. They are "Zero-Sum Games" since my gain is your loss. In cooperative activities, however, there need be no losers, since by collaborating we both do better than we would have done on our own. These are "Non-zero Sum Games". Many are of a simple unproblematic sort: there is one outcome which is better from every player's point of view, and so each has a good reason of choosing to act so as to bring it about. But some pose problems for those who construe rationality in terms of maximising one's own pay-off.

The Rule of the Road shows the importance of conventions— "Coordination Norms"—in enabling players in a many-person game to concert their decisions so as to secure outcomes that they all prefer. In driving, in communicating, in dancing and in many other social activities, we need to coordinate our actions with one another, so as to concert our efforts and avoid collisions. Schematically we represent two motorists, Mr Knight and M. Chevalier approaching each other, and needing to move over in order not to run into each other, by the matrix (with Mr Knight's pay-offs in top right of each outcome, and M.Chevalier's in bottom right):

The Rule of the Road

	Mr Knight goes right	Mr Knight goes left
M. Chevalier *va à droite*	5 each passes other safely 5	0 collision 0
M. Chevalier *va à gauche*	0 collision 0	5 each passes other safely 5

Theory of Games: Table 1

Provided both go right, or both go left, they will pass each other safely: what is essential is that they do not each decide what he, on his own, thinks best, but both abide by some convention, or rule, or law, or mutual agreement. That is to say, I should not attempt to do whatever seems to me to be productive of the best consequences, but should reliably act in the way that other people expect me to act. I should drive on the left and not cut corners, give way when the other driver has the right of way, and press forward when I have, so that other drivers know where they are with me, and can plan their own movements accordingly. There is a necessary imperfection of information about the future actions of free agents in the absence of publicly avowed rules: norm-observance— deontology—is the key to coordination. A simple maximising strategy is impossible, and each player must keep in step with others, usually by means of their all abiding by some relevant convention. Whatever the apparent attractions of consequentialism for the single operator, they are shown to be illusory, even by consequentialist standards, once the agent sees himself to be not a solipsistic loner, but one person among many, each needing to recognise others as initiators of action with minds of their own whose decisions can be anticipated only if they adhere to well-known rules.

In the Battle of the Sexes He and She want to spend their holiday together, but He would prefer to go mountaineering in the Alps, whereas She would rather they both spent it sunbathing by the sea. The matrix is:

The Battle of the Sexes

	She goes to Alps	She goes to the sea
He goes to Alps	8 lovely for him: good for her 10	4 "wish you were here too" 4
He goes to sea	0 beastly for him: beastly for her 0	0 good for him: lovely for her 8

Theory of Games: Table 2

Since for either of them the second best is so much better than the third or fourth alternatives, it would pay either to settle for that if the very best appeared unattainable. And therefore it would pay the other to make it seem so. If She can throw a fit of hysterics and say she cannot abide the Alps and will not go there at any price, then He, if he is reasonable, will abandon his hopes of an Alpine holiday, and settle for the sea, which he would like twice as much— 8—as solitary mountaineering. But equally He may see that the moment has come to take a firm masculine line, and let the little woman face up to the realities of the situation, and either come along with him or go her separate way. And if once it becomes clear that this is the choice, She will have no option but to cave in, and buy a knapsack instead of a new bikini. It is thus irrational to be guided only by the pay-offs of the outcomes that are available at any one time, because that enables the other to manipulate one's choices. If I am to retain my autonomy, I cannot be altogether a direct consequentialist. Once you know that I am guided by consequences alone, you can induce me to do whatever you want by rigging the situation in such a way that by the time I come to make a decision the least bad outcome available to me is to fall in with your plans. Rationality, rather, requires that we extend our consideration over time as well as person.

The Battle of the Sexes shows the importance not of other persons but of other times. If we are to avoid being manipulated by unscrupulous fixers, we need long-term assessments, and a guarantee of not discounting the past as being merely water under the bridge. We cannot alter the past, but we can still assess it and take it into account, and thus free ourselves from being at the mercy of anyone who can rig the outcomes at one particular time. In the Theory of Games it is often an advantage to be able to bind oneself absolutely, or equivalently to rule out certain options absolutely. The strategy of Mutually Assured Destruction only worked provided both sides believed that the other was not governed solely by consequentialist considerations, and really would retaliate if attacked, even though there would be then no advantage in doing so. In order to reinforce this expectation, mechanical devices were constructed which in the event of a nuclear attack would operate automatically without the possibility of being switched off by any consequentialist survivors. In a less grisly way the whole logic of making and keeping promises is to ensure that some actions of an agent need not be altered simply by reason of factors which had been future becoming, by the effluxion of time, past. If we discount all past considerations we not only lay ourselves open to manipulation, but give only a partial account of the context in which our decisions are made, and from which they obtain their significance. I cannot be coherently oriented towards the future alone once I recognise that all my futures will one day be past.

If it were not for existence of some transferable token of value, economic transactions would mostly be instances of the Battle of the Sexes: most of the benefit would accrue to one of the parties, and the other would have the choice of either cutting off his nose to spite the other's face or of letting the other get away with the lion's share of the cooperative cake. If, however, there are not just two stark alternatives but an almost continuous range of intermediate courses of action, the claim by the one party that his offer is the only one available, and that the other must either take it or leave it, becomes implausible, and the other can counter with an offer which is more plausible as a final offer, and which the first party would be evidently foolish to turn down out of hand. Bargaining becomes possible, and a refusal to bargain unacceptable.

The Prisoners' Dilemma was first discerned by Protagoras, and greatly impressed Plato, and later Hobbes, who made it the cornerstone of his argument for Leviathan. In its modern form it is due to A.W. Tucker. He considers two prisoners, Bill Sykes and Kevin Slob, held incommunicado, who have jointly committed a serious crime. The prosecution, however, does not have sufficient evidence to convict either of them, and they know it. But it does have evidence to convict each of them of a less serious crime, say tax-evasion, for which the penalty is six months imprisonment. The prosecution then suggests some plea-bargaining to each: if he will confess to the major crime, and give evidence so as to secure the conviction of the other, he will be pardoned for both the major and the minor crime. If he confesses, and the other confesses too, both will receive a suitably reduced sentence for having pleaded guilty, say five years. If he does not confess, but is convicted on the evidence of the other, then he will receive the full sentence of ten years. The prosecution lets each prisoner know that it has made the same proposition to the other. Each prisoner then has a strong incentive to confess: for if the other confesses too, he would get ten years unless he did, while if the other does not confess, he will get off scot-free, instead of doing six months for the minor offence. So, if they act according to their individual scale of values, they will both confess. But by so doing they will both end up worse off than if they both kept silent. If they both kept silent, they would each receive only six months for the minor offence; but by both confessing, they receive the five years for having pleaded guilty to the major crime. The matrix is given on the opposite page.

There are many Prisoners' Dilemmas in real life: tax-evasion, fare-dodging, stealing, are all familiar instances, where, other things being equal, it would seem like a good idea oneself to do them, but a very bad idea to have other people doing them too. Hence the need, argued for in Chapter 9 (§9.3), for laws backed by the sanctions of a State wielding coercive power. The importance of the Prisoners' Dilemma, howewver, lies not only in its showing the need for the State, but in its revealing the inadequacy of static

The Prisoners' Dilemma

	Sykes keeps silent	Sykes confesses
Slob keeps silent	−1 Both jailed for tax −1	0 Sykes let off: maximum jail for Slob −10
Slob confesses	−10 Slob let off: with maximum jail for Sykes 0	−5 Both jailed reduced sentences −5

Theory of Games: Table 3

ascriptions of value to individuals. For there is a sense it which it is obviously in the prisoners' interests not to confess, and this rationality the static schema employed by the Theory of Games occludes. This point is often missed, because the prisoners are *ex hypothesi* wrongdoers, and hence presumed to be selfish. If only people were unselfish, and put others before self, then, so the argument runs, all would be well: the prisoners would not confess, the tax-payer would pay his taxes, the traveller buy his ticket, and nobody would ever wrong his neighbour. That all would not be well, however, is evident once we consider the dilemma of the altruistic couple where He tries to maximise Her pay-off, and She His, with the result they both end up with something they neither want. Thus He might be keen on cars, and She on food. If He mends the car and She cooks, they have a good lunch, followed by a drive in the country. If He helps Her cook, instead of messing about in the garage, they have an absolutely super lunch, though no drive in the country, If, on the other hand, She helps Him mend the car, the car will go like greased lightning, but they will have to eat in a Transport Cafe. But if they each insist on doing what the other wants, He will try His hand in the kitchen, while She will wriggle under the car, and the result will be an indifferent lunch followed by a mediocre drive, much worse for both of them than if each had acted non-altruistically. The matrix is:

The Altruists' Dilemma

	She cooks	She helps Him mend the car
He mends the car	5 good lunch, followed by pleasant drive 5	0 record journey, with meal in Transport Cafe 10
He helps her cook	10 super lunch, but no drive 0	1 indifferent lunch, followed by mediocre drive 1

Theory of Games: Table 4

The Altruists' Dilemma is the mirror image of the Prisoners' Dilemma, and shows that the trouble lies not in one's being concerned to maximise one's own pay-off, but in being tied to just one pay-off throughout. In practice we are able to resolve or surmount the Prisoners' Dilemma because we modify our original preferences in the light of what we come to know about others', and are not confined to a single occasion. I conjugate over persons, and knowing what you want, see that we shall both be better off if we follow a cooperative strategy, and for that reason come to want it. Although other things being equal, I want to get off scot-free, and prefer a short prison sentence to a longer one, I do not want to let down my confederate. I identify with him, and begin to take his interests to heart, and consider what is best for us jointly, rather than for just me individually. I may not do so completely, and make his interests mine, as the utilitarians urge, but I do so enough to alter the balance of advantage so as to favour the cooperative strategy. Of course, in so doing, I make myself vulnerable to being let down by him; but in real life few situations are evidently and certainly one-off, and anyone who lets me down on one occasion will forfeit my trust thereafter. In the long run I shall do worse if I let people down in order to maximise my own pay-off on each occasion than if I respond to each person as he did to me the last time we met, and give those I have not met before the benefit of the doubt and trusting them to behave decently. Being reasonable seems reasonable once we conjugate over persons, and proves to be the best policy once we conjugate over time too. A completely static and purely individualist approach is inadequate and demonstrably irrational: if we are to be rational we must take the values of others into consideration as well as our own, and must be prepared to change our priorities in the light of them.

Each of these arguments is a *reductio ad absurdum*. We start by assuming, as the classical economists did, that rationality can be defined in terms of maximising future pay-offs, and then show that even within its own terms, such a definition is self-contradictory. The Rule of the Road shows that it is better to keep to the rules than to try, as the Act Utilitarians counsel, to perform the act that will have the best consequences: each of us should recognise that he is not the only pebble on the beach, that it is not for him to choose which course of events shall occur, and that often the best he can do is to fit in with what other people are likely to do. The Battle of the Sexes shows that it is irrational to have regard only to future outcomes; an agent has a past as well as a future, and should make up his mind what he is going to do with regard to what he has decided in the past as well as what will ensue in the future. The Prisoners' Dilemma shows that he should take into account not only the existence but the interests and ideals of other people, and that it is irrational to ignore the collective point of view. Contrary to the static, solipsistic, future-oriented, exclusively individualistic standpoint of the classical economists, we are forced, by thinking about these three cases, to recognise that rationality is dynamic, leading us to take a longer temporal and wider personal view of what is involved in the decisions we are called on to take.

APPENDIX B

Indian Toiletries Factory

In 1968 an international manufacturer of men's toiletries decided to set up a local manufacturing operation in India in partnership with the company's local agent. The decision was taken as a result of the Indian government's ban on the import of toiletry products.

A licence for the local manufacture was obtained whereby the basic raw material—the perfume essence—could be imported since it could not be produced in India, but on the condition that all other materials and packaging would be supplied by local manufacturers. In return the local company would provide employment for about 40 Indians. The Indian government also hoped that the local product might be exported to those markets where India had preferential access, such as certain iron-curtain countries.

The negotiations for the agreement were characterized by a bargaining process which reflected the basic trade-off between the Indian government's desire for foreign investment and the creation of local jobs, and the international investor's desire to obtain a presence in the local market, at the same time ensuring a reasonable profit through the sale into India of the perfume essence. Another advantage for the Indian government was that the toiletries factory would be on the same site as a new pharmaceutical and surgical dressings factory, thus providing a complex of manufacturing plants in an industrially underdeveloped part of India.

The question whether Indians needed toiletries, rather than medicines and fertilisers to alleviate health and food production problems, did arise but took second place to the economic consideration of increasing employment. The fact that about 40 new jobs would be created, the local population would have a product now unobtainable owing to import restrictions, and the Indian exchequer would benefit from the receipt of sales taxes on the products sold, was decisive.

Although Indian government policy at the time tended to be *dirigiste* in determining what people needed, those needs took second place in this case to the "value" of creating employment. There was no predetermined set of values which determined whether there should, or should not, be an after-shave lotion in Goa. The decision depended on the interaction between a number of different values and was the result of reaching an acceptable trade-off between them for each of the two parties concerned. Both parties benefited by the agreement, each accepting different risks: on the one hand, the Indian government risked not seeing a return on the tax incentives granted during the start-up of the new company, should the company fail to provide the 40 jobs envisaged; on the other hand, the international company risked not making a return on its investment in terms of the money and people needed to set up a viable business operation.

If the two parties had had different values and objectives they might have reached a different decision whether to go ahead or not. There was no way of deciding beforehand what the outcome would be. In that sense it was antecedently undetermined whether Indians should have a locally manufactured after-shave lotion or not.

Glossary

Aristotle Greek philosopher of 4th century B.C. He wrote about justice in Book V of his *Nicomachean Ethics*, and in his *Politics*, which have been influential ever since.

Buber: German philosopher of 20th century who, while accepting the existentialist, individual responsibility for moral actions, proposed that that should not be at the expense of treating other people as objects—the "I-it" relationship—but should recognise the value of the "I-Thou" relationship.

classical economics: the theory that markets are continually tending towards a perfect equilibrium between supply and demand, and that wages and prices must be determined by such equilibrium, and not by moral considerations.

cogent: cogent arguments are those which, while not necessarily valid in formal logic, are nevertheless weighty, and should carry conviction.

consequentialism: the assessment of actions or policies solely with regard to their consequences.

Descartes: philosopher of 17th century who started by doubting everything, but found he could not doubt his own existence, arguing *cogito, ergo sum*, I think, therefore I exist.

economics: the study of the exchange and trading of goods and services between different parties to the transaction; from the Greek word οἰκονομία (*oikonomia*) meaning 'household organization'.

Epicureans: disciples of Epicurus, a Greek philosopher of 3rd century B.C. They held that men should be free from the irrationality of superstitious religious beliefs, and that individual contentment and peace of mind was the highest good a man could attain. Their philosophy has come down to us in the Latin poem of Lucretius, *De Rerum Natura*, On the Nature of Things. They were supposed, often unfairly, to live self-indulgent lives.

Establish-
mentarians: those who support the Establishment, particularly those who supported the Church of England against the Dissenters, *i.e.* members of
Noncomformist Denominations or Sects.

ethics: from the Greek, ἔθος, (*ethos*), meaning 'custom'
or 'behaviour'.

Existentialists: Philosophers who abhor general principles, and
decide each moral question on its own, from
their individual point of view.

Gadgrind: a Dickensian character, noted for his meanness.

Gyges' ring: a ring which conferred invisibility.

Hayek: economist and philosopher of 20th century. He
wrote *The Road to Serfdom, The Constitution
of Liberty*, and *Law, Legislation and Morality*,
in which he argued against central planning,
and in favour of free markets, as being far more
efficient in providing decision-makers with the
information they needed.

Hegel: philosopher of 19th century who stressed the
importance of the State in his *The Philosophy
of Right* and *The Phenomenology of Mind*, and
other works.

Hobbes: philosopher of 17th century who was sceptical
of the effectiveness of moral argument, and in
his *Leviathan* justified a strong State as the only
alternative to the law of the jungle.

interests: interests are values that can be assigned to particular persons. Third-personal interests can be
assigned vicariously, simply on the basis of the
person's being a person—a person can be assumed to care for his health, wealth, and liberty, because that is what people naturally care
for. First-personal interests are those actually
avowed by an individual as being what he happens to be interested in. He may be interested
in French art, or ball-room dancing, but he
could not be assumed to be interested in those
things except on the basis of his own words or
deeds.

Kant: philosopher of 18th century, who based morality on the "categorical imperative", Act only
on that maxim that you can will to be a universal law of nature. He claimed that actions
were only moral if they were based solely on the
categorical imperative, and not on any pruden-

tial considerations. He maintained also that we should treat other men as "ends-in-themselves" and not as means to some other end.

Locke: philosopher of 17th century who justified political obligation on a supposed contract between the government and the governed.

Mackie: philosopher of 20th century who was sceptical of the objective existence of moral values.

Malthus: Malthus' theory of population was based on the belief that, because men reproduce faster than their resources increase, most wage earners must always earn the smallest amount possible that will keep them and their families alive. It was an important influence on those who regarded economics as a science, and opposed the optimism of those who thought that poverty and all social ills could be eradicated.

Metaphysics: from the Greek *Τῶν Μετὰ Τὰ Φυσικὰ* (*Ton Meta Ta Phusika*), meaning 'after the physics', the title of Aristotle's book in which he goes on from his account of natural philosophy to discuss the most fundamental principles of existence. In modern parlance, metaphysics is divided into ontology, the discussion of reality, and what really exists, and epistemology, the discussion of the nature of knowledge.

natural law/
positive law: laws that ought to be obeyed irrespective of whether they have been enacted by an effective regime/ laws that have been enacted by an effective regime.

normative: ought to be obeyed or observed

Physiocrats: a school of 18th century thinkers who held that only agriculture was properly productive, and that all those who did not work on the land were, strictly speaking, parasites.

omni-personal/
first-personal: moral precepts which we urge on everyone/ moral precepts which an individual may adopt for himself.

Plato: Greek philosopher of 4th century B.C. Pupil of Socrates and teacher of Aristotle. He argued strongly for the existence of objective moral values, and in his *Republic*, portrayed an ideal society, governed in accordance with those values by a class of Guardians, who held all possessions in common.

privative/
non-privative: privative goods are those, such as motor cars, which if belonging to some, necessarily do not belong to others; non-privative goods are those, like information, which can be shared, without any diminution in what is possessed by each.

Socrates: Greek philosopher of 5th century B.C., notable for his moral courage, and willingness to question accepted ideas, for which he was put to death by the Athenians. His use of dialectical method to investigate the nature of concepts like justice is described in the dialogues of his pupil Plato.

solipsist: I am a solipsist if I think I am the only person to exist.

universalisable: a precept is universalisable, if it can be expressed so as to apply to everyone.

utilitarianism: the belief that those desires or actions are good which promote the general happiness of all. Utilitarianism propounded an ethic that is democratic and egalitarian.

values: 'value' is the most general term for principles that can guide a person's actions. Philosophers differ on whether they exist independently of us—as Plato held—or are just the projections of our desires and attitudes—as Mackie held. Values are non-privative, and can be shared.

Index

Note: references are to sections, except where chapters or pages are indicated. The more important references are printed bold, and are listed first.